Building High-Performance
MUSTANGS
ON A BUDGET

GEORGE REID

S-A DESIGN

CarTech
Auto Books & Manuals

Edited By: Travis Thompson

Layout By: Joshua Limbaugh

ISBN 978-1-61325-002-0

Order No. SA75P

CarTech®, Inc.,
39966 Grand Avenue
North Branch, MN 55056
Telephone (651) 277-1200 • (800) 551-4754 • Fax: (651) 277-1203
www.cartechbooks.com

OVERSEAS DISTRIBUTION BY:

Brooklands Books Ltd.
P.O. Box 146, Cobham, Surrey, KT11 1LG, England
Telephone 01932 865051 • Fax 01932 868803
www.brooklands-books.com

Brooklands Books Aus.
3/37-39 Green Street, Banksmeadow, NSW 2109, Australia
Telephone 2 9695 7055 • Fax 2 9695 7355

Front Cover, Top Image: *The Fox Mustang is easily one of the most popular performance platforms of all time – it's a great car to use for road racing, autocrossing, and of course, drag racing, as shown here.*

Front Cover, Bottom Image: *The heart of the Fox-body Mustang is the venerable 5.0-liter engine, one of the most versatile power plants on the street today. And if that's not enough? Well, stroker kits and 351s are plentiful and easy to install as well.*

Back Cover, Upper Left: *It is time to install the new lower intake manifold. John Da Luz prefers Permatex Right Stuff gasket goop. He runs it along the fore and aft manifold rails, and around each of the coolant passages.*

Back Cover, Upper Right: *With the differential and drive pinion installed, we're ready to lap gears. This process tells us how happy the gears are with each other. The ring and pinion gears must mate smoothly. We get there by painting the ring gear teeth and running the gears through. The pattern should look like this. Do this before you install the crush sleeve for best results.*

Back Cover, Lower: *Subframe connectors, like these from Griggs, tie the front and back halves of the chassis together for added strength and stiffness. This is a great modification for any performance Fox Mustang, whether it's a corner carver or quarter-miler.*

TABLE OF CONTENTS

ACKNOWLEDGEMENTS

A book of this magnitude doesn't happen without the help of many committed people and special friends who stepped up to the plate to help me along the way. I want to acknowledge and thank John Da Luz of JMC Motorsports, and Julio Mayen of JME Enterprises, both in San Diego, California, for their invaluable assistance in the creation and publishing of this book.

I also want to thank Jim Smart, Senior Editor of *Mustang Monthly* magazine and *Mustang & Fords* magazine, who has helped me with images, ideas, and technical information on more times than I can count with this and three other CarTech titles.

I am deeply indebted to Tim Gilpin at Brothers Performance Warehouse for his help and support toward the end of this lengthy and involved book project. Tim came to our rescue with an array of ideas, technical support, staff, parts, accessories, and facilities.

There is also quite a list of people and companies who came to our rescue with product and technical support time and time again during the creation of this book. They are the Edelbrock Corporation, Trick-Flow, AFR, ARP, AMK Products, MSD Ignition, Maximum Motorsports, Griggs Racing, Holley, C&L Performance, The Dyno Shop, Steeda, Saleen Autosport, Ford Racing Performance Parts, Mustangs Plus, Classic Design Concepts, Billet Performance, Comp Cams, Federal-Mogul, Crane Cams, Canton Pans, Tremec Transmissions, LenTech Automatics, Currie Enterprises, MAC Performance Products, BBK Performance, Baer Brakes, and dozens of others too numerous to mention. Thanks one and all for your help and support.

And finally, there's Rob Kinnan of ProMedia Publishing, which publishes the *RACE Pages* for avid 4.6 and 5.0L Mustang motorsports enthusiasts. Rob has provided me with a wealth of images, including the cover image for this book.

Thank you, everyone, for your friendship, help, and support.

—*George Reid*

INTRODUCTION

The late-model, 1979-95 Fox-body Mustang has been called the 1955-57 Chevrolet of the new millennium, because it enjoys a following unequalled since the Bow-Tie struck gold in the mid 1950s. Fox-body Mustangs are successful because they're an affordable, easy to build and tune, go-fast automobile like those classic Chevys. The 1985-95 Mustang's 5.0L High Output small-block V-8s are easy to build, durable, and make a lot of power for not much money. So, out with that age-old theory that it costs more to build a Ford. There has never been an easier time to build a high-performance Ford in the company's 100-year history.

The intent of this book is to show you how to jump into late-model Mustang performance with a wide variety of budgets in mind. We're going to show you how to do it with a tight budget. We're also going to show you how to do it with a liberal budget, too, because these Mustangs sit in driveways from all walks of life, from the very poor to the decidedly affluent. Everyone likes to play with them, because they're just plain old-fashion fun.

These V-8 pony cars are successful for the same reasons their classic 1965-78 ancestors were. They're plentiful and cheap, easy to build and service, and they're a whole lot of fun when it's time for an aggressive drive.

The irony of late-model Mustangs is what automotive journalists in the 1980s predicted so long ago. Automotive writers predicted the end of the tunable automobile when Ford began fitting Mustangs with Sequential Electronic Fuel Injection (SEFI) in 1986. Because few people understood how SEFI worked, enthusiasts were quick to avoid something so new and foreign. A lot of us shied away because the fuel-injected 5.0L V-8 was so intimidating. A bizarre-looking induction system, fuel rails and injectors, throttle bodies, boxy air filters, and lots of wires and sensors were something we didn't understand back then. Those things scared us off in numbers.

But enthusiasts have embraced the fuel-injected Mustangs, quickly catching on to how they work and how to squeeze abundant performance from their castings and forgings. The 5.0L High Output V-8 has become one of the most reliable Ford engines ever, because it's designed and built to take a lot of punishment. The tunable Mustang didn't die in 1986. It was simply reborn, creating an exciting new era of hot Mustang performance. And that's what this book is all about.

Our goal with this book is to show you what's possible with your late-model tuner Mustang. Many thanks for adding this book to your Ford performance library.

FOX-BODY MUSTANG BASICS

When the first Fox-body Mustangs began rolling off the Dearborn, Michigan, and San Jose, California, assembly lines in the late 1970s, few understood the potential of these redesigned pony cars. The Fox platform got its start in the U.S. with the 1979 Mustang, even though the Fox-based Ford Fairmont and Mercury Zephyr were introduced a year earlier. Ultimately, the Fox platform became the most widely used platform in Ford history, finding its way into the Thunderbird and Cougar, Lincoln Continental and Mark VII, Granada, Monarch, LTD, Marquis and even Capri. This platform remains in production more than two decades later as the Fox-4 generation Mustang.

The redesigned, aerodynamic 1979 Mustang really didn't look like a Mustang at all. It was radically different from the Mustangs that preceded it. Underneath, it had McPherson struts and coil springs in front, with a four-bar link coil-spring suspension and tube shocks in back. Its twin-set rectangular headlamps, wedge body, and sharp European styling made it the most advanced Mustang ever at the time. TRX suspension with Metric wheels and Michelin tires debuted on the 1979 Mustang. Front four-lug discs and rear drum brakes were standard equipment.

The all-new 1979 Mustang was the Indy 500 Pace Car that year. More than 10,000 replicas were produced with distinctive graphics, ground effects, Recaro bucket seats, competition suspension, and a host of other special features. Most were fitted with the 302-2V V-8. Fewer were equipped with the 2.3L Turbo four.

From 1979-81, there were three basic Mustang models – base, Ghia, and Cobra. The Ghia was a luxury model with plush features and leather appointments. Cobra was sporty with a more aggressive suspension, performance

The redesigned, all-new 1979 Mustang was a dramatic departure from the 1978 Mustang II it replaced. Its slippery aero styling and low-to-the-ground European stance made the 1979 Mustang an immediate success. Three basic models were available: base, Ghia, and Cobra.

The 1982 Mustang GT was an exciting first step back into the factory high-performance car market. Underhood was a warmed-up 302 with a high-performance marine camshaft, Motorcraft 2150 two-barrel carburetor, cast-aluminum valve covers, dual-snorkel air cleaner, and a lot of spirit.

amenities, and a choice of either a carbureted 2.3L Turbo four or the 302-2V V-8. The Cobra was little more than a paint and tape package with a more aggressive suspension package. Not many of them survive today.

The standard engine in the 1979-81 Fox Mustang was the 2.3L OHC four-cylinder engine with a two-barrel carb, which had been in continuous production since 1974. This engine was first offered in the Mustang II, Pinto, and Mercury Bobcat. The 2.8L Cologne V-6 was an available option that appeared first in the Mercury Capri and Mustang II. This Ford of Germany V-6 was dropped in 1980 due to availability problems and replaced with an older Mustang powerplant – the 3.3L (200ci) in-line six that was standard equipment in the original 1965-70 Mustang. The 3.3L in-line six was ultimately replaced with the all-new 3.8L Essex V-6 in 1982.

Another Mustang engine option for 1979-81 was the 2.3L turbocharged OHC four, also with two-barrel carb. The 2.3L Turbo struggled with serious reliability problems due to turbo failure. Most were installed in the Mustang Cobra, but very few of them survive today.

At the top of the option list for 1979 was a 302-2V small-block V-8, also known as the 5.0L. Although we associate the "5.0L" designation with Fox body Mustangs, it first appeared on the

1978 Mustang II King Cobra. In 1979, the 5.0L carbureted V-8 wasn't much to brag about at roughly 130 horsepower at the rear wheels. It was an anemic V-8 engine short on torque, with a redline in the 4,500 rpm range. Atop the 5.0 was a Motorcraft 2150 carburetor (49-state) or the Variable Venturi (VV) carburetor (California only). Breakerless Duraspark ignition lit the fire.

In 1980, Ford introduced the de-bored 255ci (4.2L) V-8 to help improve Mustang fuel economy. We call the 255 "de-bored" because it had the same stroke as a 302 (3.00-inches with the same "2M" crankshaft and connecting rods) with a smaller 3.68-inch bore. The 255 was available only with a C4 Select-Shift automatic transmission in 1980-81, and with the C5 (a C4 with locking torque converter) in 1982. To improve emissions, Ford fitted the 255 with more rounded-port heads; this also improved intake velocity and low-end torque. Despite these features, the 255 wound up being an underpowered slug, with little in common with the 302. Buff magazines of the period weren't impressed. The best quarter-mile times were in the 16-second range at roughly 80 mph.

Mustang production ended at San Jose when the 1981 model year came to a close. California pollution standards became so strict that it became economically advantageous for Ford to produce all Mustangs at Dearborn, Michigan. It has been this way ever since. Today, the old Ford San Jose assembly plant is The Great Mall of Milpitas just a few miles northeast of downtown San Jose in Milpitas, California.

1982 – MUSTANG GT

Although it has been two decades ago, few of us who remember the period can forget the return of the Mustang GT for 1982. At a time when most of us were convinced we would never see a factory performance car again, the Mustang GT was a refreshing sight and certainly a solid effort toward a high-performance Mustang. Ford used words we hadn't heard in years – "High Output" and "BOSS." Ford told us "The BOSS is back!!!" in its Mustang advertising.

The 1982 Mustang GT 5.0L engine had a Ford 351W high-performance marine camshaft with a more aggressive profile and the 351W firing order. A rather lame single exhaust system with twin European tailpipes on the port side yielded a fresh tone. But the Mustang GT really didn't ooze with adrenaline that first year. Tubular traction bars helped the car hook up. A four-speed SROD transmission was the only gearbox available. The SROD was not a hardy transmission by any means, and would not tolerate much abuse.

On the ground were TRX metric wheels, with metric tires available only from Michelin. This is why so many 1982-84 Mustang GT models have either aftermarket or larger 15- and 16-inch 1985-93 Mustang GT wheels today. Another thing we remember about the 1982 Mustang GT was its ground effects and Marchal fog lamps borrowed from the 1979 Mustang Indy Pace Car parts bin. Just like Mustangs produced from 1979-81, the 1982 GT had modest front disc and rear drum brakes. The car was crying for better binders, but it would be many years before it would get them.

1983-84 – A BETTER GT

For 1983, Ford cleaned up the Mustang GT's appearance for a leaner look, redesigned tail lamps with amber turn signals, and Marchal driving lamps in the front fascia. Underhood, the 5.0L High Output V-8 received a Ford-design Holley four-barrel carb for a marked improvement in power. Mid-year, Ford introduced the T5 five-speed as a Mustang option. Like 1982, the 1983 Mustang GT had European design faux dual exhaust tips on the left-hand side.

Late in the 1983 model year, Ford introduced the Mustang GT Turbo, a Mustang GT with the 2.3L OHC EFI Turbo four, also available in the Thunderbird Turbo Coupe, Cougar XR-7 Turbo, and Capri RS Turbo. The 2.3L EFI Turbo four was a vastly improved mill thanks to Electronic Engine Control (EEC-IV), fuel injection, and an improved turbocharger.

The Mustang saw major changes in 1984. The 5.0L High Output engine

Since 1984 was the Mustang's 20th year, Ford produced some 5,261 limited-production 20th Anniversary edition Mustang GTs. These Oxford White hatchbacks and convertibles were produced during the spring of 1984. Most were fitted with the 5.0-liter High Output V-8. Very few had the 2.3-liter turbo four cylinder.

returned with either a four-barrel carb (five-speed), or Central Fuel Injection (CFI) with the AOD. A promised mid-year horsepower increase to 225 ponies never materialized.

In the spring of 1984, Ford produced 5,261 20th Anniversary Mustang GT hatchbacks and convertibles with 2.3L EFI Turbo fours and 5.0L High Output V-8s; most were fitted with the latter. These limited edition Mustangs received Shelby-style GT-350 stripes over their Polar White finish. Another distinctive feature for these limited edition models was the 1985 Mustang instrument panel and other interior appointments. Ford's objective was to produce 5,000 units. Some 260 additional units were produced for Canadian Ford dealers. In May, another 16 were produced for Ford executives, who wanted a piece of the action.

The Mustang GT Turbo returned for 1984, but very few were sold. Sagging sales for Mustang GT Turbo models was rooted in the availability of the 5.0L High Output V-8. No turbo lag, no waiting.

1984-86 – Mustang SVO

One oft-overlooked segment of Mustang history is the 1984-86 Mustang SVO. The Mustang SVO was a product of Ford's then newly formed Special Vehicle Operations (SVO), Dearborn's

corporate skunk works conceived in 1980 to develop factory high-performance vehicles. SVO was to the 1980s what SVE (Special Vehicle Engineering) and SVT (Special Vehicle Team) are today. SVT (Special Vehicle Team) has developed the Ford F-150 Lightning pickup, Mustang Cobra, Contour SVT, and the new Focus SVT.

The Mustang SVO was a very sophisticated, limited-production, high-performance pony car with an intercooled 2.3L OHC turbocharged four, 16-inch wheels, wide Goodyear Gatorback tires, competition suspension, special fascia and trim package, leather sports interior and more. This car was wonderful to drive because it handled so well. The Mustang SVO was conceived at a time when it was believed that turbocharged four-cylinders were the wave of the future. At the time, fuel prices were high and corporate average fuel economy (CAFE) figures were paramount. Ultimately, the Mustang SVO was dropped due to poor sales and high demand for V-8 Mustangs.

What hurt the Mustang SVO was intense interest in V-8 performance, which was making a strong comeback at the time. Fuel prices became more stable during the 1980s, which fed our appetite for the solid and predictable performance of a V-8. With a V-8, there was no turbo lag or anemic four-cylinder buzz, just snappy performance. What's more, overdrive and fuel injection brought us V-8 engines that could deliver nearly 30 miles per gallon on the highway. The Mustang SVO never stood a chance against the more affordable Mustang GT and Capri RS. Production continued through 1986 when the Mustang SVO was dropped.

1985 – ROLLER TAPPETS, QUADRA-SHOCKS & GATORBACKS

The Mustang changed significantly both inside and out in 1985 – a pivotal year. The 1985 Mustang GT had a new fascia, GT graphics, and a leaner, more slippery appearance. Inside, a redesigned instrument panel, plus all-new bucket seats with distinctive piping and plush upholstery enhanced driving comfort.

Underhood, the 1985 Mustang GT received a redesigned 5.0L High Output engine with roller tappets in an all-new block casting, which allowed for a more aggressive camshaft profile without the shortcomings of an aggressive camshaft. For the first time since 1971, a Mustang engine was equipped with forged pistons for better reliability. Holley 4180-C four-barrel carburetion returned with the same manifold and improved fast-burn "E5AE" cylinder heads. Shorty tubular headers (actually called tubular exhaust manifolds) with twin catalytic converters and pseudo dual exhausts debuted for 1985. As in 1984, Mustang GT models fitted with the AOD transmission received Central Fuel Injection (CFI) instead of the Holley atomizer. Axle ratio depended on transmission selection. If you ordered a Mustang GT with T-5 transmission, you received 2.73:1 Traction-Lok gears. An optional 3.08:1 Traction-Lok was available. Those ordered with the AOD received a 3.27:1 Traction-Lok standard, with no optional axle ratio available.

Underneath, the '85 Mustang GT had Quadra-Shock suspension in back, borrowed from the Thunderbird Turbo Coupe, which took place of traction bars. The innovative Quadra-Shock suspension design prevented rear axle hop during wide-open throttle acceleration. Revised rear link pivot points lowered the Mustang's roll center. Variable-rate coil springs improved ride and handling qualities. Rack-and-pinion power steering with a 15:1 ratio was standard on GT models. On the ground, 16-inch aluminum 10-hole wheels and Goodyear Gatorback tires gave the Mustang GT a wider footprint and better control.

1986 – THE TUNER MUSTANG ARRIVES

At a glance, the 1986 Mustang is virtually unchanged from 1985. Externally, the only difference is the third brake light, visible only from behind. More subtle changes, like matte black micro-appointments (antenna, exterior door handles, and hatch lock), were quietly worked into the styling. Inside, the 1986 Mustang is unchanged. Where the 1986 Mustang GT differs from 1985 is

The 1986 Mustang GT differs from 1985 in its use of a fuel-injected, 200-horse, 5.0-liter High Output V-8. This was the first year for SEFI (sequential electronic fuel injection). Horsepower was down 10 from 1985, but torque was up by 15 ft-lbs.

mechanically and structurally.

When the 1986 Mustang GT was introduced, we received our first look at the 5.0L High Output V-8 with Sequential Electronic Fuel Injection (SEFI). There was nothing subtle about the change. Atop the engine was something resembling a vacuum cleaner's power rug attachment – that new-fangled induction system with long intake runners, eight port fuel injectors and a large, single throttle body. Because we were so unfamiliar with port fuel injection, we were intimidated by a high-tech small-block everyone perceived as the beginning of the end of performance. Some journalists called it the end of the tunable Mustang. But nothing could have been further from the truth.

SEFI was a new form of engine management designed to both improve performance and clean up emissions. That first year, the SEFI 5.0L High Output engine was fitted with high-swirl, shrouded-valve "E6AE" heads used only in 1986. Firing the injected mixture was a new kind of Duraspark ignition system with Hall-Effect triggering and a thick-film ignition module in the distributor, which handled spark advance

signals from the engine control computer. Underneath were true dual exhausts for the first time since 1973. Twin cats fed twin mufflers and a duo of tail pipes.

Quadra-Shock suspension continued for 1986 as a means to traction management. New in back was the super-tough 8.8-inch integral carrier rear axle, with a more limited selection of axle ratios.

1987-93 – FRESH PRINCE

The 1987 Mustang brought with it a dramatic change in appearance few of us were ready for at the time. Composite headlamps made of GE Lexan plastic came to the Mustang for the first time in 1987 (the limited production Mustang SVO received them earlier in mid-year 1985).

For 1987, the Mustang fascia had less mouth and more paint. At first glance, it was very European, like the Ford Sierra coupe (sold in the U.S. as the Merkur). The Mustang GT was laced with dramatic cosmetic changes, like ground effects, a term we heard for the first time in 1987. Those bolt-on ground effects had simulated side scoops, color-

ful accent stripes, subtle pressed in MUSTANG GT graphics and more. A rear deck spoiler was also standard on the GT. Fifteen-inch turbine wheels, a throwback to the 1970s, were actually behind the times because they hurt the car's fresh appearance. They were also decidedly small in an era where 16-inch wheels were becoming the norm. Fluted tail lamps on the GT were a disappointment to journalists and enthusiasts alike. Yet, they managed to grow on us, making it hard to imagine the 1987-93 Mustang GT without them. Revised quarter windows gave the Mustang a bold, new attitude.

The Mustang changed very little from 1987-93. Most of the changes were subtle and mechanical. One significant change was the transition from speed density engine control to mass air intake sensing in 1988 for California-bound Mustangs, then in 1989 for 49-state units. With mass air came the tunable Mustang that has become the 1955-57 Chevrolet of the 1990s and beyond.

The speed density system available in 1986-88 made it impossible to perform a successful camshaft or throttle body swap without driveability problems. These modifications didn't work well with an electronic engine control module designed and programmed for only one type of engine package. Mass air allowed for modifications, like a cam or throttle body swap, because it was able to adjust for changing conditions. This has led us to a tunable Mustang that can be modified for a variety of purposes both on and off the track.

It may surprise you to know Ford didn't celebrate the Mustang's 25th Anniversary in 1989. They did, however, recognize the 25th Anniversary in 1990 with limited production Mustang convertibles in Emerald Green with white leather interiors. These Mustangs were intended for a 7-UP promotion going on at the same time, which apparently never went anywhere. Ford capitalized on the availability of these cars, working them into the belated 25th anniversary celebration.

The next significant change for the Mustang was a driver's side air bag for 1990, which eliminated the adjustable tilt steering column option. The following year, 1991, Ford stepped up to the performance plate and fitted the Mustang with five-spoke, 16-inch wheels. They were long overdue.

To help sagging Mustang sales, Ford introduced the Summer Special 1992-1/2 Mustang "feature" car, a Vibrant Red LX convertible with white leather interior, white five-spoke wheels, and a rear deck spoiler. This theme continued for 1993 mid-year with another round of "feature" cars in Canary Yellow with white leather and chrome wheels, and Oxford White with white leather and white wheels. These cars were inspired by sales of the Vibrant Red convertibles in 1992.

1993 – SVT Cobra

The Special Vehicle Team's (SVT) first effort was the 1993 Mustang Cobra introduced during the spring of 1993. The 1993 SVT Mustang Cobra was a teaser for the SN-95 redesigned Mustang to come in 1994. But it was also a punctuation mark, telling the buying public that Ford was back in the muscle car arena with exciting Mustangs.

The sole purpose of SVT was to work outside of the box, away from Ford's traditional approaches to car development and building. SVT's objective, with John Coletti's direction, was to improve division nameplates, giving them exclusivity and prestige. Ford certainly achieved important recognition in its SVT Mustang Cobra. After SVT introduced the Mustang Cobra, it fired another salvo with its high-horsepower 1993 Lightning F-150 pickup. It was a great time to be a Ford buyer.

SVT's Mustang Cobra is fitted with a GT-40-spec 5.0L High Output small-block, uprated T5 five-speed transmission (no automatics), four-wheel disc brakes, tuned dual exhausts, high-output alternator, handling suspension, heavy-duty driveshaft yoke, 17-inch wheels specific to the Cobra, and a high-performance sound system. Three colors were available – Teal, Red, and Black. A total of 5,100 were built – 1,355 in Teal, 1,891 in Red, and 1,854 in Black. Just 107 were Cobra "R" models – all in Red.

It may surprise you to know the 1993 Mustang Cobras were all hand-built. By that, we mean they received extraordinarily close attention during the build process at the Dearborn assembly plant. They were sidelined from regular production at Dearborn for close attention to determine quality, fit and compatibility of parts. There was not a better-built Mustang in 1993 than the SVT Cobra.

The 1993 Cobra was fitted with a Cobra-specific fascia with the traditional galloping pony, special rear deck spoiler, 1984-86 Mustang SVO tail lamps, SVT and Cobra badging, ground effects, and more. They're clearly recognizable at a glance. Inside, the Cobra was fitted with the same kind of bucket seats used in the Mustang GT, with the exception being stitched-in Cobra graphics and power lumbar support. A leather-wrapped steering wheel was standard. Gray leather was optional.

The GT-40 5.0L High Output engine was basically a Mustang GT powerplant with GT-40 heads and induction, roller rocker arms, special camshaft, 24 lb/hr injectors, 65mm throttle body, 55mm mass air sensor, underdrive/overdrive crankshaft pulleys, special clutch fan and more. The Cobra's 8.8-inch axle ratio was 3.08:1 in a Traction-Lok unit.

A footnote to our SVT Cobra commentary is the 107 "R" units built specifically for racing purposes in 1993. Ford decided to take on Chevy's Camaro LT-1 in SCCA and IMSA competition with a special, limited production, track-prepared Cobra-R. To do this, Ford had to meet homologation requirements by producing at least 100 street-legal examples. This they did with 107 units. All were Vibrant Red clearcoat with two-passenger seating (no rear seat), 5.0L Super High Performance V-8 (235 horsepower), engine oil cooler, heavy-duty, a two-row core aluminum radiator, recalibrated fan clutch, sport-tuned dual exhaust system, heavy-duty T5 five-speed transmission, 3.08:1 Traction-Lok, P245/45ZR17 Goodyear High Performance tires, 17 x 8-inch six-spoke aluminum wheels, handling suspension, power rack-and-pinion steering with 15:1 ratio; 13-inch dual-piston, five-lug front disc brakes; 10.5-inch, single-piston, five-lug rear disc brakes, and a special "X" frame underneath. Quite a few of these were purchased and stored for safe keeping. Others hit the racing circuit and have been successfully campaigned.

The 1987 Mustang GT had an all-new look, but still used the Fox body's original steel stampings. Ford fitted the Mustang with a new fascia with composite headlamps, ground effects, a restyled hood, and fluted taillights.

1994-95 – THE SN-95

The SN-95 Mustang, introduced on December 9, 1993, as a 1994 model, was one of the most researched and developed Mustangs ever. For one thing, Team Mustang, under the careful and passionate direction of John Coletti, had a very short time to develop the car and prove to Ford management that the Mustang was worth saving. Coletti, then head of Team Mustang, put together a very committed group of people who were not only engineers, product planners, stylists and financial people – they were enthusiasts who loved cars. Saving the Mustang was everything to them. Creating a better Mustang wasn't just a choice. It was the only choice.

Team Mustang went to work determining what the Mustang needed to be a better car. They investigated handling and braking issues. Stylists went back to the drawing board to conceive a very retro Mustang body that would remind the public of the original 30 years earlier. Interior stylists also went back to the original idea, with a pod-style dashboard that reminds us of the 1969-70 Mach 1,

more legroom, comfortable seating, and instrumentation similar to earlier generation Mustangs. Team Mustang also opted for a safer vehicle, with side impact protection, dual air bags, more padding, and improved passenger restraints. As a result of all these concerns, the car got heavier.

Body engineers stiffened up the Mustang's platform with a new "X" frame underneath, bracing between the strut towers and cowl, glued joints and seams, and the elimination of a hatchback model. The result was less cowl shake and a quieter ride. A slippery aerodynamic body also improved cabin noise levels.

The 1994 Mustang GT was disappointing in one area – power. Horsepower and torque ratings remained about the same as 1993. However, the same basic 5.0L High Output engine had more weight to carry thanks to additional structure, side impact door beams, sound deadening, air bag systems and other safety equipment. The car just didn't perform as well as it did in 1993. When the redesigned 1994 SVT Cobra was introduced in the spring of that year, it, too, suffered from weight gain.

Approximately 1,000 Indianapolis 500 Pace Car convertible Cobras were produced that year to commemorate the Mustang's selection as the official pace car of the 1994 Indy 500.

The Mustang's great success in 1994 lead to very few changes in 1995, aside from color changes and the phase out of the removable hardtop. Very few 1994-95 Mustangs were produced with the removable hardtop. In fact, for the removable hardtop to work at all, it had to have been installed at the factory.

When the Dearborn, Michigan, assembly plant produced its last 5.0L High Output small-block Mustang in the summer of 1995, it closed the door on an era of high-performance Mustangs we never thought we would ever see again. It was through the very perseverance of die-hard Ford enthusiasts behind the scenes at Ford that we have a Mustang at all in 2004. We tip our hats to those who have fought hard to save the breed from extinction, and those who continue to deliver a new generation of exciting overhead cam Mustangs we never dreamed we would see when this nameplate was first introduced in 1964.

The redesigned 1994 Mustang GT was built on the Fox-4 platform, which had a lot of improvements and revised suspension geometry.

PLANNING YOUR PROJECT

When we dream about our Mustang projects, it all looks so easy going in. When it's time to spin wrenches and screwdrivers, it suddenly becomes more complex than we ever expected. It becomes even more complicated whenever we begin a project without a plan. Your very first considerations must be facilities and budget. What can you afford and where will you carry it out? Who can you count on for help?

Believe it or not, most Mustang performance projects can be carried out in your home garage. For example, you can completely upgrade your suspension with basic hand tools, four jack stands, and a floor jack. You can even pull an engine in your driveway as long as you have access to an engine hoist. Engine hoists and other heavy equipment can be rented (or borrowed) short-term for engine swaps and rebuilds. Transmission and clutch jobs can also be performed using rented tools and equipment. The same is true for rear axle swaps and rebuilds.

One area we stress leaving to the professional is bodywork and paint. Bodywork and painting are art forms that require experience and patience. If this is something you want to try, we strongly encourage taking a shot at it. The worst that can happen are results you won't be pleased with. In which case, try again or look to a professional.

The greatest hazard with trying bodywork and painting yourself is the high cost of automotive finishes today. It can get very expensive, and you don't want to make a mistake with a $500 to $1,000 gallon of urethane paint. You also want to be safe with this very toxic paint, which means this is something you probably shouldn't do yourself in the home garage. You need proper ventilation, a legal paint booth, and conditions that prevent fallout in the paint.

Paint professionals today understand that it's no longer the good old days where you could roll a car out into the back yard and dribble some enamel on the steel. For one thing, you don't want an embarrassing Mustang – you want something that looks sharp. To get a high-quality paint job costs a lot of money not only because paint is expensive, but also because getting the surface perfect takes a lot of time. The best paint jobs aren't solely the work of a good painter, but people who understand the amount of sweat that goes into preparation. It takes countless hours to achieve a smooth finish, and this is with a good body to start with. If you have a daily beater that has seen better days, expect hundreds of hours in body prep before the paint goes on. Each hour invested adds significantly to the cost of a paint job.

On the positive side, there are also options that won't cost you much money if you do the prep work yourself. Maaco, Earl Sheib, 1-Day Paint & Body, and other economy painters offer you affordable options once the bodywork is finished. You can get into a nice looking paint job for under $1,000 if you do the bodywork yourself. To get there successfully, you must be patient and stay with the preparation until a perfect surface is achieved. If your budget allows for more than $1,000 for paint, shop local body shops to see who offers the best value for the money spent. Look at examples of their work; then make the right decision. When you're examining their work, visit with a lot of customers to get a good cross section of what you can expect. Don't just examine their showcase work.

If you're going to do the bodywork yourself, you may be surprised at how easy it is – or you might not. Bodywork is a talent that either comes naturally, or it doesn't. Seasoned body pros develop a feel for the vehicle's surface. They automatically sense irregularities and high and low areas in the surface and know instinctively what to do with them. It's an art form developed through experience. Most of the time, it's just plain persistence. That cold dogged determination that keeps us at something until it's perfect. Even when you're inclined to think it's "good enough," go back and give it more time and close inspection. You will be very surprised at what you'll find under a wide variety of lighting conditions. Most of us like to push it out in the sun for inspection. But, sunlight isn't the best light to inspect a car body with. Florescent lighting is the best light because it finds all kinds of imperfections you didn't know existed.

Bodywork occurs in layers, or in phases. If we're doing it right, we begin at the steel skin and begin with a solid foundation for our paint. We begin with filler in the shallow irregularities. We also begin by getting the steel itself as perfect as we can before laying down filler. Body filler should never be more than 1/8-inch thick at any point on the body. You should never use thick layers of filler to hide imperfections, as thick layers of filler tend to fail as outside temperatures change. If you use too much, the filler becomes apparent even under the best of paint jobs.

Good rule of thumb is to work the steel until you have a solid surface, then fill only as necessary. Use only a high-quality, two-part filler for best results. Never use body filler over rust. Ultimately, the rust is going to lift the filler and the paint, one way or the other. All rust should be completely removed before applying filler and primer.

If you have a choice between factory sheet metal and aftermarket, always go with factory sheet metal. Aftermarket sheet metal is nearly always thinner, lighter steel that doesn't have the structural integrity and corrosion protection of factory sheet metal. Aftermarket sheet metal isn't made to the strict quality standards we find with factory sheet metal. And, think about it this way. Would you want to risk your hide to anything less in a collision? Go with factory steel. If your budget won't reach new factory replacement sheet metal, go with a good, used fender, hood, door, hatch, or quarter panel.

There are a lot of misconceptions when it comes to primer and paint. Never use a primer/surfacer as a base coat over bare steel. There are two basic types of automotive primers. A self-etching epoxy primer/sealer is the best choice for a base coat finish that seals the steel. Use this as your paint's foundation. Not only does it etch the steel for good adhesion, it creates a user-friendly barrier between the paint and steel. Call it the necessary middleman between paint and steel, paint and plastic, and paint and urethane. When it's time to work the sheet metal, we use a primer/surfacer, which can be sanded and worked again and again as we massage the surface. Spot putty is used for minor surface irregularities. As a hard and fast rule, you should use body filler sparingly as you work the surface.

When it's time to choose paint, you do have a choice. Today, nearly all finishes are basecoat/clear coat urethane. We first lay down a basecoat color finish, which is dull. Then, we lay down the clear coat, which is the glossy topcoat we will live with. We can shoot the clear coat to a factory orange-peel finish. Or, we can shoot several layers of clear, then color-sand and rubout the clear to a dipped-in-clear finish. The choice is yours. The nice thing about color sanding and a rubout is the result. When we color sand the finish, it looks bad – rough and dull. But when we rub out the color-sanded clear coat, it brings the surface alive with a deep, rich finish we can feel proud of. This is something you really can do yourself.

If you have a piano-wire-tight budget, you can go with one of the economy painters and opt for additional coats of clear on top. This allows you to color sand and rub out the clear coat yourself when the job is finished. Don't be discouraged by a limited budget, because you do have options. You must first be willing to do some manual labor – it's prep time that'll make all the difference in your Mustang's paint job. Economy paint shops like Maaco, for example, lay down a nice paint job for the money. Your economy paint job stands out when you opt for those additional coats of clear, then do the color sand and rubout yourself. You'll be stunned at the result.

When you're doing the bodywork, don't forget the doorjambs and areas we don't see as often. Nothing flattens the spirits more than a nice paint job, and then opening the doors to a different color – or worse yet, gray primer. If you're going to paint your Mustang, do it all the way. And, if you're going to change the color, do it all the way. Late-model Mustangs have a body-color engine compartment. You will have to change the color there too. This means extensive disassembly of the vehicle in order to get it right. We're talking removing everything that is attached to the body. Sometimes, it's easier to live with the current color than it is to change everything. Think about this whenever you intend to change color. It may serve as incentive to leave the color alone.

If you're going to fit your Mustang with a body kit, or body bolt-ons, aim for the best quality out there. There are a lot of flimsy body kits and body bolt-ons on the market. We've seen rear deck spoilers retained with double-sided tape, and fiberglass work that left much to be desired. Aim high – you won't be sorry.

If you're contracting with a body shop to install your body kit or bolt-ons, make sure they're able to computer color-match the paint. And, be certain they know what they're doing. Few things look cheesier than body bolt-ons that don't match the paint, or worse – that fit horribly. When the paint color doesn't match, body bolt-ons look like an afterthought. And, if the paint has dust and dirt in it, it leaves the same impression. Your Mustang winds up looking cheap. People won't look at it with admiration, they'll laugh.

Body bolt-ons should be prepped and painted off of the body, not on. These components need to be worked and prepared away from the body. When it's time to paint them, they should be mounted on work stands or saw horses in a downdraft paint booth for best results. Ask your body shop if they intend to use a flex agent on urethane body parts. You need a finish that will flex with these flexible components. Otherwise, you can expect it to crack and peel.

When bodywork is complete and the body is painted, assembly is just a matter of finding time, and a place to do it. The home garage is a very doable place. So are some carports. But an apartment-building parking lot space is not. If you're thinking about a buddy's garage, be absolutely certain there's a solid commitment there. Few things are more depressing than having a car torn apart, only to learn you're going to have to move the car to a new location. Have a solid plan B for your Mustang just in case the unthinkable happens. Plan B sometimes includes renting a storage facility because there's nowhere else to assemble the car.

Truth is, there are some storage facilities where you can assemble the Mustang. Storage facility proprietors get mad whenever you make a huge mess. Sanding, grinding, engine fluids, and consuming untold amounts of space are what get you in trouble – and evicted. If you can keep a very low profile, you can probably pull it off.

Across the land, there is an untold amount of empty garage real estate available for a car project. Like the storage facility, you must keep a low profile there. No one wants their garage looking like Wally's Filling Station. How do you find this kind of real estate for your Mustang project? First, be honest. Second, run a classified advertisement in the newspaper, "Looking for garage space to store a car," and see where it goes. As the average age of our U.S. population gets higher, there will be more and more elderly couples with garage space to rent. They'll need the extra cash. You need the space for your Mustang. How much more convenient can it get?

Where else can you build a Mustang? Again, vacant garage space, often in your own neighborhood. Cruise around. Check it out. Don't be afraid to approach someone who apparently has a garage they never use. Of course, there's the ping-pong table they haven't used in 20 years, with a layer of dust to match. Convince them to push it, and the old leisure suits hanging on the garage door tracks, aside to make way for your Mustang. You can probably rent private garage space for $100 a month, depending on your area. When you consider a storage facility typically gets $200+ a month for garage-size space, depending on the area, a private garage is certainly cheaper. Some areas are more prone to storage-space sticker shock, like Man-

Successful car projects need a clean, dry workspace. Forget your apartment complex parking lot or the street in front of your house. Avoid the carport too. Full-scale car projects need plenty of protected garage space.

Your Mustang project should always begin with a plan. Professional quality work comes from following the plan and exercising discipline. Don't be tempted to wander off course because you're at a stopping point waiting on parts or services.

Whenever you're disassembling a Mustang, always catalog parts in separate, labeled containers. Don't kid yourself into believing you will remember where all those parts go if you throw them all into one box. We strongly suggest shooting images or video before/during disassembly. This makes it easier to put things back together.

hattan, Los Angeles, San Francisco, Seattle, Chicago, and Detroit. These areas are notoriously high when it comes to rented real estate of any kind. Keep this in mind when you're planning your Mustang project.

WORKING THE PLAN

It's a good idea to plan your work, and then work your plan. A plan executed in outline form will keep you on course as long as you're disciplined. If you're thinking about a whole car project, it must first begin with cataloged disassembly, with parts kept in labeled plastic containers properly stored. Bodywork and paint should always come first before any new parts are installed. Too many of us get this one backwards. We bolt on a new suspension, or install a crisp, new 5.0L crate engine, only to see it buried in body shop dust and paint over-spray. Remember, all of the dirty work comes first, then bolt on fresh parts.

The most important aspect of your Mustang project should be workmanship. It's one thing to go fast. It's quite another to look sharp and go fast. Be tasteful in your approach, planning for parts and components that work well together. So how do we get there? We get there by following a logical plan. Here's an example.

George's 20-Step, All-at-Once Mustang Project Outline

1. Evaluate the car, determine its needs, and make lists.
2. Disassemble the car, and properly store and catalog parts.
3. Take care of the bodywork and prep for paint.
4. Order needed body parts, and get it all painted.
5. Disassemble the engine and driveline, and determine its needs (while car is at body shop).
6. Order engine parts and do machine work.
7. Properly store the completed engine (plug and wrap).
8. Handle the transmission work, including clutch.
9. Rebuild driveshaft (new U-joints, yoke).
10. Rebuild rear axle, determine the desired axle ratio.
11. Inspect and replace the radiator as needed.
12. Order hoses and other engine-compartment-related parts.
13. Rebuild the suspension system (when body returns from shop).

14. Inspect and rebuild the braking system.
15. Restore and upgrade the interior.
16. Inspect the electrical system, replace/repair as necessary.
17. Install new exhaust system.
18. Evaluate your wheel and tire needs, measure carefully.
19. Perform a safety/reliability inspection on entire vehicle.
20. Spin the engine, be safe, have fun.

These are the basics. Modify this list any way you'd like. A checklist helps you organize, and it prevents you from missing anything important. Working your project successfully is a matter of discipline and know-how. Take each step and learn something from it. Tackle those intimidating projects and you'll gain new confidence in your abilities.

BUILDING YOUR MUSTANG

When you're evaluating and planning your Mustang project, you must first understand what you can personally handle and what you can't. Most car-building tasks are at least worth a try. You will quickly understand whether you can handle it or not. Most of the time, there's a learning curve with nearly anything we try the first time. And if you stumble the first time, go back and try again. Don't be discouraged when things go wrong. Seek the advice of a trusted professional, or a good friend who knows what they're doing. Sometimes, being shown how makes the going easier. And once you've done it once, it becomes easier to tackle again.

As we've already discussed, if your Mustang plan includes bodywork and painting, begin here first. Working body filler, primer, and paint creates dust and ugly fallout. Regardless of how careful you and the body shop are, dust and paint over-spray will find its way into everything. And, body shop dust and paint over-spray are one of the more frustrating clean-up tasks you will face. This is why bodywork and paint are best performed first. We cannot stress this enough because we've seen enthusiasts get it backwards all too many times.

Bodywork should always come first in any car project if you have the luxury of driving something else. Even if your Mustang is a daily cruiser, bodywork should happen first. This helps keep fresh mechanicals looking nice.

When your Mustang comes home from the body shop with fresh, expensive paint, your first goal needs to be protecting the finish. No matter what you think, you're going to nick and scratch the paint during assembly. Worse case scenario, you will dent the body with a part or tool. Your objective is to minimize the damage. Whenever you're not working on the Mustang, keep it covered with a good quality car cover. For optimum protection, you need a soft, paint-friendly car cover with padding. Not all car covers are paint friendly – some will actually scratch

When bodywork is underway, don't forget corrosion control. Always use a self-etching primer/sealer first over bare steel. Never use a regular primer/surfacer, sometimes called epoxy primer, on bare steel because it doesn't offer corrosion protection. When bodywork is complete, undercoat the wheel wells with black undercoating.

paint. And, if you live in a dusty environment, dust between the car cover and paint can do a lot of damage.

Padding protects the paint, should you accidentally bump into the body. Thin car covers don't afford you this protection. Vulnerable areas, like deck lids, rooflines, and hoods need thicker padding, like a cheap blanket borrowed from the hall closet. This protects these areas better, should an object fall from the rafters. Don't laugh, we saw this a lot

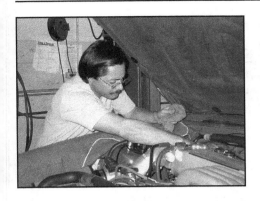

Fresh paint deserves the best protection you can give. Forget the fancy fender covers and thin membrane car covers. Protect your Mustang's body with heavy padding over the front fenders when you are working. When you are not working, cover the body with some kind of padding and a good car cover.

in Southern California during the Northridge earthquake in 1994. Falling fluorescent lights and objects stored across the rafters above damaged many vehicles. The more padding you can install between the car cover and body, the better. A good rule of thumb is to tie down everything located on top of those rafters immediately above your Mustang using bungee cords or rope. Sometimes, zip-ties work best because they're super tough and won't break. Safeguard your Mustang.

When you're working in the engine compartment, generously cover the front fenders. Forget the leather-clad fender covers with the Mustang logo to impress your friends. Opt for blankets or heavy terry cloth towels over those vulnerable fenders. When it's time to install the engine, protect the firewall from the transmission's tail shaft housing. A carelessly aimed engine/transmission will nick or gouge the firewall. You can count on it. Cover the firewall and cowl with towels and/or blankets to protect the paint. The same is true for freshly painted crossmembers and the like underneath. Being careful means not having to do it all over again, which consumes precious time.

Other areas needing protection include the rocker panels where you step into the vehicle. When you're working inside, cover the rocker panels

with blankets or towels. This protects the rocker panels from your legs and shoes. It also protects them from dropped tools. When you're working in the trunk or fold-down seat area, cover the tail panel and quarter panels with terry cloth towels or blankets to protect the vulnerable plastic finish.

As you assemble the Mustang with new tail lamps, composite headlamps and parking lamps, protect these expensive components as well with towels and blankets. It takes only a few seconds to prevent hours of damage correction or the replacement of expensive parts.

FROM THE BOTTOM UP

When we wash a Mustang, a good rule of thumb is to wash from the top down. Wash the roof first, then the hood and deck lid, then the sides. We do this because dirt and water run downhill. When we are building a Mustang, the opposite is true. We work from the bottom up. Begin assembly with the chassis and underpinnings. Install the rear axle, steering, and suspension components first. Then, the fuel system and other support equipment, like the exhaust system and brakes. The only exception to this rule might be the exhaust system. If you're installing a custom exhaust system, this needs to wait until the engine

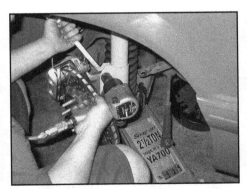

As a rule, suspension, brakes, and exhaust systems should always follow bodywork and paint. If you're thinking engine next, ask yourself how beneficial all that power is if you can't stop. Do the body, underpinnings, brakes – then engine and driveline. This approach helps keep you safe.

Always give your Mustang plenty of support whenever you're working underneath. A floor jack or bottle jack doesn't afford you the safety of a good set of jack stands.

and transmission are in place for fit reference. In fact, we can tell you no reputable exhaust shop will build and install an exhaust system without the engine and transmission in place.

We're often asked what type of suspension a person should buy. This depends on how your Mustang will be driven. Build based on how your Mustang will be driven most of the time. Daily drivers raced on the weekends need solid underpinnings. Because we're talking a daily driver, you need solid, yet friendly, underpinnings. Instead of rock-hard urethane bushings, you need polyurethane bushings, which have some "give" to their personality. Urethane bushings are rock hard, virtually void of flexibility. So are aluminum bushings. They're also noisy – they squeak and grunt, and they transmit a lot of road shock and noise. When you're selecting suspension bushings, remember this simple rule of thumb: Harder bushings make for a harsher and noisier ride. Flexible bushings give us a smoother, quieter ride. Harder bushings give us the superb handling. Flexible bushings sacrifice handling quality to some degree. The more flexible they are, the greater the sacrifice.

The reason we stress a kinder, gentler suspension with your daily driver is reality. Cruising down the freeway at speed affords us no joy when we're getting beaten to pieces by a harsh suspension system. If you're driving rough city streets, loaded with chuckholes and bumps, it only gets worse. There is some level of compromise between "stiff as a brick," and "soft as hot butter," when you're planning an effective suspension system.

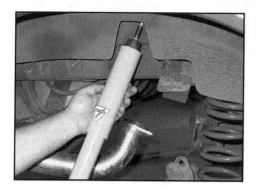

When you're shopping for shocks and struts, ride quality and handling meet in the middle. If you desire great handling, you're going to sacrifice ride quality. Road racing, even on the weekends, requires handling. This means you have to make a critical decision about which dynamic is more important. Everyone loves Koni shocks, but they're expensive and stiff, even when adjusted to the softest possible ride setting. When you're building something for the daily drive and weekend blast, you will likely have to compromise with an adjustable shock/strut that gives you a smooth ride for the commute and a stiffer ride for the road course.

Ride quality and handling go well beyond bushing stiffness. Shocks and struts are critical choices in both ride and handling quality. With each, it's about valving and bushing/seal design. Although these dampers afford us great handling, a set of racing level shocks and struts will beat you to pieces on a daily basis. This is why you need adjustable struts and shocks in any case. Koni is one of the best examples we can think of, but they don't come cheap. KYB shocks and struts are more affordable.

When it's time to go earn the bacon and you have adjustable shocks and struts, you may opt for a soft or medium stiffness. Saturday morning, you may crank the adjustment to stiff for better handling through the esses and apexes. Street Mustangs driven daily need adjustable suspension packages. So do avid racers. We want a suspension we can tune for conditions without having to swap springs, shocks, and sway bars.

The same consideration we afford bushings and shocks needs to go into sway-bar thickness – the thicker the bar, the harder the ride, especially in turns. Although there are super-thick sway bars out there, you don't always need one. Sometimes, sway bar selection depends on personal desire. You may try a sway bar and find it isn't thick enough for your handling pursuits. Or, you may have gone too far, suffering miserably

during the daily commute. Maximum Motorsports has an adjustable, tubular, torsion sway bar for the rear axle. You may adjust this torsion bar to dial in suspension performance levels and ride quality. This is one of the better suspension ideas we've seen anywhere. Now, if only someone would design an adjustable sway bar for the front.

Suspension component selection beyond bushings, shocks, and sway bars depends on extremes. How will your Mustang be driven at the extreme end of the scale? The daily commuter turned weekend racer needs control arms designed to take the weekend abuse. It also needs control arms that afford you the right kind of suspension geometry. Because there is a real difference between daily driving and weekend racing, you have to keep in mind what each will do to your Mustang.

Weekend racers need more negative front-end camber, for example, to handle the corners. Daily drivers needs less. Too much negative camber with the daily driver means excessive tire wear. Chances are good you have different tires and wheels for weekend racing. This also affects alignment issues. Alignment must be changed every time you go racing. Then, it must be changed back before you head for work Monday morning. This means you need an easy-to-align front suspension package,

The Mustang's stock suspension has a lot of room for improvement. Stamped steel control arms don't provide the strength necessary for the rigors of road racing. The geometry of a factory suspension system doesn't measure up either. Aftermarket suspension systems are designed to take abuse while keeping a consistent relationship between the tire and the road. With all of that out of the way, a good suspension also determines what the body and chassis will do as well.

beginning with a caster/camber adjustment plate. And this is the real beauty of the Fox-body Mustang. Because the struts are adjustable via a caster/camber plate, alignment is easy. Toe-in is a quick adjustment accomplished underneath at the tie-rod ends.

Believe it or not, you can do your own front-end alignment. All you need are the portable fixtures and measuring tools. You will make a lot of friends this way, once you have it down. A good idea is to align the front end, then roll the vehicle forward and backward, then check the alignment again. It can and will change. You will develop a natural feel for alignment as you practice. Late-model Mustang front-end alignment is easy to accomplish.

When you've journeyed past springs, shocks, struts, control arms, and sway bars, there is still more to consider. Because Fox-body Mustangs are unit-body vehicles, there is a lot of room for improvement in the structural integrity department. For example, 1979-93 Mustangs have a serious lacking underneath – this is a weak platform in need of stiffening. Subframe connectors and bolt-on X-frames provide substantial support for hatchbacks, convertibles, and coupes alike. In 1994-95, Ford did a good job of stiffening the Fox-4 platform. But, even in 1994-95, there is room for improvement.

Subframe connectors are mandatory for any 1979-95 Mustang that's going road racing, or even drag racing. You would be surprised at how much body flex there is without subframe connectors. Subframe connectors must be welded in place, which means carpeting and sound deadening must come out to prevent fire during the welding process. Welding should be performed well away from fuel lines. Before you weld in subframe connectors, you want to check door fit and closure operation. If door closure isn't smooth, you need to get the doors properly adjusted first. This is very important. Doors that are out of adjustment will stay out of adjustment when the subframe connectors and gussets are welded in place. Support the vehicle at the suspension members when you're welding in subframe connectors. You

want the vehicle resting naturally when subframe connectors are welded in.

Another area you may not have considered is over stiffening. We have seen enthusiasts so determined to make their Mustang platform stiff that they installed too many chassis stiffening devices. You may not see the consequences in this, but it can make your ride intolerable if you're building a Mustang for the daily commute or weekend racing. Again, it's that delicate balance between ride comfort and handling. When a platform is too stiff, there is no "give" in the body, which absorbs road shock in the same way the suspension does. Your Mustang body's flexibility is one factor in ride comfort. It gives with the irregularities in the road. When a Mustang body is stiff, the human body inside takes up the road shock instead of the vehicle. When you drive a Mustang every day, there has to be compromise when it comes to your driving comfort, or you won't enjoy your driving experience.

BRAKES

When suspension and handling issues are out of the way, and you've established a level of satisfaction with your decision-making, it's time to think about stopping. Brakes are an integral part of the handling experience on the track – and off. Naturally, you're going to want the best brakes for the money. Ever since its introduction in April of 1964, the Mustang has always suffered from braking shortcomings from the factory. Back then, Mustangs had standard four-wheel drum brakes – and without power assist! In showroom stock condition, they were at best, unsafe.

In the early 1970s, Mustangs began to see more and more front disc brakes, which was a big plus. The 1974-78 Mustang II had standard front disc brakes, with rear drum brakes. For the many years spanning 1979-93, the Mustang had decidedly small front disc brakes, and rear drum brakes that wouldn't stop a go-cart.

In 1994-95, Ford gave the Mustang what it long needed: four-wheel power disc brakes. These brakes, all by themselves, would be a welcome upgrade for

It is our opinion that you can never have too much brake. Stock factory disc brakes do the job quite well for street use. With carbon-metallic pads, factory disc brakes do the job better – but noisier. High-performance brake pads are noisy by nature, and they do their best work when they're hot. Large aftermarket disc brakes, like these from Baer and JMC Motorsports, do the job effectively, but also with noise. Not to mention that they're expensive. Again, remember that balance between the street and racetrack; you have to determine what's most important and be committed to that idea.

any 1979-93 Mustang. In fact, this is a good upgrade for any 1979-93 Mustang if you're looking for a cheap way to get into four-wheel disc brakes. Salvage yards and the aftermarket are full of answers.

Braking, like suspension, depends on how you intend to drive the car. Weekend racers need heavy-duty brakes with race pads. Strictly street drivers need good brakes, but nothing on the caliber of what we see in racing. But, daily drivers can greatly benefit from installing Baer, Wilwood, or JMC Motorsports disc brakes on all four corners. Disc brakes dissipate heat faster, so they don't suffer from fade during hard braking, like drum brakes do. If you're building a 1979-93 Mustang, you're going to need better brakes, even on the street. For 1979-93 Mustangs, a good set of high-performance aftermarket disc brakes at all four corners will make a huge difference in braking effectiveness.

Think of braking upgrades as a life insurance policy for your Mustang. Each time they keep you out of an accident, they pay for themselves. The same is true for a good suspension and tires.

Each time you steer out of an accident, these upgrades pay for themselves. This is why investing in suspension and brakes is so important to your Mustang project. Suspension, brakes, wheels, and tires should be your first priority in the car-building process.

Brake upgrades range anywhere from slotted and drilled rotors, to racing brake pads and linings, to large aftermarket disc brakes. Your budget and driving expectations should determine your choice. Daily drivers that are weekend racers need higher-end disc brakes. Baer's Claw brake systems are great street and race brakes. They keep you out of trouble en route to the office, and they're very effective on the racetrack.

Wheel and tire selection also needs to be an integral part of your planning. The choice, again, depends on how you'll be using the car. Weekend racers should have two sets of wheels and tires – one set for street driving, and another race specific set for racing. Racing mandates softer rubber for good contact patch adhesion. Street driving also calls for softer rubber if handling is a paramount issue. But, if your budget calls for a longer lasting tire, you want a harder rubber compound. Harder rubber compounds last longer because they're tougher.

While you're selecting wheels, think about wheel size and fitment issues. Not all wheels out there will fit your Fox-body Mustang. It's a good idea to measure your wheel wells, brake backing plate or axle flange location, and the like before plunking down the cash. Sometimes, it's best to put wheel/tire selection off until last. This way, you know exactly what you're dealing with in terms of fitment.

Mustang front disc brakes from 1979-93 look like this, with a four-lug bolt pattern and not much in the way of friction material or calipers. You can step up to five-lug rotors fore and aft on these Mustangs. Mix in good, slotted rotors and carbon metallic-pads to improve braking dramatically.

POWERTRAIN

Likely one of the most important aspects of a Mustang project is the engine, transmission, and rear axle: the powertrain. How will you build your engine? What kind of camshaft and induction should you choose? How about headers and exhaust system? Five-speed or six-speed? Automatic overdrive or stick? What gear ratio to choose: 3.08:1, 3.27:1, 3.55:1, 3.73:1, or 4.11:1? How far should you go?

Transmissions

Transmission selection should be based on how the car will be driven most. If you're going to do a lot of stop-and-go driving, seriously consider an AOD or AODE. Few things are more exhausting than creeping along in traffic, riding the clutch, touching the brake, working the clutch, and touching the brake some more.

If your tough city slicker commuter vehicle is going to be a weekend racer, there's a lot you can do with the AOD and AODE transmissions. LenTech builds an AOD or AODE to meet your needs, whether your Mustang is a daily commuter or die-hard racer. It's through LenTech's research and development efforts that we have a manageable AOD/AODE we can live with under virtually any conditions. Just tell LenTech what your needs are and they will build a transmission for your application.

If you love the open road, a road course, or seriously working the clutch during the daily commute, you have transmission choices out there. The World Class T-5 five-speed does a great job in weekday/weekend pavement duty. If you're going racing, and plan on racing it hard, the Tremec TKO is a good, comfortable step upward in terms of reliability. It's an outstanding transmission when durability counts.

Earlier, we mentioned the T-56 six-speed transmission. The T-56 has a lot of "wow!" potential. However, is it something your Mustang will actually need? Bear in mind that the T-56 is a manual transmission with two overdrive ranges. Having two overdrive ranges matters only when you intend to do a lot of open road driving that varies a great deal, such as mountain driving. Another issue to consider with the T-56 is fit. Transmission tunnel clearance is a problem with 1979-93 Mustangs, and you'll have to modify the tunnel to make way for the T-56. In 1994-95, the tunnel is designed more like it was meant for a T-56. Besides tunnel clearance, you also need to think about the transmission crossmember with a T-56, because its mounting location is different. We're waiting to see if the aftermarket answers this call with late-model Mustangs. It already has with classic Mustangs – you can purchase a T-56 crossmember for classic Mustangs from JMC Motorsports in San Diego, California.

Rear-End Gears

Regardless of what kind of driving you're going to do with your Mustang, axle ratio will probably be your easiest decision. Whatever transmission you choose, it will likely have an overdrive range. This means you can cheat with the axle ratio, opting for 3.55:1, 3.73:1, or 4.11:1 gears. If you like weekend racing, you're going to want 3.73:1 or 4.11:1 gears. These ranges allow you serious get up and go in lower gear ranges, without suffering wear and tear and poor fuel economy in the process. These axle ratios are especially good if you do a lot of city driving.

The open road at speed demands something less aggressive – 3.08:1 or 3.27:1 axle ratios. At 70 mph, you want a conservative engine speed of around 2,000 rpm. When you opt for lower axle ratios, like 3.73:1 or 4.11:1, engine speed at 70 mph will be closely to 3,000 rpm and higher. Though 3,000 rpm will not hurt the engine, it will adversely affect fuel economy.

We answer these "sometimes tough" questions by, again, asking ourselves how the car will be driven most often. Daily drivers call for one strategy. Weekend racers and daily drivers call for another. Full-time racers call for quite another. When we're building a driver Mustang that does weekend race duty, we have to consider how building that car affects us daily.

Engines

We all want powerful small-block engines. There's the desire for snappy on-ramp performance entering the freeway, and we want something powerful for weekend racing. Achieving a good compromise between racing and street driving should be our goal for the weekday driver.

However you build your Mustang's engine, reliability should be your first priority. We want a good combination of parts that will make a cohesive marriage. Focus your energy and cash on the

engine's bottom end. Build a solid, reliable bottom end that will serve you well for 100,000 miles. If you have a tight budget, take comfort in knowing the factory C8OE rod forging will stand up to abuse. These rods can stand a 6,200-rpm blast in a naturally aspirated engine, and good, constructive modifications to these rods to make them stronger will save you money and offer you reliabili-

ty. Hypereutectic pistons are an affordable alternative to forged. They're also quieter. If your game plan includes nitrous and/or supercharging, forged pistons become mandatory.

When you're considering nitrous or supercharging, forget longevity. Huffing a lot of air into a small block to achieve that magic 50 to 150 bonus horsepower will cost you engine life. Every time we

Engine planning involves knowing what works together and what doesn't. For example, your aftermarket cylinder heads need to be compatible with your headers. The headers you now have on your Mustang may not be compatible with the aftermarket cylinder heads you're thinking of using. Header fitment issues also include spark-plug clearance and compatibility with your Mustang's exhaust system. If you're thinking of removing the catalytic converters, keep federal and state laws in mind. It's probably illegal in your state to remove the catalysts.

Choosing a camshaft requires a lot of research. Crane and Comp Cams, for example, make camshaft selection easier by telling you what to expect from each profile. Remember, too, that even though a camshaft grinder can tell you what to expect, not all Mustang electronic engine controls are created equal. For example, 1994-95 Mustangs are more temperamental when it comes to aftermarket cams. A radical cam may not idle well in a 1994-95 Mustang. Sometimes, the engine won't run at all.

Good engine building calls for a qualified machine shop. Once an engine is completely disassembled, it takes the talents of a good machinist to get the foundation right before the build-up. Without precision machine work, all the assembly experience and talent is meaningless.

Do you need this much rod down under? Will you really need a steel or billet crankshaft, or can you get by with a high nodular iron piece? Learn to recognize overkill in your planning. Plan for the outer limits of your expected driving and use, but be honest with yourself in your planning.

When you're shopping for stroker kits, do your homework. Not all pistons are compatible with certain stroker kits. We don't always find this out until assembly begins. Ideally, your stroker kit will include pistons from the same supplier, who has built an engine or two with the kit. This is where proper planning will keep you in the clear.

How far do you build your engine? Daily drivers and weekend racers can benefit from structural integrity. This is a block girdle, which gives the main bearings strength, but not all engines need one. You only need one of these when you're spinning the crank well above 6,000 rpm, or using a power adder like a blower or nitrous.

blow squeeze through our 5.0, we're blowing the life right out of it. This happens because we're raising combustion temperatures significantly. Nitrous is very hard on pistons, rings, and bearings. The same is true with supercharging.

While we're down under, it's important to understand what kind of crankshaft will work best for your Mustang. Steel and billet crankshafts are only necessary when you're going to push your engine to its limits. For example, a race only engine getting fed nitrous and/or supercharging should get a steel or billet crank.

Nodular-iron crankshafts are more than adequate for the driver and weekend racer. Iron cranks are even acceptable for the drag racer, depending on what you intend to throw at them. Again, whenever you will be putting extraordinary forces on a crankshaft, such as nitrous, supercharging, or endurance type racing, you're going to need a steel crank. Thing is, too many of us get this one wrong. We buy too much crank – or too little.

Too much camshaft lift in a freeway commuter will hurt reliability because high-lift camshafts (greater than .500-inch lift) beat the daylights out of the valvetrain. Valvesprings, valves, and rocker arms suffer when lift increases. In daily use, they wear more quickly, making for more frequent maintenance.

Running a solid mechanical roller camshaft means you'll have to adjust the valves often. When you consider having to pull the upper intake manifold every time you have to adjust valves, running a mechanical roller doesn't make much sense, does it?

Choosing the right camshaft depends largely on your needs. Weekend racers need an aggressive camshaft, but something you can tolerate on a daily basis. For example, 1994-95 5.0L Mustangs have a narrow window of operation when it comes to camshafts. Choose too radical a camshaft and your 1994-95 5.0L engine will sputter, stall, and refuse to idle. The same is true for 1986-88 Mustangs with the speed-density system. Only a stock camshaft will work with the speed-density system. On 1988-95 Mustangs that have speed-density systems, changing the camshaft means an upgrade to mass-air metering, but that's another chapter entirely.

Our basic message with engine planning is to be realistic in your expectations. There are no low-buck 500-horsepower small-blocks. If you're seeking plenty of torque without spending a fortune, consider a stroker kit you can live with on the street and on the track. Still, you should avoid stuffing too much displacement into your 5.0L small-block. A great compromise stroker kit is the 331-ci stroker, which gives you a substantial improvement in torque, without pushing the limits of the block. The 347-ci stroker kit, depending on the kit, is also an excellent choice because it brings you greater torque, without spending all that much more on the buildup. Building a stroker, depending on the kit, doesn't cost much more than a stock displacement build.

Planning your engine build includes choosing the right machine shop. You may be able to assemble your engine, but you're going to need a seasoned machinist with engine-building skills. Crankshaft journals need precision machining. Connecting rods need their large and small ends worked. Blocks need to be checked, bored, and honed. Crankshafts, rods, and pistons have to be dynamic balanced for smooth operation. These are elements you need to think about going

in. They consume time – and cash.

Choose a machine shop based not on price, but clientele. A hole-in-the-wall machine shop that looks like a federal disaster relief zone isn't a wise choice, even if they're going to charge you half the price. When you're looking for a machine shop, ask yourself – who does business with them? A machine shop that has a large racer clientele isn't messing around. If they have a sizable racer customer base, they build good stuff. Racers don't have time for failed engines or return trips to the machine shop with broken engine parts. A reputable machine shop understands this – their goal is to please racers.

When you are planning for cylinder heads, remember two things – chamber size and piston dome design. Few things are more deflating than a chamber that's too large and compression that's too low. Talk this over with your engine builder before buying parts.

Through the years, we've been taught to rebuild our transmissions, but economics have changed with some transmissions. The Tremec T-5 five-speed transmission costs little to get into, at just over $1,000, but it costs at least $800 to rebuild one. If your T-5 is worn out, replace it and add a Centerforce Dual-Friction clutch for best results.

Reputable machine and engine-build shops have a teardown area, a machine area, and a clean room for engine assembly. A clean room is typically white, well lit, and completely separate from the teardown and machine areas. Seasoned, successful machine shops understand the hazards of having dust, dirt, and grit around engines they

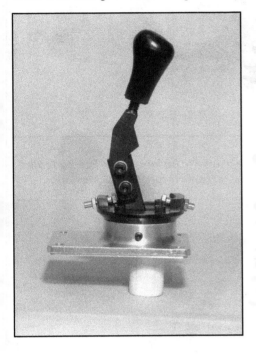

The aftermarket has brought us great shifters for the T-5 and T-56 transmissions. We like the B&M Ripper shifter, or the Pro 5.0 piece shown here. This should be a solid part of your planning because you're going to have to live with it every day and every time you hit the track.

Axle ratio should always enter into your planning. Street drivers can live peacefully with ratios ranging from 3.27:1 to 3.73:1. Weekend racers will need ratios courting 4.11:1 or lower. Much depends on your Mustang's primary duty.

are assembling. Dust, dirt, and grit can ruin an engine in short order. You would be amazed at what dust can do to new bearings in a matter of miles.

When it's time for engine assembly, you want the best parts. Avoid cheap gasket sets. Spend the money here for best results. You don't have to run racing gaskets unless you're racing. But, using a good grade of gasket will save you grief down the road. Fel-Pro gaskets are, undoubtedly, the best for performance applications. Another outstanding gasket company is SCE in Lancaster, California.

Engine hardware should always be new, and it should be the best you can afford. ARP fasteners, for example, are expensive. But, they offer you unequalled fastener integrity. ARP is top drawer because they also make aerospace fasteners. Folks who build and fly aircraft rely on ARP, so if you're going racing, step up to ARP. If ARP fasteners are too costly, see your Ford dealer for head and main bearing cap bolts. Combination daily drivers and weekend racers can get away with stock fasteners. These are the details you need to think about when planning your engine.

Mustang mechanicals, like the engine and transmission, should be worked while the body is being massaged and painted. Because bodywork and paint both take a lot of time, this gives you time to properly plan the powertrain. The completed engine should be stored with all 16 valves at rest (rocker arms loose) to prevent valve sticking if the engine sits for a while. While the engine sits, you need to oil the cylinders every three months to prevent corrosion and ring sticking. You may use WD-40 or a lightweight oil to keep the bores happy.

Let's Step Inside...

Your planning should also include what you want the interior to be. We have to plan here because the interior is where you're going to spend most of your time. If you're on the left side of crazy, you're probably thinking about a killer sound system. Maybe, you're thinking, "what's to plan?" Our answer?

Plenty. Powerful sound systems need electricity – lots of electricity. This means you need a charging system and battery that can keep up. Depending on the sound system, you may need two batteries, connected in series, to stand up to the load. Dual batteries need a powerful alternator in the 120-200-amp range to keep them charged. Sometimes, two alternators are needed to keep up with the power demand.

With important issues, like sound systems, out of the way, there's more to plan inside your Mustang. Instrumentation is a very important consideration. Mustangs come from the factory with a nice compliment of instruments – speedometer, tachometer, fuel, oil pressure, voltage, and coolant temperature. The aftermarket industry has brought us windshield pillar and dash-mounted gauges for additional engine vitals, like exhaust gas temperature, supercharger boost, transmission sump temperature, and more.

Whenever you're shopping for gauges, choose an electric oil pressure gauge rather than a mechanical oil pres-

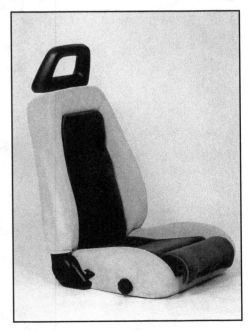

Probably one of the most comfortable Mustang seats ever was the 1985-86 GT bucket seats, with their red piping, soft upholstery, side bolsters, and adjustable head rests. You can install these seats in any 1979-93 Mustang.

sure gauge that gets its signal from fluid pressure. The reason we suggest this is the risk of line failure and one heck of an oily mess when it happens. We won't even get into what happens to an engine with zero oil pressure. Electric instruments are less prone to failure.

Seating is yet another issue that needs planning. You may find the factory Mustang seats to be quite comfortable. And this is certainly true from 1985-up. Sporting adjustable side bolsters, lumbar, and good looks, Ford seating served us quite well from 1985-95. The aftermarket brings us a wealth of comfortable seating for Fox-body Mustangs. If you decide to go with an aftermarket seat, your greatest challenge will be upholstering the rear seat to match. Most of the aftermarket seat companies have the material for that job.

There's plenty of aftermarket instrumentation available for late-model Fox-body Mustangs. The example shown here is from Saleen Autosports for 1994-95 Mustangs.

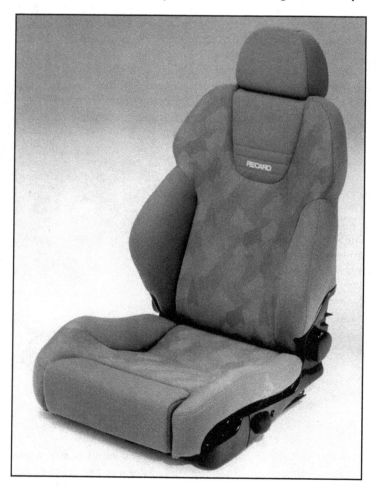

There are many aftermarket bucket seats out there for 1979-95 Mustangs. If your budget allows, shop wisely for these, and then upholster the rear seat to match.

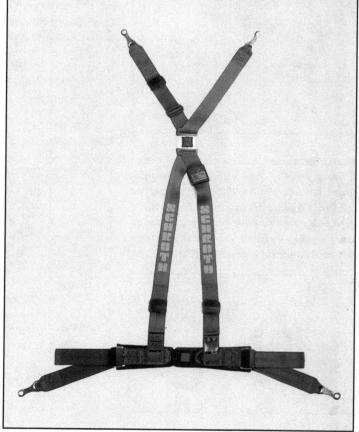

Think safety in your planning. Never disable air bags, and always use the best restraint system possible. Three-point systems work best for daily drivers where you are in and out of the vehicle a lot. Four-point restraint systems, like this one, just don't work well for daily drivers.

ENGINE BASICS

The heart of any Fox-bodied Mustang is its powerplant – that steaming, teeming, breathing mass of iron, steel, and aluminum beneath the hood that determines your Mustang's personality. The 5.0L High Output V-8 is the heart of most 1982-95 Mustangs, which makes it easy to understand and build. Because Ford built this engine for so many years, there is a wealth of cores and parts out there for your engine project. So what to do first?

First, evaluate the engine you have. Has it been rebuilt before? Is it a good foundation? A good foundation would be a 5.0L roller block with the good E5AE or E7AE heads that has never been apart. Perhaps you're doing a 1983-84 Mustang GT with its original flat-tappet 5.0L-4V engine. Time to consider a better foundation you can grow with – such as a 1985-up roller tappet engine that has never been apart. At this point, you can package your 5.0L High Output engine anyway you'd like.

The reason we stress using an engine that has never been rebuilt before is machining limitations. Your best foundation is a standard bore block that needs a .030-inch overbore, a mild decking, and modest line honing. If you begin with a .030-inch overbore block, the best you can hope for is .040-inch overbore. Although a lot of builders don't mind taking a 5.0L block to .060-

inch oversize, it's courting trouble to do so. The .060-inch overbore often leads to hotter engine operating temperatures and the risk of going into the water jackets. Regardless of what anyone will tell you, going .060-inch over is a bad idea with small-block Fords.

Along with a standard bore, you want a block with solid integrity. It needs to be a crack-free casting with a level deck. If the engine has experienced severe overheating or a catastrophic failure, there may be serious casting flaws (cracks and warping) you'll want to steer clear of. You want a good, virgin block that is well seasoned, but has never been machined. In fact, this is actually better than a brand-new block because it has the benefit of having been hot on a regular basis through regular operation. The cycling of hot and cold over the miles and through the years helps "season" the iron. Everything settles, including the cylinder walls, making the molecular structure more, well, ironclad. This is the kind of block you want for your engine build project.

DISASSEMBLY

Anytime you disassemble an engine, it's always unknown what you will find inside. If the engine has had a seemingly normal service life, you can expect normal wear patterns throughout. Because

5.0L H.O. engines are high-performance powerplants, many of them have seen abuse. Expect to see hammered rod bearings and journals. Also expect to see evidence of compression pressure and combustion gasses past the rings across the lands and piston skirt, especially if there has been nitrous use or supercharging.

First, we suggest the use of a good engine stand capable of supporting at least 1,000 pounds, with four wheels, not three. Three-wheel engine stands are prone to tipping. Mount the assembled engine on the stand using Grade 8 bolts in the interest of safety. Drain all fluids from the engine and properly recycle them at a recycling station. Remove the block drain plugs on each side to purge the water jackets of all coolant. It's a good idea to position a drip pan beneath the engine to protect your floor and keep mess to a minimum.

Rebuilding a 5.0L engine mandates having the right hand tools. You're going to need a complete SAE and metric 3/8- and 1/2-inch drive socket set that includes a breaker bar, speed handle, deep well sockets, universals, extensions, ratchets, and the like. We suggest investing in a quality 1/2-inch drive torque wrench. The most affordable type is the beam type with a needle indicator. The best type is a breakaway that clicks when the proper torque is achieved. Your neighborhood Sears store is the best place for quality Craftsman tools with a lifetime warranty.

A complete set of open and box-end wrenches in both metric and SAE sizes is suggested. Common and Phillips screwdrivers of all sizes is a good next step. Channel locks, vice grips (Vice Grip brand), pliers, diagonal cutting pliers, duckbill pliers, and needle-nosed pliers are vital to any toolbox. Thickness gauges and wire thickness gauges round out the basics. A large screwdriver or pry bar helps for stubborn pieces that won't come apart.

A PLACE TO WORK

Anytime you're going to embark on an engine rebuild, you need a clean, dry place to work. A cluttered garage will frustrate you. A carport exposes your work to the elements. An apartment parking lot or assigned space is out of the question. Your workshop should include a well-lighted workbench with a sizable vice. The workbench should be strong enough to support the weight of a cylinder block and heads, for example. We stress a clean environment because nothing kills a fresh engine more quickly than dirt, no matter how small. Dust and dirt in the air will score freshly machined surfaces quickly. This means you need to keep your engine covered, no matter how long you will be away from it.

The easiest path to clean parts is a qualified machine shop that can get those parts hospital clean in short order. While you're at it, shop for the best machine shop, not necessarily the cheapest. Check around and see who does the best work in your area. Choose on the side of quality, not necessarily cost. When you have disassembled your engine, take each of the engine's components to the machine shop and have the shop inspect and measure everything before buying parts. A good machine shop will measure all components first before the expense and wasted effort of cleaning. Each cylinder bore should be checked for taper from top to bottom, then oversize determined. The line bore across the main bearing saddles should

be checked next. Then the decks need to be checked for trueness. With each of these critical points measured, we're ready to determine a course of action.

If you have a standard bore block, it should be bored to either .020- or .030-inch oversize. Line bore is a matter of main bearing saddle alignment and size. Line boring accomplishes much the same thing reconditioning the connecting rods does. It resizes the main saddles and caps. Most blocks will have a line

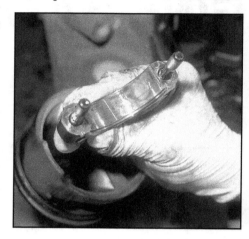

Close examination of pistons and rods during this 5.0-liter engine teardown shows abuse. These rod bearings have been hammered hard by nitrous. Piston ring and land damage tells us the same thing – nitrous abuse. These pistons are trashed. Rods need close inspection, but they'll probably be thrown away. When in doubt, throw them out.

Before any parts are cleaned, measure everything – cylinder bores, crank journals, block deck, and more. Also, check the cylinder head and block castings for cracks.

bore within specs, and line boring is rarely necessary. Most will need only a line honing to ensure main bearing stability.

Block decks typically need to be milled .005 to .010 inch, and only if there is evidence of warping. Remember that when you mill the deck, you're affecting piston deck height and compression. You're also making the deck weaker. So

All freeze and oil-galley plugs should be removed before the block and heads go into the cleaner. Call this a heavy-duty dishwasher for engine parts. All passages are thoroughly cleaned with a bottle-brush; then the castings are washed again.

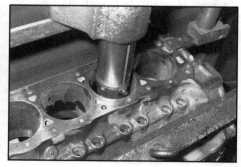

Each cylinder is bored .025-inch to make way for the .030-inch oversize pistons. Then, each cylinder is honed another .005-inch to achieve a crosshatch pattern for oil control and ring seating.

keep your milling to the absolute minimum.

Another machining step we suggest is tapping the front oil galley plugs where press-in plugs are used from the factory. Screw-in plugs offer a greater margin of safety. Also, when the block is fresh and ready for assembly, always opt for brass freeze plugs, which are less likely to corrode.

Oil galley plugs at the front of the block should be replaced with screw-in plugs. The factory uses press-in oil-galley plugs, but screw-in plugs are safer.

Cam bearings should always be removed prior to block cleaning and machining. New cam bearings should be installed before short-block assembly.

Ditch those steel freeze plugs and press in brass ones instead. Brass freeze plugs won't corrode and rot through.

UNDERSTANDING THE CRANKSHAFT

The crankshaft is your engine's backbone. The crankshaft takes the reciprocating motion of eight pistons and connecting rods, and turns this element into rotary motion and torque. To do this effectively, a crankshaft has to work hand in hand with eight pistons and connecting rods with smooth precision. To get there, we need a balanced assembly where the crankshaft counterweights are exactly the same weight as the piston and connecting rod assemblies. When we consider dynamic balancing, all elements must be included – pistons, rods, rings, bearings, and even engine oil.

When we speak of internally and externally balanced engines, we're addressing how the engine's moving parts are dynamically balanced. Internally balanced means the crankshaft and pistons are balanced separately from the harmonic balancer and flywheel. We can balance the crank, rods, and pistons independently of the flywheel and harmonic balancer. Externally balanced means the flywheel, harmonic balancer, crankshaft, pistons, and rods are all balanced as a single, unified assembly. Change the flywheel and you change the balance. Small-block Ford engines are externally balanced. This means we need to have the flywheel and harmonic balancer present for dynamic balancing. This doesn't mean we can't replace the flywheel or harmonic balancer later. When that happens, we disturb the dynamic balance. However, we don't disturb it enough for it to be of any consequence.

Prior to 1982, all small-block Fords had a 28-ounce offset balance because they had lighter rods and pistons. From 1982-up, with the debut of the 5.0L High Output engines, these engines were 50-ounce offset due to heavier rods and pistons. This means you must use a 50-ounce offset flywheel and balancer with a 1982-up 5.0L engine. Use a 28-ounce balancer and flywheel and vibration will become your greatest frustration. By the same token, use a 50-ounce balancer and flywheel on a 28-ounce offset engine and you will get the same unwanted vibration.

Ford used a number of harmonic balancers over the small-block Ford's production life. From 1962-69, a three-bolt balancer was used. In that period, there was a narrow balancer for 221, 260, and 289-2V and -4V engines. The 289 High Performance engine, produced from 1963-67, received a wide three-bolt balancer, plus a slide-on counterweight. In 1968-69, 289 and 302 engines received a wider three-bolt balancer that was marked differently than the narrow 1962-67 balancer. The 1969 Boss 302 had a wide, three-bolt balancer that's similar to the 289 High Performance balancer, but it's not the same piece.

Beginning in 1970, small-block Fords received a four-bolt balancer that was used well into the early 1980s. The 1970 Boss 302 balancer is just as odd as the 1969 balancer because it was produced for one year only. It's wide, like the 1969 Boss 302 and 1963-67 289 High Performance balancers, but with four bolt holes. With the onset of serpentine belt drive in 1979 came a new generation of four-bolt balancers for 5.0L and 5.8L engines.

Crankshaft machine work should always include chamfering the oil holes, which improves oil flow across the bearing and journal surfaces. This is performed after the journals are machined undersize, but before journal polishing and dynamic balancing.

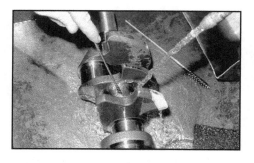

A crankshaft must be thoroughly cleaned inside and out as shown. We clean the crank before machine work, then several times afterward to eliminate any chance of dirt and debris contacting the journals.

Here, we're dynamic balancing the crankshaft to match the corresponding weight of the piston/rod assemblies. Because the 5.0-liter engine is externally balanced, the flywheel and harmonic balancer are included in the spin. Neither is shown here, but both were installed later. We remove metal from the counterweights to match the lightest piston/rod assembly.

Connecting Rods

The small-block Ford has an unmatched reputation for reliability because Ford has steadily improved this engine ever since its introduction in 1962. When Ford went to work developing the 5.0L High Output V-8 in the 1980s, it put more metal into the tried and proven C8OE rod forging first used in 1968 in the 302. Although the basic forging number hasn't changed much, the rod has become thicker at the large end. The 5.0L connecting rod is the best factory small-block Ford rod produced, with the exception being the C3AE Boss 302 rod or Le Mans rods for the older 289. The C8OE rod forgings are plentiful and cheap, which is a bonus. Fit this rod with ARP bolts and you have a tough, dependable connecting rod capable of 6,500 rpm.

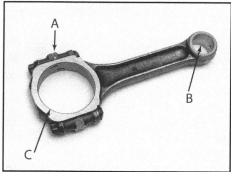

This is a typical 5.0-liter C8OE connecting rod. We recondition the rod by cutting the mating surfaces of the rod and cap (A). The small end of the rod (B) is rarely disturbed, especially with press-fit pins. The cap and rod are married using new bolts, and then the inside diameter (C) is bored (resized) to fit the bearing and journal.

Piston Selection

Piston selection is critical to the type of driving you intend to do. Most 5.0L High Output V-8 engines have been fitted with forged pistons from the factory. But here's something important you need to know about pistons. Forged pistons expand at a different rate than cast and hypereutectic. Because forged pistons expand more as the engine warms up, they mandate greater piston-to-cylinder wall clearances. This means piston noise when the engine is cold. If this doesn't bother you, and you can afford forged pistons, then specify forged pistons.

Hypereutectic pistons will work well for street engines because they withstand the high revs regular cast pistons sometimes will not. Hypereutectic pistons are cast pistons with high silicon content for strength. Where this gets shaky is when we opt for nitrous or supercharging. Cast and hypereutectic pistons will not stand up to nitrous or supercharging.

Lubrication

Your engine's oiling system should be an integral part of your engine build plan. Plan on a high-volume oil pump, chamfering the crankshaft journal oil holes, improving oil return by cleaning up the drain-back holes and painting the lifter

valley and cylinder heads, and installing a windage tray to keep oil where it belongs at high revs. These are all easy to do and cost very little to ensure engine life.

When we chamfer the oil holes in the crankshaft journals, we're providing a smoother passage to the area between the crank journal and bearing. This gives the bearing and journal more oil volume, and less chance of flow disruption. Chamfering the crankshaft journal oil holes also provides a smoother path for the oil to the journal and bearing. Chamfering should be performed by your machine shop during the crankshaft machining process. Chamfering does cost extra, but it's worth every penny.

When we clean up the oil drain-back holes in the cylinder block, we're actually chamfering them. Chamfering smooths the drain hole edges, allowing oil to return to the oil pan smoothly and quickly. If you want rapid oil return, we suggest grinding the entire lifter valley and cylinder head oil flow areas smooth for even greater oil return flow. When we grind the oil return areas, we remove the rough sand cast surfaces that impede oil return. You can accomplish much the same mission by priming these areas, and filling in the rough surfaces. This allows for smoother oil return flow.

Windage trays and baffled oil pans also do a great job of keeping engine oil where it belongs. The windage tray keeps sump oil out of the crankshaft's windage, hence the name. With a windage tray, the spinning crankshaft doesn't draw oil up out of the pan at high revs. When we have a baffled oil pan designed for either road racing or drag racing, oil stays where it belongs at high revs – around the oil pump pick-up. A road racing oil pan has baffles and doors that close in hard corners, keeping oil around the pick-up. Drag racing pans are more deep sump pans that hold a lot of oil. During racing, the deep pan keeps plenty of oil around the pick-up. If you're going either road racing or drag racing, you need to think about what type of oil sump you will need.

Cylinder Heads

Factory cylinder head choices are

Port work is expensive, costing upwards of $800. Aftermarket heads are a little more expensive than that, but will yield more power. Port work to aftermarket heads can yield impressive results if budget allows.

Beginning in 1978, all small-block Fords were fitted with bolt/fulcrum rocker arms like this one. This a non-adjustable rocker-arm setup was first used on Ford's 335-series 351C/351M/400M middle-block engines and the 385-series 429- and 460-ci big-blocks. If you're going with an aggressive camshaft, you will need to use heavy-duty roller-rocker arms with screw-in studs.

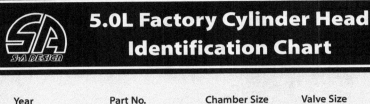

5.0L Factory Cylinder Head Identification Chart

Year	Part No.	Chamber Size	Valve Size
1979–81	D9AE-6049-AA	67.5 – 70.5 cc	1.78" Intake/1.46" Exhaust
1982–84	D9AE-6049-AA	67.5 – 70.5 cc	1.78" Intake/1.46" Exhaust
1985	E5AE-6049-CA	67.5 – 70.5 cc	1.78" Intake/1.46" Exhaust
1986	E6AE-6049-AA	62.9 – 65.9 cc	1.78" Intake/1.46" Exhaust¹
1987–95	E7AE-6049-AA	62.9 – 65.9 cc	1.78" Intake/1.46" Exhaust
	E7TE-6049-PA	60.6 – 63.6 cc	
1993–95 GT-40	F1ZE-6049-AA	60.6 – 63.6 cc	1.84" Intake/1.54" Exhaust
	F3ZE-6049-AA	60.6 – 63.6 cc	
1996–97 Explorer GT-40	F1ZE-6049-AA	63.4 – 66.4 cc	1.84" Intake/1.54" Exhaust
1997 Explorer GT-40P	F7ZE-6049-AA	58.3 – 61.3 cc	1.84" Intake/1.54" Exhaust

simple in the 5.0L camp. The GT head (E7AE or E7TE, 1987-95) is the best head to use if you're building a mild street engine. Give the GT head a little port work and you can improve flow dramatically. When the GT head isn't enough, the F1ZE or F3ZE GT-40 head is an economical alternative because it's available both new and used. Port work on both the GT and GT-40 head will net significant improvement in performance. But nothing beats a good aftermarket aluminum head right out of the box. Edelbrock, Trick Flow, Air Flow Research (AFR), Dart, and World Products all offer a great cylinder head selection for 5.0L High Output performance buffs.

CAMSHAFT & VALVETRAIN

Next to cylinder heads and induction, camshaft selection remains the most important aspect of an engine's personality. Because you're a 5.0L performance enthusiast, you know there is great potential in the roller-tappet camshaft system first introduced in the Mustang GT in 1985. A hydraulic roller camshaft enables a camshaft manufacturer to program in a lot of lift and duration without adversely affecting idle quality and driveability.

When you're selecting a camshaft profile, it's easy to get out of control because the roller cam gives us so much – just like the candy store. But too much valve lift will beat the daylights out of the valvesprings if you're building a daily driver. Limit your cam's valve lift to .500 inch and under if you're going to drive it every day to keep wear and tear to a minimum. Any lift greater than .500 inch takes a toll on the valvetrain in daily use.

In addition to valve lift issues, we want lobe separation between 108 and 114 degrees in the interest of good idle quality, driveability, and low-end torque. Compression and valve timing are other issues to keep in mind. Check with your camshaft manufacturer for more details. We strongly suggest buying matched camshaft kits that include

the camshaft, lifters, pushrods, and valvesprings. If you like a certain manufacturer, go with their parts all the way. Be uniform in your valvetrain selection.

When it comes to timing sets, the only way to go is the same way Ford did to begin with in factory 5.0L High Output engines – a double-roller timing set with steel gears. A double-roller set offers reliability and precision timing; there's no better choice when you're on a budget.

The camshaft and valvetrain directly determine not only an engine's personality, but also how reliably an engine performs throughout its service life. When it comes to camshafts, there are probably more misconceptions then there are facts. We're here to dissolve most of the myths and get you headed in the right direction on your stroker project.

To understand how to pick a camshaft and valvetrain, you must first understand how it all works. Choosing a camshaft profile is rooted in how we want an engine to perform. Are we building a streetable engine, where low and midrange torque are important? Or are we building a high-revving racing engine that makes peak torque at high RPM? A camshaft manufacturer's catalog lists dozens of camshaft types for the same type of engine. This is where it gets mighty confusing for the beginner. We see words like lift, duration, lobe separation, base circle, lobe centerline angle, and valve overlap. Our job here is to teach you what it all means so you can get back to your Mustang project.

Based on everything we've seen through the years, the best street performance cams are ground with a lobe separation between 108 to 114 degrees. When we have our lobe separation above 112 degrees, we improve driveability because the engine idles smoother and makes better low-end torque. This is the kind of performance we want from a street engine. Anytime lobe separation is below 108 degrees, idle quality suffers. But there is more to idle quality and low-end torque than just lobe separation.

Compression and cam timing must be considered because one always directly affects the other. Valve timing events directly affect cylinder pressure. Long intake valve duration reduces cylinder pressure. Shorter duration increases cylinder pressure. Too much cylinder pressure can cause detonation (pinging) and quite possibly engine damage. Too little cylinder pressure and you lose torque – that grunt you get coming out of a traffic light. You can count on cam manufacturers to figure stock compression ratios into their camshaft selection tables, which makes choosing a camshaft easier than it's ever been. The greatest advice we can offer the beginner is to be conservative with your cam specs if you want reliability and an engine that will live a long time. Keep with a conservative lift profile (under .500 inch lift). High-lift camshafts are very hard on valvesprings. They also increase the chance of valve-to-piston clearance issues. Watch duration and lobe separation closely, which will help you be more effective in camshaft selection. With street engines, we need to take a different approach to valvetrain logic than we would a racing engine. Instead of opening the valve more (lift), we want to open it longer (duration) and in better efficiency with piston timing (overlap or lobe separation).

Always think about what you're going to have for induction, heads, and exhaust. The savvy engine builder understands that in order for an engine

Aftermarket Cylinder Head Quick Reference Guide

Manufacturer	Type/Number	Intake Valve	Exhaust Valve	Chamber
AFR	Street 165 cc	1.90"	1.60"	58 or 61 cc
AFR	Street/Strip 165 cc	1.90"	1.60"	58 or 61 cc
AFR	Street 185 cc	2.02"	1.60"	58 or 61 cc
AFR	Street/Strip 185 cc	2.02"	1.60"	58 or 61 cc
AFR	205-cc SBF Race Head	2.08"	1.60"	60 or 71 cc
AFR	225-cc SBF Race Head	2.08"	1.60"	60 cc
Edelbrock	Performer #60319 Bare #60329 Assem.	1.90"	1.60"	60 cc
Edelbrock	Performer #60349	2.02"	1.60"	60 cc
Edelbrock	Performer #60279 Assem. Loc-Wire	2.02"	1.60"	60 cc
Edelbrock	Performer #60219 Bare #60229 Assem. Non-Emissions	1.90"	1.60"	60 cc
Edelbrock	Performer #60249 Bare #60259 Assem. Non-Emissions	2.02"	1.60"	60 cc
Edelbrock	Performer #60259 Assem. Loc-Wire	2.02"	1.60"	60 cc
Edelbrock	Performer #602159 Polished	2.02"	1.60"	60 cc
Edelbrock	Performer 5.0L/5.8L #60369 Bare #60379 Assem.	1.90"	1.60"	60 cc
Edelbrock	Performer 5.0L/5.8L #60289 Assem. Loc-Wire	1.90"	1.60"	60 cc
Edelbrock	Performer 5.0L/5.8L #60389 Bare #60399 Assem.	2.02"	1.60"	60 cc
Edelbrock	Performer 5.0L/5.8L #60299 Assem. Loc-Wire	2.02"	1.60"	60 cc

Aftermarket Cylinder Head Quick Reference Guide

Manufacturer	Type/Number	Intake Valve	Exhaust Valve	Chamber
Edelbrock	Victor Jr. #77169 Bare #77179 with valves only #77189 with valves, springs, and keepers. #77199 with valves, springs, and keepers for mechanical roller cams.	2.05"	1.60"	60 cc
Edelbrock	Victor Jr. #77389 Bare	2.05"	1.60"	70 cc
Edelbrock	Victor Jr. CNC #61269 Bare Std. Exhaust Pattern	2.10"	1.60"	60 cc
Edelbrock	Victor Jr. CNC #61279 Bare J302 Pattern	2.10"	1.60"	60 cc
Edelbrock	Glidden Victor CNC #61099 Bare	N/A	N/A	56 cc
Edelbrock	Glidden Victor CNC #77099 Bare For 9.2" Blocks with 9.5" manifold.			56 cc
Edelbrock	Victor Ford #77219 Bare	N/A	N/A	47 cc
Edelbrock	Chapman Victor CNC 276-cc Head #61299 Bare	N/A	N/A	60 cc
Edelbrock	Chapman Victor CNC 255-cc Head #77289 Bare	N/A	N/A	50 cc
Edelbrock	Chapman Victor CNC 255-cc Head #77299	N/A	N/A	61 cc
Ford	GT-40 "Turbo-Swirl" Aluminum M-6049-Y302 (Bare Head) M-6049-Y303 (Complete)	1.94"	1.60"	64 cc
Ford	GT-40X "Turbo-Swirl" Aluminum M-6049-X302 (Bare Head) M-6049-X303 (Complete)	1.94"	1.54"	64 cc
Ford	GT-40X "Turbo-Swirl" Aluminum M-6049-X304 (Bare Head) M-6049-X305 (Complete)	1.94"	1.54"	58 cc
Ford	Sportsman Short Track Cast Iron M-6049-N351	2.02"	1.60"	64 cc
Ford	"Z" Head Aluminum	2.02"	1.60"	64 cc

to work effectively, there have to be matched camshaft and valvetrain components. In fact, cam, valvetrain, heads, intake manifold, and an exhaust system must all work as a team or you're just wasting time and money. If you're going to use stock Ford cylinder heads, which we expect with a budget street engine, your cam profile needs to be less aggressive. Opt for a cam profile that will give you good low and midrange torque. Torque doesn't do you any good on the street when it happens at 6,000 rpm. Choose a cam profile that will make good torque between 2,500 and 4,500 rpm. Otherwise, you're just wasting engine.

The most important thing to remember with camshaft selection is how the cam will work with your engine's cylinder heads. We need to take a close look at valve lift with a particular head and determine results. Some camshafts will actually lose power with a given head because there's too much lift or duration. You can actually flow too much air through a cylinder head and lose power. Or, you can change when the power happens. This is why we want to understand a cylinder head before choosing a camshaft.

What type of fuel are you going to run and how will the vehicle be used? This also affects camshaft selection. We can actually raise compression if we're running a mild camshaft profile or using a higher-octane fuel. It all has to work together. Camshaft timing events must be directly tied to compression ratio. The longer our duration, the lower the cylinder pressure and resulting compression. The shorter the duration, the less air we're going to bring into the cylinder, which also affects compression. Our objective needs to be the highest compression without detonation. With this in mind, we want the most duration possible without compression extremes. Duration is what gives us torque as long as compression is sufficient.

Valve overlap, as we have stated earlier, is the period between exhaust stroke and intake stroke when both valves are slightly open. It improves exhaust scavenging by allowing the incoming intake charge to push remaining exhaust gasses out through the closing exhaust valve. It's a very necessary sequence in valve-timing events. Were the exhaust valve completely closed, we wouldn't get scavenging. The greater the overlap in a street engine, the less torque the engine will make down low where we need it most. This is why we want less valve overlap in a street engine and more in a racing engine, which will make its torque at high RPM. Increased valve overlap works best at high RPM.

Street engines need 10 to 55 degrees of valve overlap to be effective torque makers. When valve overlap starts wandering above 55 degrees, torque on the low end begins to go away. A really powerful street engine will need greater than 55 degrees of valve overlap, but not much greater. To give you an idea of what we're talking about, racing engines need 70 to 115 degrees of valve overlap – that's a lot.

For a street engine, we want valve overlap to maximize torque, which means having a conservative approach in the first place. Push overlap as far as you can without compromising torque. We also have to figure in lift and duration with valve overlap.

Lobe separation angle is another area to consider when selecting a street cam. This camshaft timing element is chosen based on displacement and how the engine will be used. Consider lobe separation based on how much displacement and valving you're going to be using. The smaller the valves, the tighter (fewer degrees) lobe separation should be. However, tighter lobe separation does adversely affect idle quality. This is why most camshaft manufacturers spec their cams with wider lobe separations than the custom grinders. Much of it depends on what you want the engine to do.

Duration in a street engine is likely the most important dynamic to consider. We increase duration whenever less lift is desired. Why? Because we get airflow into the cylinder bore two ways: lift and duration. We can open the valve more and for less time to get airflow. Or we can open the valve less and keep it open longer via duration to get airflow. Each

Aftermarket Cylinder Head Quick Reference Guide

Manufacturer	Type/Number	Intake Valve	Exhaust Valve	Chamber
Trick Flow	Twisted Wedge Aluminum TFS-51400002	2.02"	1.60"	61 cc
Trick Flow	Twisted Wedge Aluminum TFS-51400003	2.02"	1.60"	61 cc
Trick Flow	Track Heat Aluminum TFS-52400010	2.02"	1.60"	61 cc
Trick Flow	Track Heat Aluminum TFS-52400011	2.02"	1.60"	61 cc
Trick Flow	R-Series Aluminum TFS-52400001	2.08"	1.60"	61 cc
Trick Flow	R-Series Aluminum TFS-52400101	2.08"	1.60"	61 cc
Trick Flow	R-Series Aluminum TFS-52400201	2.08"	1.60"	61 cc
Trick Flow	R-Series Aluminum TFS-52400100	2.08"	1.60"	61 cc
Trick Flow	R-Series Aluminum TFS-52400200	2.08"	1.60"	61 cc
Trick Flow	High Port Aluminum TFS-51700001	2.02"	1.60"	64 cc
Trick Flow	High Port Aluminum TFS-51700002	2.02"	1.60"	64 cc
World Products	Windsor Jr. Cast Iron 053030 (Bare)	1.94"	1.60"	58 cc
World Products	Windsor Jr. Cast Iron 053030-1 (Hydraulic)	1.94"	1.60"	58 cc
World Products	Windsor Jr. Cast Iron 053030-2 (Hydraulic Roller)	1.94"	1.60"	58 cc
World Products	Windsor Jr. Cast Iron 053030-3 (Solid Roller)	1.94"	1.60"	58 cc

Aftermarket Cylinder Head Quick Reference Guide

Manufacturer	Type/Number	Intake Valve	Exhaust Valve	Chamber
World Products	Windsor Jr. Lite Aluminum 023030 (Bare)	1.94"	1.60"	58 cc
World Products	Windsor Jr. Lite Aluminum 023030-2 (Hydraulic Roller)	1.94"	1.60"	58 cc
World Products	Windsor Jr. Lite 023030-3 (Solid Roller)	1.94"	1.60"	58 cc
World Products	Windsor Sr. Lite Aluminum 023020 (Bare)	2.02"	1.60"	64 cc
World Products	Windsor Sr. Lite Aluminum 023020-2 (Hydraulic Roller)	2.02"	1.60"	64 cc
World Products	Windsor Sr. Lite Aluminum 023020-3 (Solid Roller)	2.02"	1.60"	64 cc
World Products	Roush 200 Cast Iron 053040 (Bare)	2.02"	1.60"	64 cc
World Products	Roush 200 Cast Iron 053040-1 (Hydraulic)	2.02"	1.60"	64 cc
World Products	Roush 200 Cast Iron 053040-2 (Hydraulic Roller)	2.02"	1.60"	64 cc
World Products	Roush 200 Cast Iron 053040-3 (Solid Roller)	2.02"	1.60"	64 cc

way has a different effect on performance. Duration is determined by how much cylinder head and displacement you have, and how the engine will be used. Excessive duration hurts low-end torque, which is what we need on the street. So, we have to achieve a balance by maximizing duration without a loss in low-end torque. We do this by using the right heads with proper valve sizing. Large valves and ports don't work well at all for street use. Mix in too much duration and you have a real slug at the traffic light.

So, what does this tell us about duration? Plenty. We want greater duration whenever displacement and valve sizing go up. Increasing duration falls directly in line with torque peak and RPM range. And this does not mean we necessarily gain any torque as RPM increases. It means our peak torque simply comes in at a higher RPM range. For example, if our engine is making 350 ft-lbs of torque at 4,500 rpm and we increase duration, we may make that same amount of torque at 5,200 rpm. In short, increased duration does not always mean increased torque.

Compression has a direct effect on what our duration should be. When we're running greater compression, we have to watch duration closely because it can drive cylinder pressures too high. Sometimes we curb compression and run greater duration depending on how we want to make power. When we have greater duration, our engine is going to make more power on the high end and less on the low end. This is why you must carefully consider duration when ordering a camshaft. Higher compression with a shorter duration helps the engine make torque down low where we need it most in a street engine. The thing to watch for with compression is detonation and overheating. Maximum street compression should be around 10.0:1.

Valve lift is another issue that depends on an engine's needs. Small blocks generally need more valve lift than big blocks. As we increase lift, generally we increase torque. This is especially important at low and mid RPM ranges where it counts on the street. Low-end torque is harder to achieve with a small block because these engines generally sport short strokes and large bores. Your objective needs to be more torque with less RPM if you want your engine to live longer. Revs are what drain the life out of an engine more quickly.

To make good low-end torque with a small block, we need a camshaft that combines effective lift and duration. As a rule, we want to run longer intake duration to make the most of valve lift. We get valve lift via the camshaft. But, rocker arm ratio is the other half of the equation. The most common rocker arm ratio is 1.6:1, which means the rocker arm will give the valve 1.6 times the lift we have at the cam lobe. When we step up to a 1.7:1 ratio rocker arm, valve lift becomes 1.7 times the lift at the lobe.

When we're spec'ing a valvetrain, it's best to achieve balance all around. If you run a high-lift camshaft with a 1.7:1 rocker arm ratio, you may be getting too much lift, which means excessive wear and tear. It's best to spec on the conservative side, especially if you're building an engine for daily use. Whenever you opt for an aggressive camshaft with a lot of lift, you're putting more stress on the valvestem, valve guide, and valvespring. The constant hammering of daily use with excessive lift is what kills engines without warning.

We will take this excessive wear logic a step further. It's vital that you ascertain proper centering of the rocker arm tip on the valvestem tip when you're setting up the valvetrain. We do this by using the correct length pushrod for the application. Buy a pushrod checker at your favorite speed shop if ever you're in doubt. A pushrod checker is an adjustable pushrod used to determine rocker-arm geometry. If the pushrod is too long, the tip will be under-centered on the valvestem, causing excessive side loads toward the outside of the cylinder head. If the pushrod is too short, the rocker-arm tip will be over-centered, causing excessive side loading toward the inside of the head. In either case, side loads on the valvestem and guide cause excessive wear and early failure. This is why we want the rocker arm tip to be properly centered on the valvestem for smooth operation.

One accessory that will reduce valvestem tip wear and side loading is the roller-tip rocker arm. Roller-tip rocker arms roll smoothly across the valvestem tip, virtually eliminating wear. Stamped steel, roller-tip rocker arms are available at budget prices without the high cost of extruded or forged pieces.

A dual-pattern camshaft runs different lift and timing profiles on the intake and exhaust side; this is useful whenever we're pushing the revs up. Typically, a dual-pattern camshaft runs shorter exhaust valve duration due to less time required to scavenge the exhaust gasses at high RPM. This is also beneficial whenever we're running nitrous or supercharging/turbocharging where exhaust scavenging is rapid and furious. Running a dual pattern camshaft on the street doesn't make much sense because

---

Understanding Camshaft Technology

Lift is the maximum amount a valve-lifter-pushrod combo can be raised off the base circle. Lift is measured in thousands of an inch (.000"). Lobe profile determines how quickly lift occurs. It can either be smooth or abrupt depending on lobe profile.

Duration is the amount of time the valve is open, beginning when the valve unseats. By this, we mean the number of degrees the camshaft will rotate between when cam lift begins, and when the valve closes. Duration typically begins at .004 inch of cam lift or when the lifter begins to ride the ramp coming off the base circle. "Duration at fifty," means duration begins at .050 inch of cam lift. Duration at fifty is the industry standard for determining camshaft lobe duration. When you're reading camshaft specs, this is the spec you'll most likely see.

Lobe Separation (also known as lobe centerline) is the distance (in degrees) between the intake lobe peak and the exhaust lobe peak. Lobe separation generally runs between 102 and 114 degrees (camshaft degrees).

Intake Centerline is the position of the camshaft rotation in relation to the crankshaft rotation. For example, an intake center-line of 114 degrees means the intake valve reaches maximum lift at 114 degrees after the crank reaches top dead center (ATDC).

Exhaust Centerline is basically the same thing as intake centerline. It's when the exhaust valve reaches maximum lift before top dead center (BTDC) in degrees.

Valve Overlap is the period of time when the intake and exhaust valves are both open to allow for proper cylinder scavenging. Overlap occurs when the exhaust valve is closing and the piston is reaching top dead center on the exhaust stroke. The intake charge from the opening intake valve pushes the exhaust gasses out. Valve overlap is also known as lobe separation. Camshaft grinders can change lobe separation or valve overlap to modify the performance of a camshaft. Sometimes they do this rather than change lift or duration.

Adjustable Valve Timing is being able to dial in a camshaft by adjusting valve timing at the timing sprocket. By adjusting the valve timing at the sprocket, we can increase or decrease torque. Advance valve timing and you increase torque. Retard valve timing and you lose torque.

---

we lose torque and fuel economy at low and mid RPM ranges. Keeping the exhaust valve open longer is what helps a street engine.

If you're building an engine for racing, you're going to build it differently than you would a street engine. Camshaft profile in a racing engine depends on the type of racing you're going to do, vehicle weight and type, even the type of transmission and rear axle ratio. Drag racing mandates a different camshaft profile than road or circle track racing. A short track racing engine will need to be able to produce huge amounts of torque in short order, for example. The same is true for a drag racer. These issues teach us something about engine breathing. Breathing effec-

tiveness is determined by camshaft profile.

Lobe separation for the drag racing camshaft should be between 104 and 118 degrees – a broad range actually, because drag racing needs can vary quite a bit. This is where you have to get very personal with a trusted camshaft grinder. Most camshaft grinders have computation charts that show the right cam for your application. As your needs change, so must the camshaft grind.

If you're going road racing, lobe separation will be in the 106-degree range. Some cam grinders push lobe separation higher for the circle track engine. Generally, the higher the lobe separation, the broader the torque curve (more torque over a broader RPM range).

Degreeing Your Camshaft

Making power isn't just about a longer stroke, large-port heads, big carburetor, and a high-performance camshaft – it's about the science of setting up your engine. Why do we degree camshafts after they're installed? What will we accomplish?

Degreeing a camshaft is like a police investigation. Call it, "just one more question …" in your quest to learn the truth about power. The reason for degreeing a camshaft is to determine that you have the correct cam profile for the job. Camshaft grinders today employ the most advanced technology available. As a result, very few faulty camshafts ever make it to the consumer. However, camshafts do get mispackaged at times, which means you could receive a completely different grind than appears on the cam card and packaging. All the more reason to degree the cam going in.

We degree a camshaft by bolting a degree wheel to the crankshaft, cranking the number-1 piston to top dead center, and installing a timing pointer. You can get a degree wheel from Comp Cams, Crane Cams, or Performance Automotive Warehouse.

We find top dead center with a bolt-on piston stop that screws into the spark plug hole or at the top of the block with the head removed. We suggest doing this with the cylinder head removed, which provides the greatest accuracy. Begin this process by turning the crankshaft clockwise until the number-1 piston rises to top dead center. With the cylinder head installed, hold your thumb over the spark plug hole and listen to the air being forced out by the piston. The air will stop when the piston reaches top dead center.

At this point, both timing marks on the crank and camshaft sprockets should be in alignment at 12 and 6 o'clock. Install the degree wheel next and align the bolt-on timing pointer. With all of this accomplished, the number-1 piston should be at top dead center, with the degree wheel and pointer at zero degrees. This becomes our base point of reference. Everything from here on out becomes BTDC (before top dead center)

Camshaft selection should always be in kit form, with matched components including lifters, pushrods, and valvesprings designed for the cam profile. Any time you start mixing camshafts, lifters, valvesprings, and like valvetrain components, you may run into serious performance and reliability issues.

Small-block Fords built prior to 1985 can still benefit from roller-tappet technology with a conversion kit from Lunati Cams. Two types are available. The most economical type is the spider system that anchors to oil drain holes in the lifter valley. The more expensive type ties pairs of roller lifters together with a bar.

The best bang for the buck is the double-roller timing set, which is exactly what Ford used to begin with. Use a fuel-pump eccentric if you're building a carbureted engine. You would be surprised how many people forget that.

or ATDC (after top dead center). The intake valve will open at a given number of degrees after top dead center and close at a given number of degrees before top dead center. The exhaust valve will open at a given number of degrees before top dead center and close a given number of degrees after top dead center. Much of this depends on valve overlap.

FORD CASTING IDENTIFICATION

Ford makes it easy for enthusiasts to identify corporate castings – just understand that Ford casting numbers aren't always the same as part or engineering numbers. Identifying a casting is a matter of knowing what Ford part and casting numbers mean. Here's what you can expect to see:

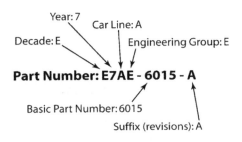

Year: 7
Car Line: A
Decade: E
Engineering Group: E

Part Number: E7AE - 6015 - A

Basic Part Number: 6015
Suffix (revisions): A

It's easy to identify Ford castings once you understand the system because there's not only a casting number, but a casting date code that tells you exactly when the piece was cast. Not only that, a date code is stamped in the piece, which tells us the date of manufacture. With these two date codes, we know when the piece was cast and when it was ultimately manufactured.

Ford part numbers can be found in the Ford Master Parts Catalog on microfilm at your Ford dealer, or in one of those obsolete 900-pound parts catalogs from the good old days. Because Ford has obsoleted a great many parts for vintage Fords, these part numbers don't always exist in present-day dealer microfilms. This is called "NR" or "not replaced," which means it's no longer available from Ford. However, casting numbers on parts tell us a lot about the piece.

Here's how a typical Ford part/casting number breaks down.

First position (E7AE-6015-A) means **Decade**.

B = 1950-59
C = 1960-69
D = 1970-79
E = 1980-89
F = 1990-99

Second position (E7AE-6015-A) means **Year of Decade**.

Third position (E7AE-6015-A) means **Car Line**.

A = Ford
D = Falcon
G = Comet, Montego, Cyclone
J = marine and industrial
M = Mercury
O = Fairlane and Torino
S = Thunderbird
T = Ford truck
V = Lincoln
W = Cougar
Z = Mustang

Fourth position (E7AE-6015-A) is the **Engineering Group**.

A = chassis group
B = body group
E = engine group

If the item is a service part, the fourth position then indicates the applicable division as follows.

Z = Ford
Y = Lincoln-Mercury
X = Original Ford Muscle Parts Program
M = Ford Motorsport SVO or Ford-Mexico

Four-digit number (E7AE-**6015**-A) indicates the **Basic Part Number**.

The basic part number tells us what the basic part is. For example, "6015" in the example above is a cylinder block. The number "9510" refers to carburetors, and so on. Each type of Ford part, right down to brackets and hardware, has a basic part number. This makes finding them easier in the Ford Master Parts Catalog.

The last character (E7AE-6015-**A**) is the **Suffix**.

The suffix indicates the revision under the part number. "A" indicates an original part. "B" indicates first revision, "C" second revision, "D" third revision, and so on. During Ford's learning curve with emissions in the 1970s, it was not uncommon to see "AA", "AB" and so on in cylinder-head casting suffix codes.

DATE CODES

Date codes can be found two ways in Ford castings. When the four-character date code is cast into the piece, this indicates when the piece was cast at the foundry. When it's stamped into the piece, this indicates the date of manufacture.

Month = B
Year = 7   Day = 26

7 B 26

Another area of interest to Ford buffs is where the piece was cast or forged. With Ford engines, we've seen three foundry identification marks. A "C" circled around an "F" indicates the Cleveland Iron Foundry. "DIF" indicates Dearborn Iron Foundry. "WF" or "WIF" indicates Windsor Iron Foundry. Single- and two-digit numbers typically indicate cavity numbers in the mold.

BUILDING OPTIONS

You don't always have to rebuild what you have. So lets look at options. The aftermarket industry offers us a wealth of options beginning with the crate engine. Ford Racing Performance Parts (FRPP), Performance Automotive Warehouse (PAW), Summit Racing, Jasper Engines, Speed-O-Motive, and even some regional engine builders offer crate engines, short blocks, and kits you can assemble yourself.

When it comes to engine kits, PAW offers the most affordable engine kits in the industry. These are complete kits that include a machined block, crank, reconditioned rods, new pistons, bearings, gaskets, rebuilt cylinder heads, a performance flat-tappet camshaft with lifters and pushrods, and more. All you have to do is check tolerances (always check tolerances, never assume anything), thoroughly clean the parts, and assemble the engine. If you desire a roller-tappet engine, PAW comes through for you there too. The thing to remember about PAW is that you can equip an engine kit anyway you like depending on budget. Check with PAW for more details on availability and cost.

Another option quite a few of us should consider is the stroker kit. Stroker kits cost roughly the same as a conventional engine kit (unless you're seeking a steel crank and H-beam rods). You can get into displacements upwards of 331, 347, and 355 ci in a 5.0L block using affordable stroker kits. Call this free horsepower and torque for the price of a rebuild. Aftermarket companies do this using a 400M cast crankshaft (347 and 355 ci) and any number of off-the-shelf connecting rods available. Sometimes simply offset grinding a 302 crank will yield 320+ cubic inches. This is what makes these kits so affordable.

The main thing you want in an engine kit or crate engine is quality parts and assembly. Some kits and crates are cheap because you're not getting quality

Ford Racing Performance Parts offers a variety of complete and partial crate engines that you can complete and install in a weekend. This is the M-6009-B58 short-block displacing 351 cubic inches. 5.0-liter versions are also available.

parts. This is where you must do your homework. Examine each engine kit or crate engine to determine what's inside. Not all kits are created equal. Much depends on how you will use your engine. If you're going to run it hard, then spend the money now for better parts. Cutting corners now can mean greater misfortune and expense later. For example, don't build an engine with cast pistons to save money today and expect it to live with nitrous later on. Build your engine for the long haul. If you're planning nitrous, supercharging, or weekend drag racing, then spend the money now on a dependable bottom end you can live with in the future.

While you're looking at engines and kits, think about an engine life insurance policy. Engine life insurance includes a supportive cooling system, extra heavy-duty parts that will live through abuse, a good oiling system, and redundant safety systems. Two things help an engine run cooler – a high-flow water pump and a good cross-flow radiator. A productive electric fan or fans keep things cool. If electric fans aren't to your liking, then opt for the factory thermal fan clutch, which doesn't consume much power and cools effectively. Aftermarket flex fans cool well, but they consume power. The humble clutch fan is superior to every kind of cooling fan known, except the electric fan, when it comes to power consumption.

Another safety feature widely overlooked is the cooling system filter. Rebuilt engine castings shed iron particles and rust that will clog a new radiator. Use a cooling system filter between the thermostat and radiator to catch those loose particles that will hinder cooling. Periodically clean the filter to ensure proper coolant flow.

Stroker kits offer same-price engine building – which means free horsepower – if you're content with a cast crankshaft and stock rods. Most have forged pistons, as well as quality bearings and rings.

Spend your money wisely on a new high-flow water pump. The Edelbrock water pump, for example, is dyno-tested to outperform virtually every pump in the marketplace. Plus, a cooler-running engine will live longer.

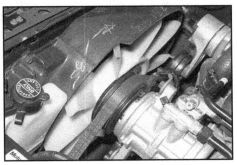

Although clutch fans have the stigma of being for grandpa cars, they're the best performing mechanical fans available for 5.0-liter Mustangs. The factory clutch fan works best if you're not fond of electric fans. Flex fans and huge multi-blade fans consume more power.

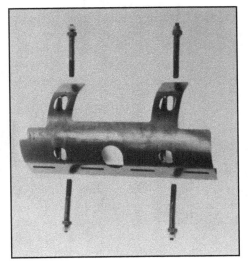

A windage tray is a good idea if you're planning to spin your 5.0L to 6,000+ rpm. This keeps oil in the pan and off the spinning crank. Remember that not all windage trays will work with all aftermarket oil pans.

High-performance Mustangs need generous cooling systems. A good cross-flow radiator from Griffin will pull great amounts of heat from your engine under the toughest of conditions. A radiator's purpose is to remove engine heat via the coolant inside. The coolant serves as a medium for heat transfer. The more radiator we have, the more heat we remove.

Electric cooling fans save horsepower, and they're more efficient in many cases.

STEPPING UP TO STROKER PERFORMANCE

A stroker is an engine with increased stroke. By increasing an engine's stroke, we gain the displacement necessary to make more power. Short-stroke engines like high RPM, where they make their greatest torque. Stroking an engine does more than just increase displacement. It increases torque by giving the engine more of an internal mechanical advantage. When we increase stroke, we increase the engine's crankshaft arm or lever, which makes the most of a combustion cycle. The longer the stroke, the greater the torque or twist.

Stroke comes from the length of the crankshaft's rod journal arm. Then, we double that length to come up with the engine's stroke. We double the length of the crankshaft's arm because we get that arm in two directions: top dead center, then bottom dead center. This is a simple 2:1 ratio. If the crank's rod arm is 1.5 inches, you have a 3-inch stroke.

Factory stock small- and middle-block Fords have had four basic strokes since their introduction in 1962. The 221-, 260-, and 289-ci engines have a 2.87-inch stroke – which is something few of us into 5.0L Mustangs are concerned with. The 302 (5.0L) and Boss 302 have a 3.00-inch stroke. The raised deck 351W engine has a 3.50-inch stroke, as do the 351C and 351M middle-blocks. The 400M has a 4.00-inch stroke. None of these latter engines (C or M series) have ever been factory installed in a Fox Mustang.

So how do we get more power from a stroker? We get power from the greater mechanical advantage of a longer crankshaft arm. But there's more. We are also filling the cylinder with a greater volume of air and fuel, which gives us more power all by itself. From stroke, and cylinder swept volume, we get torque. Torque is the truest measure of an engine's power output.

When we consider the crankshaft's arm – the distance from the crankshaft centerline to the center of the rod journal – this is where torque is born. Torque is an engine's grunt, that physical pressure at your backside when the accelerator is pressed. Think of the crankshaft's arm as a simple lever, like you were taught in high school physics class. Torque equals the downward force of the stroke times the length of the lever or arm. If we look at a 5.0L engine's 240 ft-lbs of peak torque, this means each cylinder bore is producing 480 pounds of pressure on each power stroke. We increase torque when we increase the length of the arm. When we increase the length of the arm, we increase stroke.

We know a stock 5.0L engine's arm is 1.5 inches. This means it has a 3.00-inch stroke. If we add .25 inch to the arm, this increases the arm to 1.750 inches. Double the 1.750 inches and you have 3.50 inches to achieve 351ci with the standard 4.00-inch bore. This gives us 40 additional foot-pounds of torque. Overbore the cylinders .030 inch and you have 355 ci. Push the bore to 4.060 inches and you're courting 360 ci.

Despite the advantages of a stroker, there are disadvantages too, especially if you're bent on pumping the most displacement possible into a 302. When we stroke a 302 to its limits, piston skirts have to be shorter, which hurts stability. We also push the piston pin into the piston ring land area, which weakens piston design. It also puts the pin close to the piston dome, which exerts too much heat on the pin and boss. These disadvantages shorten engine life.

Another factor with strokers is rod length. When we bring the piston deep down into the cylinder bore, we are also bringing it closer to the crankshaft counterweights, which creates conflict. This means we need a longer connecting rod to get the piston down there without interference with the counterweights. Sometimes, we can find off-the-shelf connecting rods to complete our stroker. And sometimes, we are forced to custom make connecting rods that will work. More expensive stroker kits have custom parts, like rods and pistons. More affordable kits have off-the-shelf parts that have made the kit possible without expensive tooling costs.

Whenever we have to custom make connecting rods, this drives the cost of a stroker kit up. The same is true for custom pistons. Stroker kits often mandate custom pistons to keep things friendly at the top of the bore. A 347- or 355-ci stroker, for example, has custom pistons with pin bosses pushed way up into the ring lands. This drives the cost up and shortens engine life, for reasons explained earlier.

Whenever we increase the stroke length, we are squeezing more volume into the same combustion chamber. This means we need to concern ourselves with an increase in compression. With that increase in stroke and compression comes an increase in cylinder volume. In that volume comes an increase in air and fuel, which gives us more power.

For more info on building a stroker small-block Ford, check out my other book, *How To Build Big-Inch Ford Small Blocks*. It's an entire book dedicated to making big power with big cubes.

COMPRESSION RATIO

So, what is compression ratio all about and how do we understand it? One popular misconception is that pistons alone determine compression ratio. This isn't true. Compression ratio comes from piston dome features – as well as stroke, bore, gasket thickness, and combustion chamber size. Compression comes from piston travel from BDC to TDC with both valves closed. We're simply squeezing the cylinder volume (displacement) into the combustion chamber. Compression ratio is cylinder volume at BDC versus cylinder volume with the piston at TDC. If cylinder volume with the piston at BDC is 10 times more than it is with the piston at TDC, then we have a compression ratio of 10.0:1, or simply 10 to 1.

Five basic facts affect compression ratio: cylinder swept volume, piston dome shape, head gasket thickness, clearance volume, and combustion chamber size. Swept volume is how much air or volume the piston displaces during its journey to the top of the bore. If we enlarge the swept volume by boring the cylinder oversize or increasing stroke, we increase compression ratio.

We may also increase or decrease compression ratio by changing the piston dome. If we dish the top of the piston, we lose compression. This is common with stock pistons, which are often dished to reduce compression. Late-model 5.0L High Output engines sport compression ratios of 10.0:1 with flattop pistons and valve reliefs, which are added to maintain piston-to-valve clearances.

To raise compression ratio, we can dome the piston, with a surface shaped like the combustion chamber. This reduces clearance volume at the top of the bore. When we reduce clearance volume, we increase compression ratio. Thinner head gaskets will also increase compression ratio.

Compression ratio may also be increased by reducing combustion chamber size. For example, older 289/302/351W heads have smaller chambers, which means plenty of compression with a stroker kit. While this has its power benefits, it also can cause engine damage. A 347-ci stroker kit with a 289's 57-cc chambers can yield too much compression, with catastrophic results. For one thing, a 289 head wouldn't be an intelligent choice for a 347-ci stroker. Port size would greatly limit the engine's potential. This leads us to a better aftermarket cylinder head for the 347. And don't discount the 351W head for your 347-ci stroker either. It makes for a stealthy factory cylinder head for the 347.

Whenever you step up to an aftermarket head, keep combustion chamber size in mind. Most aftermarket heads have chamber sizes around 64 cc. If you desire greater compression, you can make adjustments with proper piston selection.

Figuring Cylinder Volume

Cylinder volume is figured using a simple formula. Using a standard 351W or 351C bore and stroke (4.00 x 3.50 inches), work the following numbers.

Cylinder Volume =
0.7853982 x bore2 x stroke

When we apply this formula, we come up with 43.982-ci per cylinder. Multiply this number by eight and you have 351 ci. Truth is, you have 351.858, which is closer to 352. If we bore the 351 to 4.030 inches, we then have 44.644-ci

per cylinder, which comes out to 357 ci. This is cylinder volume. See the following table for easy answers.

Displacement Chart

BORE SIZE	STROKE	ACTUAL DISPLACEMENT
3.500"	2.87"	220.90 ci (221 ci)
3.800"	2.87"	260.39 ci (260 ci)
4.000"	2.87"	288.52 ci (289 ci)
4.030"	2.87"	292.86 ci (293 ci)
4.040"	2.87"	294.32 ci (294 ci)
4.060"	2.87"	297.24 ci (297 ci)
4.000"	3.00"	301.59 ci (302 ci)
4.030"	3.00"	306.13 ci (306 ci)
4.040"	3.00"	307.65 ci (308 ci)
4.060"	3.00"	310.70 ci (311 ci)
4.000"	3.20"	321.69 ci (322 ci)
4.030"	3.20"	326.54 ci (327 ci)
4.040"	3.20"	328.16 ci (328 ci)
4.060"	3.20"	331.42 ci (331 ci)
4.000"	3.25"	326.72 ci (327 ci)
4.030"	3.25"	331.64 ci (332 ci)
4.040"	3.25"	333.29 ci (333 ci)
4.060"	3.25"	336.60 ci (337 ci)
4.000"	3.40"	341.80 ci (342 ci)
4.030"	3.40"	346.95 ci (347 ci)
4.040"	3.40"	348.67 ci (349 ci)
4.060"	3.40"	352.13 ci (352 ci)
4.000"	3.50"	351.85 ci (352 ci)
4.030"	3.50"	357.15 ci (357 ci)
4.040"	3.50"	358.93 ci (359 ci)
4.060"	3.50"	362.49 ci (362 ci)
4.000"	3.75"	376.99 ci (377 ci)
4.030"	3.75"	382.66 ci (383 ci)
4.040"	3.75"	384.56 ci (385 ci)
4.060"	3.75"	388.38 ci (388 ci)
4.000"	3.80"	382.01 ci (382 ci)
4.030"	3.80"	387.76 ci (388 ci)
4.040"	3.80"	389.69 ci (390 ci)
4.060"	3.80"	393.56 ci (394 ci)
4.000"	4.00"	402.12 ci (402 ci)
4.030"	4.00"	408.17 ci (408 ci)
4.040"	4.00"	410.20 ci (410 ci)
4.060"	4.00"	414.27 ci (414 ci)
4.000"	4.20"	422.23 ci (422 ci)
4.030"	4.20"	428.58 ci (429 ci)
4.040"	4.20"	430.71 ci (431 ci)
4.060"	4.20"	434.99 ci (435 ci)

Computing Clearance Volume

If we take a standard 4.000-inch bore and overbore it by .030 inch, compression will increase by a fraction of a compression ratio point. If we have compression ratio of 10.0:1, compression will increase by less than a point with a .030-inch overbore. We compute the compression increase (or decrease) by figuring the clearance volume, which is the area left above the piston when it reaches top dead center. It's important to understand that the piston doesn't always reach top dead center flush with the block deck. In most applications, the piston comes within 0.005 to 0.020 inch below the deck surface. It looks more flush with the block deck than it actually is. This is called piston deck height. Piston deck height affects compression because it determines clearance volume at the top. If we have a lot of clearance volume, we have less compression. The greater the piston deck height, the lower the compression ratio.

The following is a formula for figuring clearance volume.

Clearance Volume =
0.7853982 x bore2 x deck height

Displacement

Again, let's look at our 351-ci small-block with a 4.000-inch bore and 3.50-inch stroke. Let's say our 351 has a piston deck height of 0.015 inch below the block deck. When we use our formula of (0.7853982 x 4.000)2 x 0.015, we get 0.188 ci, or just a fraction of the cylinder's 43.98 ci. If the deck height increased any amount, compression would drop. If deck height decreased any amount, compression would increase.

After figuring how to compute displacement in each cylinder and how to figure in piston deck height effect on compression, it's time to figure in the piston's role in all of this. Remember that if we dish the piston, we lose compression. If we dome the piston, we increase compression. Most piston manufacturers will give you the specifications on a piston. If it's dished or domed, the manufacturer will tell the volume of the dish or dome in cubic centimeters (cc's).

If you're baffled by cubic centimeters versus cubic inches, you're not alone. A lot of us are confused by metric versus SAE. Follow this formula and end your confusion.

Cubic Inches = cc's x 0.0610237

Cubic Centimeters = ci's x 16.387064

Figuring Head Gasket Volume

Back to our 351-ci engine. Lets say our 351 has dished pistons with 4.00-cc dishes. Using our formula, we come up with a dish volume of 0.244 ci. This lowers compression ratio because we have more clearance volume above the piston. If we dome the piston by the same amount, we increase compression accordingly.

The next factor in compression ratio is cylinder head gasket volume, which adds to clearance volume above the piston. The thickness of the head gasket affects compression ratio. Thick head gaskets increase clearance volume, which lowers compression. Thin head gaskets decrease clearance volume, which increases compression. To figure the head gasket volume, use the following formula.

Cylinder Head Gasket Volume = 0.7853982 x gasket bore^2 x gasket's compressed thickness

Let's look again at our 351-ci engine with a 4.000-inch bore. We have a cylinder head gasket that, when compressed, is 0.040 inch thick. We take 0.7853982 x 4.000 x 4.000 x 0.040, to arrive at 0.502 ci of gasket volume.

Understanding Chamber Volume

With all of these issues out of the way, it's time to focus on combustion chamber volume. Combustion chamber volume is the actual size of the chamber in cubic centimeters (cc's). Think of the combustion chamber as the ultimate

clearance volume. Chamber sizes for small-block Fords (289/302/351W) range from 53 cc to 64 cc. For the 351C/351M/400M, chamber sizes run much larger. The 351C4V head has small wedge chambers. The 351C-2V, 351M, and 400M head has larger open chambers.

Combustion chamber volume is figured with a graduated cylinder using fluid. We meter fluid into the chamber and figure how many cc's of fluid it takes to fill the chamber. Our sample cylinder head has 64-cc chambers. Use the previous cc-to-inch conversion formula to convert to cubic inches.

At Last, Compression Ratio!

Based on our formula above at 64 cc, we have 3.90 ci of volume in the chamber alone. Now, we have all of the information needed to compute compression ratio in our 351-ci engine. Add up all of the numbers for bore and stroke, piston deck height, head gasket thickness, and combustion chamber size. Use the following formula.

Cylinder Vol. + Clearance Vol. + Piston Vol. + Chamber Vol. + Gasket Vol.

Clearance Vol. + Piston Vol. + Head Gasket Vol. + Chamber Vol.

Our 351-ci engine, with its 4.00-inch bores and 3.50-inch stroke, 0.020-inch deck height, 0.040-inch head gasket thickness, 64-cc chamber heads, and 4.00-cc dished pistons winds up like this. (Note: You have to change all figures to either cubic inches or cubic centimeters, before you can work the formula. Don't mix and match!)

43.982 ci + 0.188 ci + 0.244 ci + 3.90 ci + 0.502 ci

1.504 ci + 0.244 ci + 0.502 ci + 3.90 ci

When we work this formula, we are taking cylinder volume, clearance volume, piston volume, chamber volume, and gasket volume, and adding them together to arrive at 48.816 ci. Then we add up clearance volume, piston volume, head gasket volume, and chamber vol-

ume to get 4.834 ci. Then, we take 48.816 ci and divide it by 4.834 ci to arrive at 10.098, which, rounded off to the nearest tenth, is 10.10. So, our compression ratio is 10.10:1

LONG RODS AND GENERAL ENGINE THEORY

What are the benefits of a longer connecting rod? A longer connecting rod improves combustion efficiency by allowing the piston to dwell longer at the top of the cylinder bore. When the piston stays at the top of the bore longer, this allows us to pull more power from the same amount of air and fuel and more time to extract the energy.

Speed-O-Motive, as one example, offers a variety of long-rod stroker kits designed to make the most of your small-block power project. Lets use a 351W engine as one example. In box-stock form, the 351W has a 5.956-inch long connecting rod. It has been proven that you can stroke the 351W to as much as 429 ci in a factory block. We can fit as much as 6.580-inches of connecting rod into a 351W stroker. This gives us 0.62-inch more rod, which means more time at TDC and BDC.

Because internal combustion engines tend to waste approximately 70 percent of the heat energy they create (most is absorbed by the coolant or lost out the tail pipe), allowing the piston to dwell longer at the top of the bore enables us to capture some of this wasted heat energy.

To learn how to make more power, we have to understand how power is made to begin with inside an engine. How much power an engine makes depends on how much air and fuel we can pump through the engine, plus what we do with that fuel and air mixture during that split-second it lives and dies in the combustion chambers.

We have to think of an internal combustion engine as an air pump. The more air and fuel we can "pump" through the cylinders, the more power we're going to make. This is why racers use big carburetors, manifolds, heads, superchargers, turbochargers, and nitrous oxide. Racers understand this air pump theory and practice it with reckless abandon – sometimes with catastrophic results. But good racers also understand the "too much of a good thing" theory. Sometimes it can cost you a race; sometimes it can cost you an engine.

To get power from our "air pump," we need to get liberal amounts of air and fuel into the chambers, and then squeeze the mixture as hard as we can without damaging the engine. When we raise compression (i.e., the squeeze), we increase the power our mixture makes. It's the intense heat of compression coupled with the ignition system spark that ignites the energy. The more compression we have, the greater the heat we have to ignite the mixture.

Problem is, when there's too much compression and accompanying heat, the air/fuel mixture can ignite prematurely, resulting in preignition and detonation. So we have to achieve the right compression ratio to get the most from the fuel we have. Today's street fuels won't tolerate much over 10.5:1 compression. This means we have to look elsewhere for answers in the power equation, like more aggressive camshaft profiles, better heads, port work, hotter ignition systems, exhaust headers that breathe better, state-of-the-art intake manifolds and carburetors – even EFI where we never thought of using it before.

The thing to remember about gasoline engines is this: the air/fuel mixture does not explode in the combustion chambers, it "lights off" in a quick fire, just like your gas furnace or water heater. Because the mixture is compressed and ignited, it lights more rapidly. Combustion in a piston engine is just that, a fast light-up that sends a flame front across the top of the piston. Under ideal circumstances, the flame front will travel smoothly across the piston dome, and the heat and pressure will act on the piston and rod uniformly to create rotary motion at the crankshaft.

A bad "light off" that originates at two opposing points in the chamber is called pre-ignition or detonation. The opposing ignition fronts collide, creating a shock that hammers the piston dome, which is the pinging or spark knock we hear under acceleration. The objective is to get a smooth, quick fire, with the flame front traveling in one direction for maximum power. Call this common sense power management.

Power management is having the right balance of ignition timing, fuel mixture, compression ratio, valve timing events, and even external forces like blower boost or nitrous input. All of these elements have to work together if we're to make productive power.

For one thing, the science of making power must tie in with your intended vehicle usage. Street engines for the daily commute need to be approached for good low and midrange torque. Drag racing engines need to make power at mid- to high-RPM ranges. Road racing engines need to be able to do it all – down low, in the middle, and at high RPM, because they're going to live in all of these ranges while racing.

We've long been led to believe horsepower is what "power" is all about. But horsepower is rooted more in Madison Avenue advertising rhetoric than fact. In the power picture, horsepower doesn't count for much. What counts is how much torque we have, and when we have the most of it. A good friend of ours, John Baechtel of Westech Performance in Ontario, California, said it best when he said, "Torque is the grunt that gets us going, and horsepower is the force that keeps us moving…" Well said, John.

Engines are doing their best work when they reach peak torque, where they are making the most grunt. John tells us that when an engine is below the torque peak, it has more than enough time to completely fill the cylinder with air and fuel. He adds that when engine RPM rises above the torque peak, there isn't enough time to completely fill the cylinders with air and fuel.

The horsepower we feel from an engine's spinning crankshaft is torque multiplied by engine speed (RPM) to produce a number that tells us something about the engine's output. This theory dates back to steam engines and an inventor of steam engines named James Watt. Watt's theory was simple. It compared the work his steam engine could do with the same work an equal number of horses could do. Watt determined a single horse could pull a 180-pound load 181 feet in one minute. This formula figured out to 32,580 ft-lbs per minute. Watt rounded it off to 33,000 ft-lbs per minute. He divided this figure by 60 seconds, which worked out to 550 ft-lbs per second. This became the standard for one horsepower.

We're not going to bore you with the math, but from that definition of horsepower, it's pretty easy to figure out how to calculate horsepower if you know the torque that an engine generates at a given RPM. The formula is:

$$HP = \frac{Torque \times RPM}{5{,}252}$$

That 5,252 figure is a constant that's derived mathematically from Watt's definition and a little geometry (like we said, we won't bore you with the math), and it's an important number. Anytime you know an engine's torque and speed, you can use this formula to determine horsepower. By putting an engine on a dyno and measuring torque and speed as an engine revs up, we can then plot a graph of torque and horsepower.

Which leads us to an often-asked question: Why are torque and horsepower always equal at 5,252 rpm? Well, let's do the math. Say HP and Torque are equal, at 1 apiece. That gives us this:

$$1 = \frac{1 \times RPM}{5{,}252}$$

To solve for RPM, we can multiply both sides by 5,252, like so:

$$5{,}252 \times 1 = \frac{5{,}252 \times 1 \times RPM}{5{,}252}$$

On the right side of the equation, 5,252/5,252 equals 1 and is cancelled out, which leaves us with:

$$5{,}252 = RPM$$

So, when torque and horsepower are equal, RPM will always be 5,252.

When we look at torque alone, it's the measure of an engine's work. Horsepower is a measure of how quickly the engine does the work. Torque comes from displacement and stroke mostly. This means the real power we derive from an engine comes in the torque curve. The broader the torque curve, the better our power package. A broader torque curve comes from making the most of the air/fuel mixture across a broader RPM range. Truth is, we're never going to get the best of everything, even with fuel-injected engines. Our engines need to be planned and built based on the way we're going to use them. What we choose in terms of a camshaft, cylinder heads, and induction system determines how our engine will perform.

Exhaust System

Believe it or not, you can pick up a lot of power by making key changes in your Mustang's exhaust system. Before we go any further, we do not endorse removal of the factory emissions system, such as the catalytic converters, in your pursuit of power. Hollowing out the catalytic converters or installing test pipes does little for performance. Add to that the penalties in many states for altering the emissions system and we find it just isn't worth the consequences. Though this may contradict traditional hot-rodder thinking, aftermarket high-performance catalysts do more for performance than you might think because the engine and electronics are designed to work with them. Leaving those cats in place does a lot for peace of mind and the environment.

The exhaust system is an area we fail to get right all too often. You can spend a fortune on an induction system, force feed it with a supercharger, and squeeze a ton of nitrous through it, but if your exhaust scavenging isn't up to the task, you're pouring good money after bad. The exhaust needs to be able to scavenge exhaust gasses effectively.

Whether to go with long- or short-tube headers depends largely on how you intend to use the vehicle. Short-tube headers work well on the street because they're clean and simple, like factory headers. They also tie right into a catalyst, so most are emissions legal.

Long-tube headers are more suited to racing because they scavenge and flow better. Of course, they may or may not be street legal, depending on how strict the emissions laws are in your area.

Although there is speculation about header coatings – chrome versus ceramic versus paint – the best header coating is ceramic. Ceramic is best because it contains heat inside the header where it belongs. It also gets rid of heat quickly after engine shutdown, which makes it easy to change spark plugs without getting burned. Ceramic coatings also prevent rust.

Another area of speculation is header and exhaust tube size. Bigger isn't always better. For street use, you don't need 3-inch exhaust tubes, and you don't need huge primary header tubes either. It's called right sizing. On the street, and even on the race track, tube size needs to be directly proportional to engine dynamics. Header and exhaust tube size selection should be based on the type of engine you're building and the kind of driving you will be doing most of the time.

Popular myth says larger tubes and pipes mean more power. Truth is, larger pipes work well with high-revving engines with aggressive camshafts and heads. Large pipes are for the race track and drag strip. They don't serve a valuable purpose on the street. On the street, smaller tubes and pipes help your engine make more torque where it's needed at lower RPM. Smaller tubes help maintain the greater exhaust velocity needed to make low-end torque. The objective is to achieve a balance of breathing and tube size.

Free Power!
Nitrous Oxide Injection

Nitrous oxide, also called "squeeze," is popular today for those looking for quick and easy power (50 to 150 horsepower) on demand. But nitrous can be very harmful to an engine that isn't properly prepared and tuned, especially your pistons and rings. It hammers rod and main bearings, resulting in severe wear. And no matter what the nitrous oxide advocates will tell you

about "laughing gas," nitrous can and does shorten engine life. So don't be drawn into believing it's a magic horsepower pill without a down side. If you're going to be using nitrous oxide, be prepared. Accept the fact that nitrous will shorten engine life no matter how it's used. The more aggressively you use nitrous, the shorter your engine will live.

So what, exactly, is nitrous oxide and what does it do? Nitrous is a physics lesson in how to generate greater amounts of power from the air/fuel charge we introduce to the combustion chambers. Nitrous oxide is a very simple gas composed of two nitrogen atoms and one oxygen atom. Chemists call it $N2O$. Contrary to what you may believe about $N2O$, it's not a poisonous gas, nor is it harmful to the atmosphere. This doesn't mean you should breathe it, however. Because $N2O$ is an asphyxiate, it can suffocate you if inhaled in heavy quantities. It would have a similar affect on you as carbon dioxide ($CO2$), called oxygen deprivation.

Nitrous oxide is available in three basic grades: medical, commercial, and high-purity. Medical grade is what's commonly known as laughing gas used by dentists and surgeons. It has to be very pure for human consumption, and you must be licensed as a medical professional to get it. Commercial-grade

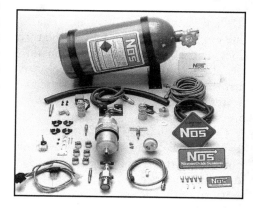

Nitrous makes for great bolt-on horsepower. NOS, for example, offers us kits that deliver various levels of power. But remember: too much nitrous equals engine destruction. All that power at the punch of a button comes with the price of reduced engine life.

nitrous oxide is what we use in our engines for performance gains. High-purity is also a medical grade nitrous oxide that is extremely pure, and it's priced and controlled accordingly.

The commercial grade nitrous oxide is marketed as Nytrous+ and sold by the Puritan-Bennett Corporation. You can find it all across the country. It's a mix of 99.9 percent nitrous oxide and 0.01 percent sulfur dioxide. Puritan-Bennett adds the sulfur dioxide to give its N2O gas odor just like we experience with natural gas. This is another reason you wouldn't want to inhale it.

When you buy nitrous oxide, it's pumped into a storage tank that you provide the supplier. You need an appropriate tank capable of holding at least 1,800 pounds per square inch (psi). To play it safe, your tank(s) must have a visible certification date from within the past five years. Inside the tank, nitrous oxide exists in liquid form because of the extreme pressure. As it leaves the tank, it becomes a gas. When it leaves the tank quickly, it leaves very cold, just like refrigerants and propane. For nitrous oxide to become a liquid in an unpressurized environment, the ambient temperature has to be –127 degrees F. At 70 degrees F, nitrous oxide needs to be pressurized to 760 psi to become a liquid. Warm things up to 80 degrees F and you need 865 psi to make nitrous oxide a liquid.

Using nitrous oxide to make power is nothing new. In World War II, it was used to help aircraft engines make power. The principle then was much the same as it is now. Nitrous was stored under pressure in tanks, much as it is today. Nitrous oxide stored under pressure must be anchored securely in the interest of safety. We stress safety because a carelessly handled nitrous oxide bottle with nearly 1,000 psi of pressure behaves like a bomb if the bottle fails. It can explode, maiming or killing you.

To get the nitrous we need for performance use on demand, we meter the gas leaving the bottle via electrical solenoids that are fired when we hit the button. Of course, it involves more than this. Nitrous oxide should be administered on demand at a time when it's safe to do so. Too much nitrous oxide and not enough fuel can destroy an engine. For one thing, nitrous oxide should never be administered to the intake ports unless the throttle is wide open. Set up properly, the throttle should close a nitrous oxide solenoid switch when in the wide-open position. Closing the switch activates the nitrous oxide solenoid, releasing the nitrous oxide into the intake manifold.

So how do we get nitrous oxide into the intake ports? We do it a number of ways, depending on how the engine is set up. Carbureted engines get their nitrous oxide diet through a fogger plate located beneath the carburetor. Pin the butterflies and the nitrous oxide "fogs" the intake plenum, assisting the air/fuel mixture en route to the chambers. Carbureted engines may also use nozzles at each intake port to administer the nitrous oxide. The nice part about this design is being able to tune each cylinder bore based on the needs of that cylinder. On carbureted engines, the center ports typically receive more fuel and air than the perimeter ports. The outers tend to run leaner than the centers, which is very critical when you're running nitrous oxide.

Port fuel-injected engines also use nozzles off of a common tube manifold to administer nitrous oxide at each port. Here again, the port-injected nitrous oxide arrangement can be port-tuned for better performance. This is especially true when you think of your V-8 engine as eight separate engines operating on a common crankshaft.

One popular misconception is that we get power from the nitrous oxide itself, but this isn't true. Nitrous oxide works hand-in-hand with the air/fuel mix to make power in each cylinder bore. Nitrous oxide brings out the best in the fuel. Not only is the nitrous oxide mist cold (good for thermal expansion), it's also loaded with oxygen, which gives the igniting air/fuel mix a bad attitude. It makes the air/fuel mix burn faster, which creates a powerful thermal expansion experience in each combustion chamber.

Where we have to be careful with nitrous oxide is how we feed it to our engines. Perhaps this isn't the best parallel, but think of nitrous oxide the same way you would cocaine, crystal meth, or nicotine. The more powerful the nitrous oxide experience, the more an enthusiast wants. So, we keep feeding our engine more nitrous oxide in our quest for power until it fails under the stress. You must recognize your engine's limits before even getting started on a nitrous oxide diet.

Using Nitrous Oxide

The first thing to remember with nitrous oxide is that it makes fuel burn faster. This means you must be mindful of what it can do, both productively and counterproductively.

Let's start with engine tuning. Nitrous oxide should not be administered to the combustion chambers with reckless abandon. Use too much of it and you burn pistons. You have to think of nitrous oxide and your air/fuel mixture just like you would oxygen and acetylene. When we're using oxygen and acetylene to weld or cut steel, we use lots of oxygen to blaze a path through the steel. Similarly, it's possible to burn right through the piston like a cutting torch if you use too much nitrous. And aluminum pistons aren't as forgiving as steel either, they melt at 1,300 degrees F.

When we're tuning a small-block Ford to run on nitrous oxide, we have to get air/fuel mixture and spark timing where they need to be or face certain destruction. So how do we get there? First, we have to control fuel delivery to where it jibes with the flow of nitrous oxide. If we get too much N2O in there and not enough fuel, we overheat the chamber and melt pistons. We have to control fuel and nitrous oxide flow to a finite point where we get the most power possible without causing engine damage. This takes practice.

The key to getting the most power from nitrous oxide is getting spark timing, fuel delivery, and peak cylinder pressure going at the same time. Ideally, we light the air/fuel/nitrous mixture at the time when we have peak cylinder pressure, which makes the most of the incoming charge. When everything is working well together, we get a smooth, firm light-off that nets us a lot of power.

Things go wrong when the light-off resembles an explosion, exerting a shockwave on the top of the piston. This is the spark knock we hear as a multiple "rapping" under acceleration.

When fuel, air, and nitrous ignite violently, why don't we net more power from the explosion? The answer is simple. When an engine is running smoothly, we get that "quick-fire" mentioned earlier in this chapter. A smooth light-off smoothly applies pressure to the piston dome, which forces it downward in the cylinder bore, turning the crank and completing the power stroke. Detonation is what occurs when we get a spontaneous light-off, especially from two points in the chamber. The two waves of power collide, causing spark knock or pinging under acceleration. The problem with this kind of light-off is that those violent combustion spikes don't really yield much power – not to mention that they hurt parts.

So how do we safely make the most of nitrous oxide? We should first address the fuel system because we need to have enough fuel to meet the demands of nitrous oxide. Without enough fuel, we toast the engine. The next issue is fuel octane rating. What octane rating do you expect to use? Then there's ignition timing. Where does yours need to be? And finally, what is your engine's compression ratio? Too much compression with nitrous will cause destructive detonation. Getting each of these elements dialed in is crucial to productive performance.

Compression has to be thought of in two ways: static and dynamic. Static compression is the compression ratio we often think of. This is the swept volume above the piston, with the piston at bottom dead center, versus the clearance volume left when the piston is at top dead center. If we have 100 cc of volume with the piston at bottom dead center and 10 cc left with the piston at top dead center, then we have a static compression ratio of 10.0:1 – 100 cc to 10 cc.

Dynamic compression is what happens with the engine operating. This is the kind of compression that happens with pistons, valves, and gasses in motion through the engine. We get dynamic compression when we're huffing lungfuls of air through the engine during operation. With the engine running, we're pumping more volume through the cylinders and chambers than we would by simply hand-cranking the engine. This actually increases the compression ratio, which means dynamic compression is higher than static compression. So, what does all of this mean for your engine? It means you need to consider the dynamic compression ratio as your engine's actual compression figure when you're planning nitrous oxide. A lower dynamic compression ratio is generally safer when you're using nitrous, as it gives you a little more leeway in your tuning.

Camshaft selection is also important when using nitrous oxide. Nitrous-burning engines need different camshafts than those that are naturally aspirated or supercharged. Dynamic compression ratio is affected by camshaft profile. A camshaft profile with a short duration will give us greater dynamic compression. When we lengthen the duration, we tend to lose dynamic compression.

On the exhaust side, duration is a very important issue with nitrous. Because the air/fuel/nitrous charge coming in expands with fury during ignition, it needs a way to escape when the exhaust valve opens. We need a longer exhaust valve duration with nitrous for good scavenging and thorough extraction of power.

While we're thinking about exhaust valve duration, we must also remember overlap in all of this. Less overlap means more dynamic compression. More overlap, less dynamic compression. Overlap is the point in the power cycle when the exhaust valve is closing and the intake valve is opening. The incoming charge helps scavenge the outgoing hot gasses through the overlap process. This means the exhaust valve needs to open earlier in the cycle and stay open longer for adequate scavenging.

Fuel octane plays into the power process because we need to understand when and how the fuel will ignite. The higher the octane rating, the more slowly it ignites and burns, which reduces the chances of detonation and pre-ignition.

With a higher octane rating, we get a smooth, more predictable light-off in the chamber. When we opt for a lower octane rating, we get a more unstable fuel that will light quickly and cause pinging. When we throw nitrous oxide into the equation, we can count on a quick light that can be violent. This is why a higher octane rating is so critical to a cohesive performance package.

Next, we're ready to address the all-important air/fuel mixture, sometimes called the air/fuel ratio. This ratio is set by adjusting jet size in the carburetor or controlling fuel injector pulse width. Jet size and pulse width both determine how much fuel goes into the chamber.

If your Fox-body tuning effort involves a carburetor, you have to get jet sizing down to a science to help your engine live on nitrous oxide. As a rule, carbureted engines live happily with an air/fuel ratio of 12.5:1 to 13.0:1. If we go any leaner, we can cause engine damage and will also lose power. Any richer and we lose power as well.

When we're working with fuel injection, like the majority of Fox-body owners, we can control fuel mixture by reprogramming the electronic control module or changing injector size. With nitrous, we typically go up one injector size and fine tune from there. Too large is better than too small. Of course, you'll need to tune on a dyno to get it right. Factory fuel-injection systems run a fuel manifold pressure of 30-45 psi. If you're running nitrous oxide, you're going to need a lot more fuel pressure to get the job done safely. Around 80 psi is considered the norm. This is when you need to step up to high-pressure Earl's hoses and fittings.

Most nitrous experts we have consulted suggest a nitrous-to-fuel ratio of 5.0:1 as a starting point for engine tuning. Starting here means going decidedly rich, but it's the safest approach. Begin at 5.0:1 and work your tuning toward 6.0:1 for optimum results. If your power goal is 500 horsepower on nitrous oxide, you're going to need 37.94 gallons an hour or 0.63 gallons a minute to run productively on nitrous oxide. Of course, we're not going to stay on nitrous oxide for one hour, but it gives you an idea about how much fuel you're going to need.

Ignition timing is the next big hurdle because it can kill an engine as quickly as a lean fuel mixture or too much compression when we're running nitrous. We want the spark to occur in advance of peak cylinder pressure because it takes time for the air/fuel/nitrous mixture to ignite. Under normal circumstances, without nitrous, we want full spark advance around 36 to 41 degrees before top dead center. Exactly where the spark occurs depends on how the engine is equipped and how it performs at full spark advance at 3,500 rpm. Full advance varies because every engine is different.

When we add nitrous oxide into the equation, we have an air/fuel/nitrous mixture that is going to ignite more rapidly than the conventional air/fuel mix. The pros suggest retarding the ignition timing to approximately 12 degrees BTDC because the air/fuel/nitrous mixture ignites much more quickly. With the full spark advance at 36-41 degrees BTDC, we would waste the engine in short order. Retard timing to 12 degrees BTDC and go from there. Twelve degrees BTDC at 3,500 rpm should be your baseline, with ignition timing advancing slowly from there. Test it out at wide-open throttle under a load, beginning at 12 degrees BTDC, then advance from there one degree at a time.

There are other points to consider when running nitrous. To be effective, fuel has to atomize (vaporize) properly. This means the fuel has to "mist" as it enters the intake manifold and, ultimately, the combustion chamber. The problem is that nitrous comes out of the fogger or nozzle ice cold. This makes it very difficult to atomize the fuel effectively. When nitrous comes out at a frigid −100 degrees F, fuel tends to exist as large droplets, rather than the mist we need for good ignition and combustion.

Nitrous system manufacturers have dealt effectively with the issue of fuel atomization by designing systems that allow the gasoline to atomize with the nitrous oxide fog or mist. The finer we can get the mist, the more power we're going to pull from the mixture. The

objective is to keep the fuel in suspension as long as possible.

CarTech Books publishes an excellent nitrous oxide book (*How To Install and Use Nitrous Oxide Injection Systems for Maximum Horsepower*, SA-50), authored by respected and well-known automotive writer, Joe Pettitt. For more detailed information on nitrous oxide, pick up this book at your favorite bookstore.

SUPERCHARGING

Supercharging, like nitrous oxide injection, was conceived a long time ago to generate as much power as possible from a given displacement. Unlike nitrous oxide, supercharging is more involved, yet easier to tune and manage. Supercharging is easier to tune because you know you're getting into trouble before trouble arrives. Knowing you're in trouble comes from the sound of detonation. Superchargers and turbochargers don't come on as strong as quickly as nitrous oxide. For the most part, they cannot damage the engine as strong and fast as nitrous oxide, because you can come off the power in time to prevent engine damage. There is also a safety device called a waste-gate that prevents overboost with superchargers and turbochargers. With nitrous oxide, damage,

and certain engine damage, are instantaneous if you deliver too much of it without enough fuel, or with too much ignition timing.

Supercharging and turbocharging both accomplish the same objective. They each force air into the cylinders to make the most of a combustion power cycle. They mechanically increase cylinder pressure, which, given enough fuel, makes more power. Superchargers are driven by the engine's crankshaft. Turbochargers are driven by exhaust gas pressure. A supercharger's compressor, driven by the crankshaft, moves the air we're feeding into the intake manifold. A turbocharger's compressor, driven by exhaust gas pressure, does the same thing.

Superchargers give engines nearly immediate power. The power comes on stronger with higher RPM – the compressor turns faster, forcing more air pressure into the intake manifold, which gives us the power. We prevent overpressure by fitting the supercharger with a waste-gate, which vents excessive pressure.

Turbochargers take a certain amount of time to give us induction pressure when we step on the gas. This is called turbo lag. Because it takes the turbocharger time to spool up during acceleration, there is a certain amount of lag before we get the boost or pres-

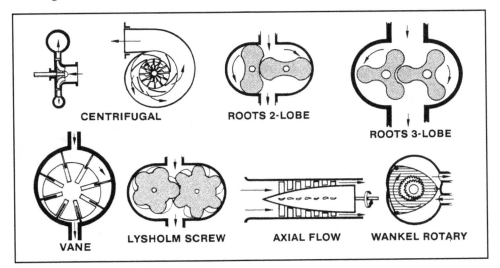

These are the six different types of superchargers. The most common for small-block Fords are the Roots two- and three-lobe, and the centrifugal. Roots blowers typically mount on top of the induction system or off to one side. Centrifugal blowers mount at the front of the engine. Both types are belt driven off the crankshaft.

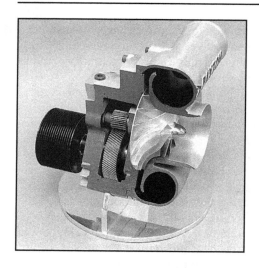

This is a cutaway of a Paxton Novi supercharger. Air is drawn in through the intake at the center of the impeller and thrust outward through a pressure housing to the tubing. This is the high-tech Paxton Novi centrifugal supercharger for small-block Fords. Thanks to its roller bearing design and step-up gearing, it gets the job done reliably.

sure, and the resulting power. Turbochargers have a waste-gate, which also bleeds excessive boost pressure, and prevents engine damage.

There are six basic different types of superchargers. Centrifugal, rotary, axial flow, Roots two-lobe and three-lobe, vane type, and Lysholm screw. Probably the most common type we see out there on small-block Fords are centrifugal and Roots lobe types. Centrifugal types are typically hung on the front of the engine, driven by the crankshaft pulley. Roots blowers, also driven by the crankshaft pulley, are normally an integral part of the intake manifold, with the carburetor mounted immediately upwind of the blower. With fuel injection, the throttle body is mounted in any number of locations before the Roots blower's intake. Fuel injectors are positioned in each of the intake ports, downwind of the Roots blower.

Which type of supercharger should you choose and why? This depends on your needs. Roots and centrifugal superchargers both have significant purposes. Let's talk about the Roots blower first.

The Roots lobe-type supercharger

has served many purposes during its service lifetime. Probably the most common Roots supercharger duty has been to feed hungry Detroit two-stroke diesel engines. You've undoubtedly heard the term "6-71 blower" in hot-rodding circles. Detroit two-stroke diesel engines, once manufactured by General Motors, are named based on displacement, number of cylinders, and cylinder arrangement. The Detroit 6V-71, for example, is a V-6 with 71 cubic inches of displacement per cylinder. A Detroit 8V-92 is a V-8 with 92 cubic inches per cylinder. The Detroit 6-71 is an in-line six, with 71 cubic inches per cylinder. So when you see a huge 6-71 blower atop a well-fed small-block Ford, it's a blower originally designed for huge Detroit Diesels that power semi-trucks.

What makes a Roots blower quite effective is its positive displacement design, which a Detroit two-stroke diesel engine needs for proper ingestion of air and scavenging of exhaust gasses. This kind of positive displacement design ascertains plenty of cylinder pressure when and where it counts in a high-performance V-8 engine. The "positive displacement" in a Roots blower is the result of its design not allowing much, if any, air to escape en route to the cham-

bers. Roots blowers have two- and three-lobe rotor designs in which rotors interlock to ensure consistent airflow, under pressure, into the engine.

Ford has been using the Roots design on factory production engines for many years, beginning with the 1989 3.8L Essex V-6 Thunderbird. Today, it's used atop the 5.4L SOHC V-8 engine in the Lightning and Harley-Davidson F-150 trucks, as well as the 2003-04 Cobra. This reliable, highly successful supercharger design will work quite well on your small-block Ford.

A more common type of supercharger is the centrifugal, which we see on a lot of newer 5.0L OHV and 4.6L SOHC and DOHC Mustangs. You may have heard the familiar whistle associated mostly with the Vortech and Paxton superchargers. Instead of the interlocking rotors used in the Roots positive displacement supercharger, centrifugal superchargers employ a fan that draws air into its center and rings it outward into a duct where it enters the intake manifold. Centrifugal force is defined by The American Heritage Dictionary as "the component of an apparent force or a body in curvilinear motion, as observed from that body, that is directed away

This Paxton Novi setup features a very heavy-duty mounting plate and a ten-rib belt. This keeps belt slippage down and boost up.

from a curvature or axis of rotation."

To make this easier to understand, centrifugal force is the energy of a spinning object that tends to throw the object, or parts of the object, outward. In this case, air is the object we sling outward from the spinning fan (compressor). The compressor takes the air in through its center and blows it outward with the whirling blades or fins that thrust it outward into the shell into the intake tube. Not only does the compressor move the air outward from its center, it also squeezes the air in the shell, feeding it to the intake tube. Think of the centrifugal style blower like your hairdryer, in which air is drawn into one side and blown out the other side. A hairdryer is a compressor of sorts. Even the humble blower in your Ford's air conditioning system compresses air to some degree before it exits your dashboard outlets. Most home vacuum cleaners are also of a centrifugal blower design.

Turbochargers work much like the centrifugal supercharger. Instead of being belt-driven, they're driven by a turbine that is propelled by hot exhaust gasses. As we accelerate, hot exhaust gasses drive the turbocharger's single-stage turbine, which drives the centrifugal compressor. Jet engines work on this same basic principle. We drive a turbine or turbines with hot exhaust gasses. The turbine or turbines drive a compressor or compressors that ram air into combustors. In the case of piston engines, we compress air, ramming it into the combustion chambers and making power.

Anytime you're going to raise your engine's stress level with nitrous oxide, supercharging, or turbocharging, you should remember the importance of cylinder sealing. Opt for only the best competition head gaskets. Be prepared to spend more than $100 for a set. If you're going to blow a ton of squeeze or boost into the chambers, think seriously about O-ringing the block for adequate cylinder sealing.

For more information on supercharging your Fox Mustang, check out *A Do-It-Yourself Guide To Street Supercharging*, by Pat Ganahl. It is available from CarTech books.

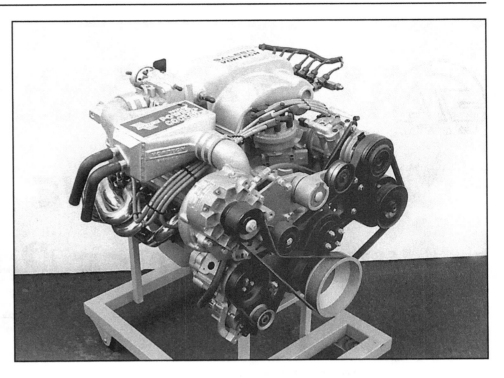

The Vortech V1 for the 5.0-liter small-block has a high-output T-trim impeller and a water-to-air aftercooler. The result here is more power.

This is a cutaway of the Powerdyne supercharger, which has a quiet belt-drive inside the case instead of gears.

ENGINE
PERFORMANCE PROJECTS

We're going to try actual experience in our efforts to teach you how to build a better 5.0L V-8 engine and outfit it to make the most of your building efforts. First, we want to talk about power, how power is made, and how you can achieve more of it. Internal combustion engines make power from thermal expansion inside of the combustion chambers. We mix vaporized fuel and air, compress and ignite this mixture, then use the heat and expansion and convert it to rotary motion inside the short block.

Think of your engine as an air pump. In theory, the more fuel and air we can pump through the chambers, the more power we should net. But it's more than just pumping fuel and air; it's how and when we pump it that matters most. For example, where do we want our engine to make the most power? If we want good low-end power for street use, then we want a nice compromise between small and large intake ports, with a mild cam profile that does its best work down low and in the midrange. We also want an intake manifold with long runners in order to get increased air/fuel velocity into the intake ports and chambers. If we want power on the high end like we see in a racing engine, we want shorter intake runners and larger intake ports where we will have velocity (and volume) at high RPM.

Whenever we're building an engine, we want something planned and executed to best suit our needs. For example, it makes no sense to build a high-revving race-track screamer if you're going to use it for the daily commute. By the same token, why fail to build enough into your engine if you're going to the races?

Proper planning should always include the long-range picture. If you intend to fit your Mustang with nitrous or a supercharger later on, then build a bottom end designed to take the punishment to come later on. Forged pistons, a steel or billet crankshaft, race bearings, shot-peened and properly bolted rods, proper compression ratio, and other issues should play into the plan. We need to plan these things in because we don't want the disappointment and expense of engine failure. Engine failure happens whenever we throw more at our small block than it's designed to handle safely.

Whenever we supercharge or turbo-charge an engine, we're increasing cylinder pressure and combustion temperatures. Cast pistons don't do well with high cylinder pressures and temperatures. The greater the boost we throw at cast pistons, the more quickly they fail under extreme pressures and temperatures. And don't kid yourself. There is a solid reason why the

automakers run forged pistons in supercharged applications. In fact, you'll never see a reputable engine builder opt for cast pistons in a supercharged or nitrous application. Why forged or hypereutectic pistons in supercharged and nitrous applications? Because forged and hypereutectic pistons stand up to extreme pressure and temperature better than cast.

Another important consideration is piston design. Piston ring location is everything in a supercharged or nitrous application. When we're ramming air and fuel into the chambers with a supercharger or turbocharger, we're raising temperature and pressure, which is also hard on piston rings. Supercharged and turbocharged applications need pistons designed for the task, where rings are moved further down the piston, away from extremes in pressure and temperature. The more boost we intend to throw at the piston, the more we need to think about piston tolerance, even with a forged piston. How we stack the rings in a piston matters a lot more than most of us understand.

If you're like most of us building carbureted engines, you probably won't be running a supercharger or turbocharger. Carbureted engines are harder to dial in when we're using a supercharger or turbocharger because fuel delivery is harder to program and adjust. That's the beauty of fuel injection. It's very precise. We can get carburetor jetting close, which works well in a naturally aspirated environment. The minute we start blowing air through that carburetor, a lot of unknowns come into play. If we're going to be driving our Mustang in a variety of environments ranging from high elevation to sea level, carb-jetting theory goes right out the window, but it's easy with fuel injection.

If you just want a snappy performer for street use only that will never be aggressively driven, then opt for hypereutectic pistons, 10.0:1 compression, and a more conservative cam grind and heads. This way, you will save money for other areas of your Mustang project. In any case, be realistic about how you intend to drive your Mustang.

Because you're most likely building a street engine, or a combination of street and track, we're going to show you a variety of mainstream engine projects that will be useful to you. Our first engine build project is for 5.0L enthusiasts who have older carbureted applications. From 1979-84, 5.0L engines were little more than mild-mannered small-block Fords with flat-tappet hydraulic camshafts.

The first project in the pages to follow is a warmed-up version of the 1985 5.0L roller-tappet engine that debuted that year. From the factory, it was topped with a Ford-design Holley carburetor that couldn't be tampered with. But, you get the idea of what we are trying to build here. We're building a powerful 5.0L-4V small-block engine that can go in any 1979-85 Mustang and actually pass a smog check.

Passing a smog check, of course, depends on where you live and how your engine is tuned before heading to the smog certification station. When we tune an engine to pass a smog check, we're inviting it to run horribly, especially if it's carbureted. Carburetor fuel systems don't afford the flexibility of electronic fuel injection with mass-air sensing. However, there's always tuning you can do that will make a difference in performance, with some sacrifice in the emissions department. We just don't get the same kind of efficiency and flex-ibility with a carburetor that we witness with fuel injection. In fact, we've become so spoiled that we expect carburetor fuel systems to give us the same fringe benefits we see with fuel injection. It simply won't happen.

How do we build a solid, reliable carbureted street engine that will make a real difference in our Mustang's performance? We get there by supplying our small block with the basics – good cylinder heads and induction, just the right cam profile, good exhaust scavenging, a hot ignition system, and the wisdom to know how to get it all to work together.

PROJECT 1:
TRANS AM RACING 5.0L-4V

We're going to try something decidedly unconventional with our first late-model Mustang power project – a carbureted 5.0L V-8 engine. As we stated earlier, this is the perfect power platform for a 1979-85 Mustang. If you build and tune this one correctly, you can even get it through a smog check without cheating. Although we have chosen a combination that has worked well for us, you can opt from a smorgasbord of performance equipment out there that's not only California smog legal, but will yield the same kind of performance we have witnessed here. When you're shopping for the right combination of components for your engine project, you want a cohesive package that works in harmony. And that is what this simple, carbureted small-block buildup is all about.

You can build a good carbureted small block using stock iron heads and still gain a lot of power. Power Heads is one good source for stock iron heads with port work that makes them comparable with more expensive aftermarket aluminum heads. You may also take your 5.0L engine's iron heads and do your own minor port work to improve power and save money. Just don't go too far with the grinder. GT-40 iron heads are also an affordable option, as are the GT-40P heads for the Explorer.

You may also opt for older 351W heads with larger ports. Just remember smog laws in your area. Older small-block heads aren't affected by the air pump provision, which didn't happen until 1975. This could hurt you during a smog check. Be mindful of combustion chamber sizing while you're shopping heads. Most older heads have smaller chambers ranging from 53 to 57 cc, which can raise compression too high in some applications. Our goal here is to empower you when it comes to your Mustang's engine build-up. There is a lot of it you can do yourself – including making the right decisions for your project.

Instead of doing a completely low-buck project, we're going to turn up the flame a little to show you what can be done using the right parts. Our platform is a brand new 5.0L roller block from Summit Racing Equipment. We've opted for a Scat 302 nodular-iron crankshaft. Federal-Mogul TRW hypereutectic aluminum flattop pistons will squeeze the mixture. Shot-peened C8AE connecting rods with 3/8-inch bolts marry piston and crankshaft with solid integrity. On top, we've opted for Trick Flow heads and an Edelbrock Performer RPM dual-plane intake manifold, fitted with a 600-cfm Holley carburetor. An MSD ignition system will ignite the mixture reliably. The result is approximately one horsepower per cubic-inch of displacement. Your result may vary significantly, depending on how closely you follow this example.

1. We're going with a good combination here – Edelbrock's Performer RPM intake manifold and a 600-cfm Holley carburetor. This combination gives us good low-end torque for the street coupled with breathing at high revs.

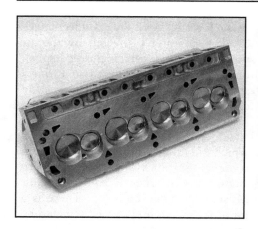

2. Trick Flow's Twisted Wedge aluminum cylinder head has 1.94/1.60-inch valves and 61-cc chambers.

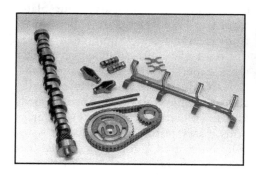

3. Valvetrain components should always be chosen as a package from one manufacturer. We're going with race-proven components from Comp Cams. Everything, from the camshaft to the valvesprings, is Comp Cams. We're running a mild street grind with roller tappets. We will achieve a smooth idle, coupled with a broad torque curve between 2,500 and 6,000 rpm.

4. AMK Products has provided us with all of the factory-type fastening hardware necessary to assemble our 302.

5. Federal-Mogul is our vendor of choice for bearings, gaskets, pistons, and more. Bearings should always be installed dry, void of lubrication between the bearing and block/rod. This reduces the chances of a spun bearing. Always lubricate the bearing heavily before installing the crank and rods. This is a Speed-Pro bearing from Federal-Mogul. In this application, we have a new nodular-iron crankshaft from Coast High Performance that calls for standard main and rod bearings.

6. Late-model small-block Fords have this one-piece rear main seal that is less likely to leak. Our builder, Mark Jeffrey of Trans Am Racing in Gardena, California, uses sealer around the perimeter to ensure leak-free performance.

7. Mark suggests generous amounts of assembly lube on main and rod bearing surfaces. This is good engine life insurance for the first fire-up.

8. Main bearing caps should be torqued carefully and checked repeatedly. Torque them in third values from #3 cap outward. The first torque should be 1/3 of the full torque value, beginning with #3 cap, then #2, then #4, then #1, then #5. Check the crankshaft for freedom of movement between each torquing sequence.

9. We're opting for an aggressive street roller Comp Cams camshaft here. This cam will give us good low-end torque, then come alive at high RPM. We want a broad torque curve that begins to come on strong from 2,500 through 6,000 rpm.

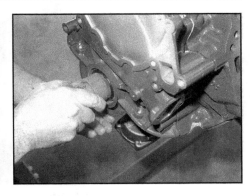

10. *When pistons are installed, always take care to ensure the large end of the rod doesn't nick the cylinder wall or crank journal. Use generous amounts of lube on the bearing. Coat the cylinder walls with SAE 30 weight engine oil. Torque the connecting rod bolts in half values. Make sure the crank rotates smoothly after each installation.*

13. *Be careful when installing the timing cover. Use a thin film of gasket sealer on both sides of the gasket. Center the timing cover using a harmonic balancer. Mark uses a special tool here, but you won't need it. Centering the timing cover prevents unnecessary front seal wear and leakage.*

11. *Oil pump installation is next. Always remember the pump shaft first. You would be surprised how many forget it. The C-clip always goes at the top of the shaft. Bolts need Loc-Tite on the threads before installation.*

14. *Like the timing cover, installing the oil pan requires great care. Use a thin film of gasket sealer on both sides of the gasket; you don't need much. Many people use too much sealer, which can contaminate your engine if the excess circulates throughout the engine. Make sure you have plenty of sealer where the rubber end gaskets meet the side rail gaskets, as this is a common leak point. Gently torque the pan bolts in a crisscross fashion. Don't over-torque them.*

12. *Fox-body Mustangs use a different type of oil pickup than classic Mustangs. Fox bodies use a rear-sump pickup fastened at the pump and at the number-3 main cap. Use Loc-Tite on the bolt threads.*

15. *Freeze plugs don't always get the careful attention they need. Use a thin film of gasket sealer around the perimeter, and then drive the plug in until the lip is flush with the block.*

16. Never cut corners on head gaskets, especially when you're using aluminum heads. Use the best gaskets you can. Position the head gasket coolant passages at the rear of the block. "FRONT" means FRONT! Torque the heads in third values. Remember to recheck your torque values.

19. Intake gaskets need your close attention. Make sure coolant passages are clear at the gasket. Run a bead of silicone sealer along each end of the block. Torque the manifold in third-values.

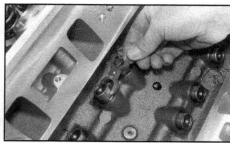

17. Roller lifters must sometimes be installed before the cylinder heads are installed, depending on the head. The Trick Flow heads give us clearance to get the roller lifters installed.

Trans Am Racing 302-4V Dyno Test

RPM	Horsepower	Torque	VE%
2000	122	319	75.00%
2500	156	328	78.20%
3000	195	342	81.30%
3500	237	355	85.20%
4000	278	365	89.20%
4500	314	**366**	91.00%
5000	338	355	90.90%
5500	**348**	332	89.20%
6000	345	302	85.70%

IT'S ABOUT FORDS – AND MORE!

So, what are we learning about small-block Ford performance? We are finding you can successfully build a small-block Ford and make lots of power, without giving away your first-born. It takes no more cash to build a small-block Ford than it does a small-block Chevy. We've also learned we can get factory small-block Ford heads to flow just as well as the Chevrolet.

Years ago, *Hot Rod* magazine pitted three sets of cylinder heads in a flow bench matchup. It was a bench race between the 351W head and Chevrolet's LT-1 and Bow-Tie heads. The results were surprising. At .600-inch valve lift, the 351W flowed 76 and 51 percent of the air through a 300-cfm orifice, intake and exhaust respectively, at 28 inches of water. Chevrolet's LT-1

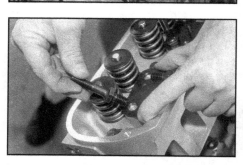

18. Comp Cams roller-tip rocker arms are a nice compromise between high end and low-budget. The rocker-arm stud, guide plate, and rocker arm must first be fit-checked and adjusted before the installation becomes permanent. The pushrod must clear the guide plate. The rocker arm must be centered on the valvestem. Hand crank the engine and adjust each rocker arm with the valve closed. Tighten the rocker arm until the tip contacts the valvestem, then tighten it 1/2-turn.

head flowed 79 and 57 percent, intake and exhaust. Although the Chevy head did perform better, performance was only marginal. We're convinced some port work time on the Ford 351W would have netted even higher numbers. And keep something else in mind: the Chevrolet LT-1 head has 2.02/1.60-inch valves – the 351W has 1.94/1.60-inchers. It's virtually impossible to get 2.02-inch valves in a 351W head.

Camshaft profile is another issue we have to be mindful of. In this age of roller camshafts, it's easy to get carried away with valve lift and duration. But valve lift is still valve lift. Street engines need conservative valve lift of .500 inch or less. Any more than this, and we're pounding the poop out of the valves and valvespring, costing us reliability. It's better to keep valve lift around .450 inch and keep the valves open longer. Valve overlap is another important issue when we are planning for power. Overlap can yield us even greater amounts of power if it's dialed in properly. Consult your cam grinder for details.

Whenever we're planning and building our engines, we tend to focus on the top end – cylinder heads, intake manifolds, and camshafts. We too easily forget the bottom end and what it can do for us in terms of power. Piston design determines power output. How are we going to stack our piston rings? How much piston skirt will there be? How much compression are we going to run? The less skirt we have, the less cylinder wall drag there will be. But, we have to find that ideal compromise where piston stability isn't compromised. Instability leads to certain wear and destruction.

Another way to increase power from the bottom end is by increasing bore and stroke. Stroker kits enable us to generate more power than the stocker. And this is what we're about to learn with Project 2. We're increasing the stroke marginally. Ditto for bore size. We're also going to pull more horsepower and torque from our small-block Ford from the use of electronic fuel injection. Let's face it, EFI is better; it not only allows us to meter fuel delivery more precisely, it also allows us precise spark timing. Let's look in on John Da Luz at JMC Motorsports in San

Diego, California, and see what he's been able to do with a fuel-injected 331.

PROJECT 2: JMC MOTORSPORTS 331-ci SEFI HIGH OUTPUT

We're going to build the Scat budget 331-ci stroker kit from JMC Motorsports in San Diego, California. The Scat 331 kit includes a new nodular iron hardened crankshaft, forged I-beam connecting rods with 3/8-inch rod bolts, forged Ross pistons, Total Seal piston rings, Clevite 77 bearings, and more. John Da Luz of JMC Motorsports is building this 331-ci stroker for a '94 Mustang GT with a 5-speed and 3.55:1 gears. Of course, the stroker bottom end is a luxury, but making power with extra cubes is often easier and more affordable than using a bunch of one-off race parts.

John intends to do some road racing with the hollowed-out shell he snapped up for $2,500. When John stripped the Mustang and sold most of its usable parts, like the interior, some body parts, the engine, transmission, and rear axle, he got back his $2,500 and a whole lot more. He found a solid, undamaged race-car platform that didn't cost him a penny, with a sound factory-original paint job he can take racing after a light splash of JMC Motorsports graphics.

JMC Motorsports is building this engine with Edelbrock Performer RPM heads and induction for late-model 5.0L Mustangs. Here again, the Edelbrock pieces are a luxury, but they aren't really that much more expensive then properly machining/rebuilding your stock pieces. The nice part about the Edelbrock Performer 331-ci stroker from JMC Motorsports is its emissions-legal status. John isn't concerned with building an emissions-legal engine because he won't be licensing this Mustang. However, everything John is using here will get you through a smog check, thanks to the E.O. status of a lot of these components. Edelbrock Corporation works very hard to ensure its cylinder heads and induction systems will pass a tough California smog check. In fact, Edelbrock is so committed to smog-legal performance parts that it has invested heavily in the necessary equipment to

test and certify its speed performance parts. You can pump displacement into your 1986-95 Mustang GT or LX with ease thanks to this engine package from JMC Motorsports, Scat, and Edelbrock.

What we learn from following John Da Luz in an engine build is that no detail is ever too small. John is very methodical in his work, checking each step two and three times in the interest of integrity. Few things frustrate John more than sloppy workmanship and important points getting missed in the interest of speed. And we're not talking vehicle speed either. John speaks of the failed engines he has seen in his career that would have survived, given closer attention to detail and a second look by the builder. One way to keep costs down is to only do things once – so get it right the first time.

Not only does John stress attention to detail, but also cleanliness along the way. A tiny, nearly invisible piece of dirt can score a bearing or seize an oil pump. If that tiny piece of dirt scores the bearing, it hurts oil pressure in the process. If the oil pump fails, especially at high-RPM, the engine will seize in a split second. These facts keep John committed to close inspection and cleanliness with every engine he builds. You should have this same level of commitment to your personal engine project.

With everything hospital clean, John focuses on fit and precision dynamic balancing. So, what about fit? How does your engine measure up? Piston-to-cylinder-wall clearances. Piston ring fit. Piston drag. Bearing clearances. Connecting-rod side clearances. Crankshaft endplay. Deck height. Compression height. Combustion chamber size. John checks these clearances again and again during the machining and build-up process. This is why he has successfully spun a stock 302 bottom-end with a cast crankshaft and C8OE rods to 8,000 rpm without failure. We saw this first-hand in his '66 Mustang fastback.

It should come as no surprise that John is going to build a Scat 331 stroker with the same level of attention he gave his 8,000-rpm 302, and he will do so with the dozens of other engines he builds every year. Now we're going to show you how it's done.

1. This is the Scat 331-ci stroker kit from JMC Motorsports. Included, depending which kit meets your budget, is a high nodular iron crankshaft with a 3.250-inch stroke, forged I-beam rods, forged Ross pistons, Total Seal piston rings, and Clevite 77 bearings.

3. John Da Luz places very strict emphasis on checking tolerances throughout a short-block build. Ring end gaps are custom-fitted and checked on each bore. Some folks check one bore and assume the rest will be identical, but John tells us that's foolish. He says it's rare that any of them match.

4. Summit Racing has provided our new 5.0-liter roller block. Although we have a new block, John's going to check everything. He has decided to bore the block .030-inch oversize. The cylinder skirts have been notched to clear the 331's rods.

2. The Crane hydraulic roller camshaft is lubricated and prepped for installation. This cam has an aggressive amount of lift above .500-inch because it's going into a road-race '94 Mustang.

5. We're using Clevite 77 street bearings. Because John is going road racing, you would think he would opt for race bearings. But John brings up an important fact: Race bearings are much harder than street bearings. This works well if your crank is forged steel or billet steel, both of which are harder than nodular iron. If the bearings are harder than the crank, then it's your crank that will get damaged if something comes between them. Stick with street bearings with nodular cranks, even if you're going racing.

6. John stresses using an abundance of assembly lube throughout the engine. This protects moving parts for that initial fire-up before there is enough oil flow and pressure. Also, if the engine is going to sit for an extended period of time, assembly lube will prevent corrosion. We suggest priming the oiling system before fire-up.

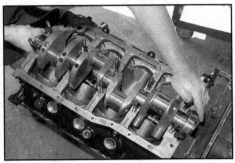

11. Total Seal rings are rolled onto the piston. Compression ring end gaps should be 180 degrees opposite as well, but not in alignment with the oil ring gaps. Gaps should be at 9, 12, 3, and 6 o'clock.

7. You need to check crankshaft endplay with a dial-indicator at the front of the crankshaft. When we check endplay, we are checking side clearances at the thrust bearing shown here. It should be .0004 to .0008 inch.

8. John uses a fish scale to check piston-to-cylinder-wall friction, which comes from oil ring tension. He installs the piston upside down with only the oil rings installed. Then, he uses a fish scale to pull the piston out of the bore. On a street engine, if drag is any less than 15 pounds, you need to try some different oil rings.

12. John coats the piston rings and cylinder walls in engine oil. He gently pushes the piston into the bore with two thumbs. Rod bearings have already been installed, seated, and lubed. John suggests watching the connecting rod's big end to make sure it doesn't nick the crank journal. Torque each rod bolt to spec.

9. We're using a Coast High Performance stud girdle to stiffen the block. No matter what any stud girdle manufacturer will tell you, some modifications have to be made to the main caps to clear the girdle. John torques the mains in three steps. First, 1/3 of the full torque value. Then 1/2. Then the full amount. Crankshaft endplay must be checked again.

10. John installs the pistons on the rods using a new-fangled clip that won't come out. It offers a fail-safe design that keeps your cylinder walls out of harm's way.

13. Check the rod side clearances. Clearances should be .010 to .020-inch.

14. We're using a Melling high-volume oil pump. Our pump has to clear the stud girdle and the crankshaft counterweight. You can expect the oil pump to interfere with the girdle, which will require some milling in places.

17. John installs a new crankshaft seal in our new timing cover from JMC Motorsports. Remember, the lip and spring must always go toward the inside. John positions the timing cover using an SCE gasket. We suggest using a very thin film of silicone sealer around the coolant passages.

15. We're using a Crane dual-roller timing set on John's 331. Because we're using a Crane cam, everything is Crane all the way up to the valvesprings.

18. We're using a one-piece rubber oil pan gasket/seal combo from SCE. This makes installation easier. Lay the gasket in place, using silicone sealer at the trouble spots in the corners of the pan rails. A new double-sump Fox-body Canton pan from JMC Motorsports is installed next. John snugs the corners first, and then tightens all of the bolts in a crisscross fashion.

16. John degrees the camshaft in with a Comp Cams degree wheel. This step determines proper valve timing and cam specs.

19. John has chosen AFR 185 cylinder heads for this particular build. This is a nice street/strip cylinder head with 2.02/1.60-inch valves. D-shaped exhaust ports improve exhaust scavenging.

20. John installed some ARP head studs. He opted for studs because he eventually wants to supercharge this engine. SCE provided the gaskets for this build-up. After checking the deck and cylinder head surfaces for scoring and debris, John is ready for the AFR 185 heads.

21. John installed the AFR 185 cylinder heads. When John received these heads from Airflow Research, he disassembled them and performed port and bowl work. It will be interesting to see what this does for power.

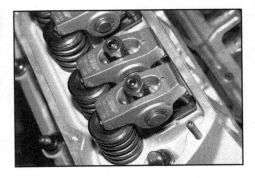

22. We're using Crane roller rockers with a 1.6:1 ratio. Rocker arm angle is checked. Because we're running a hydraulic camshaft, John runs down the rocker-arm stud nuts to where the rocker contacts the valvestem (off the cam lobe). Then, he tightens the rocker arm nut 1/2 turn.

23. Next, we're installing SCE intake manifold gaskets. A large bead of silicone works quite well at the end rails if you don't trust cork gaskets. John installs the Edelbrock Performer RPM lower intake manifold.

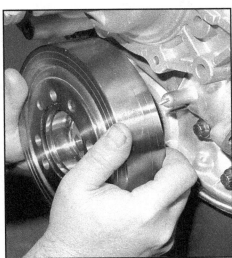

24. John is using a Ford Racing Performance Parts harmonic balancer. The excessive weight in some aftermarket balancers can break the crankshaft. Do your homework before purchasing one.

JMC Motorsports 331 Dyno Test

RPM	Horsepower	Torque	VE%
2000	134	332	69.9
2500	174	342	73.3
3000	220	365	76.9
3500	270	384	81.8
4000	320	391	86.2
4500	367	408	89.0
5000	391	387	90.0
5500	401	373	89.7
6000	434	362	87.2

5.0L ENGINE PERFORMANCE BOLT-ONS – 1988-93

We're going to show you how to improve your 5.0L High Output V-8's performance. When we remember that our engine is an air pump, the rest comes easier. The more air molecules we can feed into the chambers, the more power we're going to make. For example, your Mustang's hot underhood environment robs you of power. That's because hot air is thinner, with those air molecules dancing the jig far apart. When the air is colder, those molecules dance a lot closer together. When we feed those molecules into a hot combustion chamber, they expand rapidly, dancing outward with fury, making the most of those fuel molecules accompanying them. When we install cold-air induction, this helps our Mustang's engine produce more power. The installation of cold-air induction is an economical upgrade that can give you some power.

Denser, cooler air is the most affordable performance modification you can make in your quest for power. Getting more of it inside your engine is the next step. We do this with a larger throttle body and mass-air sensor. We're doing both here with a 76-mm C&L mass-air sensor and a MAC 70-mm throttle body. We get this done for well under $400.

When you're feeding an engine more air, that air has to have somewhere to get out. The Mustang GT's stock dual exhaust system will not get the job done effectively. But MAC's True-Fit dual exhaust system, with 2-1/2-inch pipes, and our JBA shorty headers, will improve our 5.0L engine's exhaust scavenging and performance.

We're also going to install one of the most basic upgrades – underdrive pulleys. They are easy to install, even if the results aren't overwhelming. Underdrive pulleys also benefit you by slowing down your accessories, which helps them last longer and keeps them from over revving.

It's important to remember that none of these modifications will give us great power yields; these are all baby steps. You can get into better induction and exhaust efficiency for not much money. That's the nice part. A supercharger, and nitrous, cost quite a bit more than basic induction and exhaust upgrades. Those are basic upgrades, but those basic upgrades help us get started. A supercharger or nitrous can punctuate our message later on.

Our foundation is a stock '93 Mustang GT 5.0L High Output engine with 60,000 original miles. This one is unusual because not many Mustangs out there have less than 100,000 miles, and most have been dogged to death with pedal-to-the-metal experiences. So, your results could vary. Let's get started.

COLD-AIR, 76-MM MAF, AND 70-MM THROTTLE BODY (1988-93)

Performance improvements don't always have to cost a bundle. We're installing a MAC cold-air induction. Nothing spectacular, but performance wars are won in baby steps, not quantum leaps. Hopefully this can get us 5-10 horsepower closer to victory.

Our next step is a larger 70-mm throttle body from MAC and a 76-mm mass-air meter from C&L. The larger throttle body and MAF will help improve power, and the mass-air meter can also be programmed for future modifications. When ordering your C&L mass-air meter, you need to relate your injector size in order to get the sampling tube sized right. Later, when we grow

our engine with stroking or a larger cam and heads, the C&L mass-air meter can help keep things running right. The other nice thing about the C&L mass-air meter is its compatibility with Ford electronics – just plug it in and it works.

The cold-air intake, larger-than-stock MAC throttle body, and innovative C&L mass-air meter move us in the right direction. They all contribute to power gains for not much money.

1. Here are our weapons of choice. The C&L 76-mm mass-airflow sensor is programmable in its own way, adjustable to your mission requirements. We like the way it looks and functions. Complementing our C&L mass-airflow sensor is a MAC 70-mm throttle body and EGR plate. Gaskets are included.

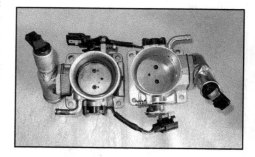

2. On the left is the stock throttle body. On the right is the MAC 70-mm throttle body. The difference is obvious. The objective is increased airflow, horsepower, and torque. You can get there for well under $200.

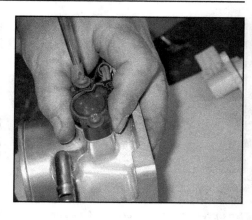

3. The new MAC 70-mm throttle body needs to be dressed for success. We're installing a new throttle-position sensor for best results. You may transfer the old one to the new throttle body if your budget is prohibitive.

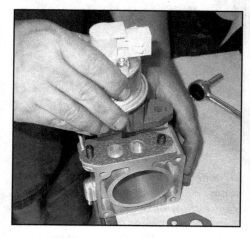

4. We're installing a new EGR valve and sensor assembly on the MAC EGR plate. We trust you're going to want to be emission legal, so don't forget to install this assembly.

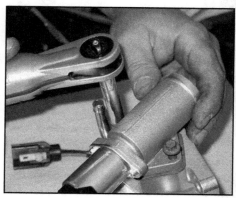

5. The idle speed motor is installed next on the EGR plate.

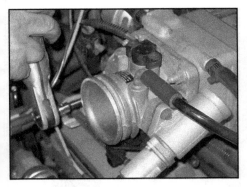

6. The stock throttle body and EGR plate assembly is disconnected at this time. Take note of all vacuum hose and electrical connection locations. This will be very important when it's time for assembly. And don't kid yourself – you can easily forget.

7. The throttle body and EGR plate are removed as an assembly.

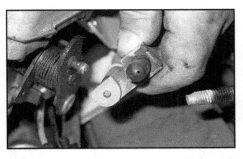

8. Both the throttle linkage and EGR sensor plug are disconnected next, which frees up this assembly for removal. Put the old throttle body and EGR plate on the shelf for safekeeping. You never know when emission laws will change in your area. We suggest keeping everything you remove.

9. Install a new gasket on the upper intake as shown. Then, install the new MAC EGR plate.

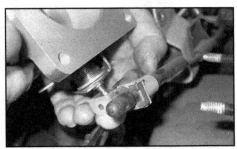

10. Install the gasket first between the throttle body and the EGR plate – then, install the 70-mm MAC throttle body. Connect the throttle linkage. Shown here is the throttle valve cable for the AOD transmission. This is adjustable to control shift points and pressure.

11. Next, install the brackets, vacuum hoses, and all electrical connections. We presume you took notes during disassembly. The installed MAC throttle body shows us that size really does matter. This nice-looking piece will improve performance considerably for under $200.

12. Installing the C&L programmable 76-mm MAF begins with removing the factory sensor, which is considerably smaller. The actual mass-airflow sensor must be transferred to the C&L sensor body, along with the bracket.

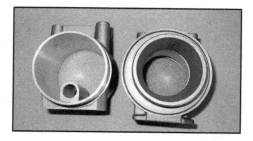

13. When we place the stock mass-airflow sensor (right) next to the larger C&L 76-mm mass-airflow sensor (left), the difference is clear. Our goal is to flow more air through the intake system prior to reaching the throttle body downstream. The C&L sensor enables us to do that effectively.

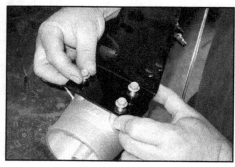

14. The MAF is transferred to the C&L 76-mm mass-air body. So is the bracket. This is a simple task. Don't forget to transfer the O-ring between the actual sensor and the body.

15. We want to go all-MAC with this change in induction. This is a MAC air filter, being installed just ahead of the C&L mass-airflow sensor.

JBA HEADERS AND MAC EXHAUST (1988-93)

With our 5.0L High Output foundation breathing in quite well, and making more power, we're ready to rise to the next phase: the exhaust system. When Ford first fitted the 5.0L High Output V-8 with headers in 1985, we were impressed because there had never been a factory Mustang exhaust header ever, including anything made of iron in

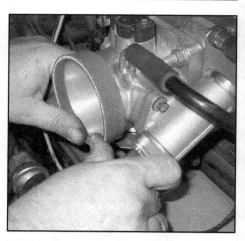

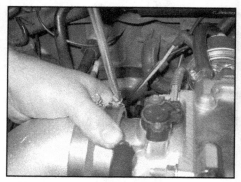

16. The C&L induction system is next and last. Begin at the throttle body and work your way back to the air filter. The installed package should look like this.

the 1960s. Even the old 289 High Performance V-8 available in the 1965-67 Mustang really didn't have an exhaust header. It had less-restrictive cast-iron exhaust manifolds. They did virtually nothing for performance.

When we look at the shorty factory exhaust headers installed on the Mustang GT and Cobra from 1985-95, they make about as much sense as the 289 High Performance exhaust manifolds of 40 years ago. They do virtually nothing for performance. Not only are the header tubes small, barely accommodating the thumb of an average person, they're kinked and poorly bent, which also adds restriction.

We're going to install some ceramic-coated JBA shorty headers and a complete MAC exhaust on our '93 GT. If you've done your homework on the intake side (like we have), improving the exhaust system will also give you more power. Dollar-for-dollar, the exhaust is one of the best places to make power.

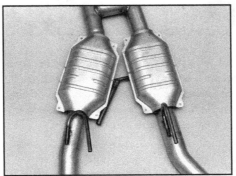

1. The MAC True-Fit exhaust system, as its name implies, fits the Mustang GT like a glove. We're adding something even more beneficial to this Mustang GT: MAC Flow Path mufflers, which will reduce backpressure considerably. This cat-back system delivers a throaty sound and yields an improvement in performance.

5. Remove the mufflers and tailpipes. If you're working with a factory exhaust system, your only choice is to cut the pipes at the mufflers where they join the tailpipes.

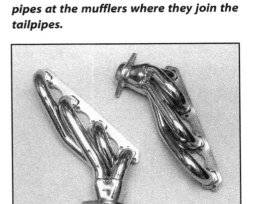

2. Our 1993 Mustang GT has Hooker mufflers, which are poorly fitted, and actually too large for this application. The right muffler rubs the driveshaft and touches the frame rail, which makes for a noisy ride. This brings us to a valuable point: When is large, too large? Size your mufflers to the application. When mufflers and pipes are too large, they touch the body, which transmits noise to the cabin. Trust us, the noise will drive you nuts.

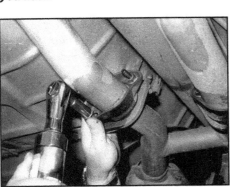

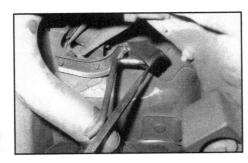

3. Begin removing the old exhaust system by taking off the catalytic converters and H-pipe.

4. Late-model Mustang exhaust systems are hung by rubber hangers, which are easy to remove and install. These hangers also isolate exhaust system resonance quite well.

6. JBA ceramic-coated shorty headers are a good fit for this application. When you compare the JBA headers (bottom) to factory equipment, you can see the difference in pipe sizing and flange construction.

7. Header removal takes some insight. On the driver side, you won't have much trouble removing the factory header through the top. The JBA header will need to be installed through the bottom, though that means disconnecting the steering shaft to get it through.

8. The passenger-side header goes in and out through the top as shown.

9. Header installation takes practice. Get each header started with a couple of bolts at each end. These bolts have lock washers, which keep them from backing out.

10. With a couple of bolts loosely in place at each end of the header, drop the header gaskets in place as shown. Then tighten the header bolts in a crisscross fashion to ensure uniform torque.

11. JBA's ceramic-coated shorty headers look nice and perform a solid function. They keep heat inside the tubes, where it belongs, and they scavenge spent gasses very well.

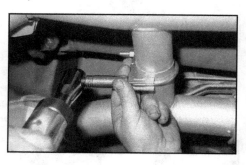

12. The H-pipe with catalytic converters is next. Don't forget the oxygen sensors and connections. In fact, install new O2 sensors while you are here. This is the air pump tube, which is very important for cleaning emissions and passing a smog check. This is a two-piece H-pipe for ease of installation.

13. Both mufflers and tailpipe assemblies are installed next. These assemblies are hung via rubber hangers. The hangers are tied to the catalytic converter/H-pipe assembly in front, plus there's one at each muffler.

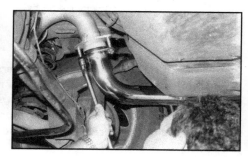

14. Tailpipes bolt to the muffler and tailpipe assemblies. Like the mufflers, the tailpipes slip into rubber hangers on the body.

UNDERDRIVE PULLEYS (1988-93)

What purpose do underdrive pulleys really serve on a 5.0L High Output Mustang GT? Underdrive pulleys are sized to change the crank-pulley-to-accessory-pulley drive ratio. When we make the crankshaft pulley smaller and the accessory pulleys larger, we slow down the accessory speed, which saves wear and tear on the accessories by slowing them down. We also make it easier for the engine to turn the accessories, which frees up a little power.

Most Mustang enthusiasts start off with pulleys because they're affordable and easy to install. You literally just take off your belt, take off the pulleys, put on the new pulleys, and put the belt back on – it's that easy. Remember to follow the manufacturer's instruction if it's your first time.

5.0L ENGINE PERFORMANCE BOLT-ONS – 1994-95

They are hot-rodding tricks as old as the automobile itself – those basic engine performance upgrades we can do right in the car to enhance performance. These are nice upgrades you can perform in your home garage in weekend increments. If you have a local dyno shop, you can test the worth of these modifications and see the gains for yourself. In Southern California, specifically San Diego, we have The Dyno Shop in suburban Santee. We're going to test these bolt-on upgrades step-by-step on the DynoJet chassis dynamometer at The Dyno Shop to show you how much difference each upgrade makes in the power picture.

We're going to install cold-air induction to see what a cooler, denser air charge will do for performance. After that, we're going to fit our Mustang with a MAC cat-back exhaust system and some new, smog-legal JBA shorty headers. We will strap our used '95 Mustang GT beast to the dyno for a real-world look at what these simple power upgrades do for power. The result may surprise you.

After the exhaust system upgrade and an aggressive dyno test, we're going to take our 81,000-mile 5.0L Mustang and change its personality considerably. We're going to install an Edelbrock Performer package that includes cylinder heads, induction, and a hotter camshaft.

We're looking to John Da Luz of JMC Motorsports in San Diego, California, once again, for a closer look at the installation of the bolt-on upgrades. Here's how our GT did, box-stock, fresh out of the San Diego used-car classifieds.

At the rear wheels, John's 1995 Mustang GT with an AODE transmission yields 191 horsepower and 245 ft-lbs of torque. That's roughly 240 horsepower and 308 ft-lbs of torque at the crankshaft. What has surprised us most throughout the life of this project was torque. It has remained very consis-

Baseline Dyno Test '95 Mustang GT

RPM	Horsepower	Torque
3,900	182	245
4,000	181	239
4,100	184	236
4,200	188	235
4,300	189	231
4,400	191	228
4,500	189	221
4,600	189	215
4,700	189	211
4,800	189	206
4,900	188	201
5,000	186	196
5,100	184	190
5,200	180	182
5,300	177	175
5,400	172	166
5,500	167	159

tent in the mid 200s. It started at 245 didn't dramatically improve until we step up to heads, induction, and camshaft. Of course, it jumped even higher later on because of our Power-dyne XB-1 supercharger.

MAC COLD-AIR KIT (1994-95)

Cold-air induction is a lesson in common sense. What will cold-air induction do for your Mustang's power output? It'll improve torque right off the bat because it provides your 5.0L engine with a denser air charge. Even if the optimistic gains people expect from cold-air induction are rarely realized, especially in hot weather, it's a proven fact that colder air makes a difference in power output. We experience this most in the hot Southwest. When the outside air temperature is in excess of 100 degrees, our Mustangs fall flat on their faces. They don't climb a grade very well, which means we have to lean on them harder. When you add insult to injury with extremely hot underhood air, power output becomes even more pathetic. Cold-air induction doesn't

necessarily give us "cold" air in all cases, but the air outside is usually cooler than what's under the hood.

The 1994-95 Mustang GT induction system tends to be more restrictive due to the very nature of its design. Ford moved the mass-air sensor inside the air cleaner, adding to the restriction. This is why MAC's cold-air system stands to improve things considerably.

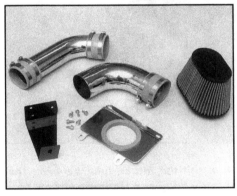

1. Underhood on a 1994-95 Mustang GT, you will find a different air cleaner-silencer set-up (top) than you would on a 1987-93. The mass-airflow sensor is located inside the air cleaner for '94s and '95s. MAC's cold-air kit (directly above) for the 1994-95 Mustang simplifies the induction system and makes it less restrictive.

2. Remove the air cleaner assembly.

3. With the air cleaner assembly open as shown, access the mass-airflow sensor located inside and remove it.

4. Install the intake tube between the throttle body and the mass-airflow sensor. Don't tighten the clamps until the entire assembly is installed. You need flexibility for adjustment purposes.

5. After installing the new mass-airflow sensor and intake elbow, you install the air cleaner mount. The air cleaner installs up inside the fender once we have the elbow installed.

MAC Exhaust and JBA Headers (1994-95)

We're going to bolt a MAC True-Fit exhaust system onto John Da Luz's Mustang GT and see what the dyno tells us. JBA shorty headers will also replace the stock manifolds. We aren't showing another MAC/JBA installation photo sequence because the process is so similar to the one detailed earlier in the chapter – plus there isn't exactly a lack of photos in this book!

So what have we learned from John Da Luz about making power? John has installed the MAC cold-air system to get a denser air charge into the intake plenum. This helps power just a bit. Then John went underneath and installed a MAC exhaust system with JBA headers just off the cylinder heads. For these relatively simple mods, he gained 18 horsepower and 27 ft-lbs of torque at the rear wheels. At the crank, that equates to about 20 and 32 respectively. Remember, we don't gain lots of horsepower and torque all at once when we are chasing power. It happens in baby steps.

MAC Cold Air, MAC Exhaust, and JBA Header Dyno Test

RPM	Horsepower	Torque
3,900	191	**272**
4,000	198	261
4,100	200	260
4,200	201	256
4,300	204	251
4,400	206	249
4,500	207	245
4,600	**209**	240
4,700	208	239
4,800	208	233
4,900	207	228
5,000	206	223
5,100	203	217
5,200	200	202
5,300	198	196
5,400	193	189
5,500	188	180

Cylinder Head, Camshaft, and Intake Manifold Swap (1994-95)

When the Mustang GT became fuel-injected in 1986, we were convinced that we had lost the tunable pony. Opening the hood yielded a mass of aluminum and complex electronics. We didn't understand any of it. In the years since, we've learned how to live peacefully with fuel-injected Mustangs. Along the way, we've learned how to tune them and modify them for more power, and with great results. A case in point is John Da Luz's

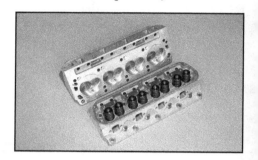

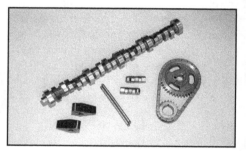

1. Step up and bolt on the powerful Edelbrock Performer RPM cylinder head and induction package. There's even a camshaft kit available that goes with it. We're using the Comp Cams hydraulic roller camshaft kit shown here because John Da Luz wanted to fine-tune the grind. We've come to find that the camshaft tuning is very important in 1994-95 Mustang GTs and Cobras due to the limits of the ECM. Anything too radical does not run well.

'95 Mustang GT. When John found this one in the classified ads for chump change, he knew it had potential. To prove its potential to himself and to us, he dyno-tested it in stock form. Then, he tried proven hot-rodding tricks, like cold-air induction, shorty headers and deep-breathing dual exhausts.

John's Mustang GT has gone about as far as it can go with factory iron cylinder heads, induction, and camshaft. To make more power, John knows he needs to get more air and fuel into the cylinders. He also understands that the way air and fuel enter and leave the cylinders will have to change as well. John's going to make this happen with a pair of Edelbrock Performer cylinder heads and intake manifold, and an aggressive roller camshaft from Comp Cams.

Let's look at the Edelbrock Performer 5.0L cylinder heads. These are the PN 60329 aluminum cylinder heads with 1.90-inch intake valves and 1.60-inch exhaust valves. The chambers are 60 cc, while stock Ford heads, by comparison, have 1.76-inch intake valves and 1.46-inch exhaust valves. Chamber size on those heavy iron heads is 60-63 cc. With the Edelbrock Performer 5.0L heads, we gain airflow in and out of the chamber, and we may actually gain some compression. Plus, the aluminum head will carry heat away, enabling us to push the engine a little harder. And, considering where we are headed with this engine, we're going

to need heads that can manage heat and cylinder pressure issues wisely.

On top, we're going with the PN 3821 Edelbrock Performer 5.0L upper and lower intake manifolds. This is an induction system designed to work very well between 1,500 and 6,000 rpm, which is where most street 5.0L smallblocks live. Truth is, our 5.0L smallblock, even with everything we're going to throw at it, will make its peak power around 5,500 rpm. Peak torque consistently comes in around 4,000 rpm.

Comp Cams has provided us with an XE264HR roller hydraulic camshaft. At .050-inch lift, we get 212/218 degrees

of duration. The cam also features .512 inch of gross valve lift, which keeps us safely out of the pistons, while lobe separation is 114 degrees, and intake centerline is 110 degrees. John believes we could make even more power by working the duration a pinch. Every seasoned engine builder has a little bit of cam grinder in them, including John Da Luz.

Here's how you make real power with a stock bottom end. And because the 5.0L H.O. has a strong factory bottom end, it's not really our main concern here. Now, if only we could figure out how to get around the factory electronics. The Dyno Shop will show us how.

4. The 1994-95 5.0-liter engine's front dress with air conditioning looks like this. We're giving you this as a visual reference.

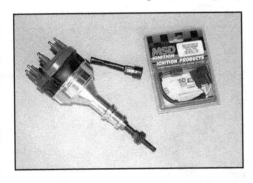

2. MSD's Pro-Billet distributor for 5.0-liter High Output engines brings the quality and reliability we've come to expect from MSD. Installation is a snap, since you can plug it into the 1994-95 Mustang harness using an adapter plug. The MSD Digital-6 Plus amplifier gives us a consistent, hotter spark.

3. Since we're going to be dealing with the front of the engine, we have to remove the radiator. For 1986-93 Mustangs, this is fairly simple, but for 1994-95 Mustangs, it's quite involved. The plastic radiator cover is retained with simulated plastic screws, which really aren't screws at all. Turn them counterclockwise for removal. Install them by simply pushing them in. Once the cover is removed, work your way through the cooler system control module and radiator retaining brackets. Drain the radiator by opening the petcock on the right-hand side. Disconnect the radiator hoses and automatic transmission cooler lines (if equipped). The coolant recovery reservoir also needs to be disconnected and removed.

5. The upper intake manifold is next. Disconnect the throttle cables as shown. Because we're going to use this BBK 70-mm throttle body on the new Edelbrock Performer RPM manifold, it will need to be transferred. There are lots of vacuum hoses and sensors to disconnect, and the intake hose needs to be removed at this time. Take pictures or make a video of these installations before you disconnect everything, since you'll need references later. Remove the engine identification cover on top, which is held in place by four screws. Six bolts retain the upper intake.

6. With the upper intake removed, the induction system looks like this. Eight ports feed eight cylinders. There are eight fuel injectors on two fuel manifolds or fuel rails. Again, photograph all of this before disassembly. Disconnect all sensors and hoses. The fuel manifold is disconnected from the fuel lines with a special tool available at your local auto parts store. This is a quick-connect fitting designed for fast factory connection. Remove the distributor at this time, but only after cranking the number-1 piston to top-dead-center on compression/ignition stroke, taking note of rotor positioning. Use that camera. Remove the ten bolts that retain the manifold and lift the manifold off. Watch out for coolant, which can get into the engine oil.

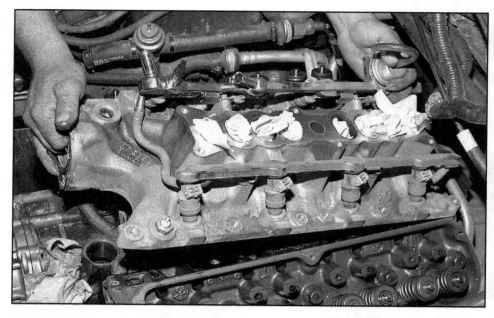

7. The power-steering pump pulley must be removed with a puller before the pump can be removed.

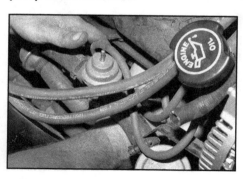

8. Air pump plumbing must be disconnected at the headers. Then, remove the headers. You can leave the headers tied to the exhaust system; however, access is improved when we completely remove the headers. If you haven't done so, this is a good time to upgrade to new aftermarket JBA shorty headers for smooth compatibility with the Edelbrock heads.

9. The accessory drive package is next. There are two basic assemblies. On your left, as you face the engine, is the subassembly that holds the alternator, air pump, and idler pulley. On your right is the subassembly that holds the power-steering pump and A/C compressor. Disconnect and remove the alternator. Remove the air pump. Detach the power-steering pump and safely swing it out of the way. There is no need to disconnect the lines. The same is true for the A/C compressor. Just secure the compressor and get it out of the way. Remove the subassembly.

10. Now its time to remove the cylinder heads. Start by pulling the valve covers and removing the rocker arms and pushrods. Remove the head bolts and heads. Be careful when lifting the heads; remember, they're made of iron.

11. This really is a lackluster job, but it has to be done. Clean up the block deck surfaces, removing all old cylinder head gasket material. You want a clean deck surface. Do not use a grinding wheel or disc. Gently use a wire wheel for the final cleanup.

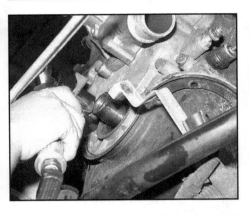

12. After you have removed the harmonic balancer with the proper tool, the timing cover and water pump are next. Remove all of the bolts in front and at the oil pan. Remove the timing cover.

13. We're going to remove the timing set and camshaft now. In the lifter valley, the spider assembly, which retains the lifters, comes out with two bolts. Remove the lifters, and then remove the timing chain and sprocket. Two bolts retain the camshaft. Gently slide the camshaft out of the block, taking extra care not to score any of the cam bearings, as they nick easily.

14. Our new Comp Cams roller camshaft offers an aggressive profile, without adversely affecting idle quality. The 1994-95 5.0-liter High Output engine has a more limited operating range inside its ECM. Cams that are too radical do not perform very well with this ECM, as idle quality suffers greatly. In some cases, the engine will not run at all. Lube up the camshaft with assembly lube and install, and again, watch those cam bearings. Loc-Tite is used on the cam retainer bolts.

15. Comp Cams has provided our timing set. We all know this one, right? The timing marks go at 12 and 6 o'clock as shown.

16. The Comp Cams roller tappets are installed next. Use Loc-Tite on the spider bolts. Lube the lifters with assembly lube.

17. SCE competition head gaskets are used here, just in case we decide to blow squeeze or install a supercharger. Edelbrock's Performer RPM cylinder heads are good street heads, giving us great low-end torque. Plus they're good up to 6,000 rpm. The heads are installed and torqued to Edelbrock's specifications. Torque your heads in third values. Begin at the two center head bolts and work outward in twos.

18. Install the pushrods and rocker arms. These are fully adjustable roller rockers. Check the geometry and ascertain a proper relationship between pushrod and valve.

19. Prepare the timing cover next. We're installing a JMC Motorsports high-flow water pump for improved cooling. Make sure the surfaces are cleaned before you install a new gasket. Use a conservative amount of silicone gasket sealer between the timing cover and gasket only. Then, use sealer around the coolant passages on both sides of the gasket. Install the timing cover. Lubricate the harmonic-balancer seal contact surface with assembly lube. Make sure to lube the seal and install the harmonic balancer.

20. Use Loc-Tite on the harmonic balancer bolt threads. The installed harmonic balancer and underdrive pulley look like this. Note the timing mark and marker. The number-1 cylinder should be straight up at top-dead-center on the compression stroke.

21. The lower intake manifold is next. John Da Luz prefers Permatex Right Stuff gasket goop. He runs it along the fore and aft manifold rails, and around each of the coolant passages.

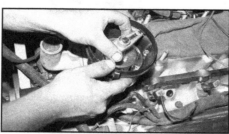

23. Our new MSD billet distributor goes in next. If you have trouble getting the distributor to seat, hand crank the engine once the distributor is down to 1/4 inch from seating. This turns the distributor shaft and aligns the oil pump shaft. The distributor should drop right into place.

24. The upper intake manifold is next. A lot of assembly is required before this manifold is installed. Remember the throttle body, fittings, hoses, sensors – there's a lot to consider here.

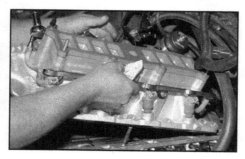

22. The JBA shorty exhaust headers are installed next. Gasket installation is simplified by first installing two header bolts at the cylinder heads, then dropping in the gaskets and installing the rest of the bolts.

25. There is more to install and connect than we have room to show you here. The Fluidyne radiator is installed, along with all cooling system hoses and connections. This is why it is important to photograph your setup before it comes apart. In the old days, engine compartments were simple and easy to remember. Today, they're more involved; you need pictures or video.

Cylinder Heads, Intake, and Camshaft Dyno Test

RPM	Horsepower	Torque
3,900	207	279
4,000	214	281
4,100	216	277
4,200	216	271
4,300	221	267
4,400	225	265
4,500	228	263
4,600	235	261
4,700	242	260
4,800	248	257
4,900	254	254
5,000	256	247
5,100	263	242
5,200	266	238
5,300	272	236
5,400	277	236
5,500	273	236

These results just cost us the better part of a weekend in John's San Diego shop. A period of 48 hours and a lot of wrenching has netted us 277 horsepower and 287 ft-lbs of torque at the rear wheels. We are up 59 horsepower and 49 ft-lbs of torque at the wheels. These are nice, acceptable gains in power for some relatively affordable bolt-on modifications.

POWERDYNE XB-1 SUPERCHARGER INSTALLATION (1994-95)

When John Da Luz of JMC Motorsports was planning his Mustang's performance agenda, he knew what he wanted from the start. Not only did he know what he wanted, he went after it knowing the result in advance. Because John has a lifetime of experience making all kinds of vehicles go faster, this Mustang was no exception. He knew it would go faster, but only with a realistic plan for power.

John knew his Mustang was never going very far with stock cylinder heads and induction. He also knew it needed a more aggressive camshaft and an exhaust system that would allow the breathing necessary to make real power. Because John had a lot of faith in the stock 5.0L block and internals, he was prepared to top his engine with ported Edelbrock Performer cylinder heads and induction, and a more aggressive hydraulic roller camshaft from Comp Cams. He was also prepared to throw supercharging at it. Why so much courage? Because John understands just how much boost he can huff at the stock 5.0L bottom end without failure.

The stock 5.0L short block is very durable because Ford engineered it that way. Inside it has a very strong 2M nodular iron crankshaft, hypereutectic (sometimes forged) pistons, and the most current evolution of the C8OE connecting rod. You wouldn't want to use a 1968-vintage C8OE rod. The best rod to use is a current-generation, broad-shouldered C8OE rod, with 3/8-inch ARP bolts. Because John's 5.0L engine is a dead stocker, he's going at it knowing just how far he can go without losing the bottom end. And since we

have great faith in John's judgment, we're convinced he's going to step up the power without disappointment.

John has opted for the new Powerdyne XB-1 blower for his mild-mannered 5.0L. Because John wants a nice balance of power and reliability, he plans on keeping the boost conservative at 7-8 pounds. This shows respect for the stock bottom end, with its hypereutectic pistons, rings near the top of the piston, and a compression ratio courting 9.0:1. Let's get started on the final stretch of our power project.

1. This is the Powerdyne XB-1 supercharger for 5.0-liter H.O. Mustangs. Everything we need for a complete installation is here, not including the MSD boost-retard electronics. If you're installing the XB-1 with a stock induction system, installation is a snap. Aftermarket induction systems and radiators can sometimes create fitment and clearance issues.

2. Steeda 36-lb/hr injectors are just what we need to safely operate our 5.0-liter H.O. powerplant. Stock injectors are 19 lbs/hr each, which isn't enough fuel to meet boost demands. Running lean under boost can cause permanent engine damage.

Now that we understand what we have for bolt-on power, it's time to get started. Before we go any further, we want you to know this is not an easy installation. The Powerdyne XB-1 supercharger is an outstanding blower. Everything you could ever need to complete the installation is included in the kit. Where this installation becomes challenging is custom installations. The XB-1 kit really is a contradiction in terms. It fits stock applications perfectly. But, how many of us are going to install an XB-1 supercharger in a stock application? Certainly not John Da Luz. John has installed Edelbrock heads and induction, which really don't present any fitment issues. But his wider-than-stock Fluidyne aluminum radiator does. This creates fitment problems that Powerdyne didn't encounter during research and development of this kit. John figured out a way

3. We first disconnect the battery and remove the air intake system.

4. The upper intake manifold has to be removed to upgrade the fuel injectors. Stock applications have 19-lb/hr injectors. With the Powerdyne supercharger huffing 7-8 psi at full throttle, we need Steeda's 36-lb/hr injectors. Remove the upper intake manifold to expose the eight fuel injectors.

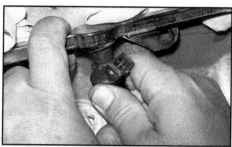

5. The engine's eight fuel injectors are positioned along two fuel rails, one down each bank of four cylinders. Remove the fuel rail bolts and pull the fuel rails. The injectors are ganged along the fuel rail as shown. Gently remove each fuel injector. Lubricate each new injector with petroleum jelly on both ends. Gently insert the new injectors into each fuel rail. Reinstall the fuel rail and injectors as a unit. Then reinstall the bolts.

around these problems, and managed to find his way to the dyno anyway.

Our Powerdyne XB-1 installation isn't going to be a step-by-step because there isn't enough page space in this book. However, we're going to guide you through the installation process, giving you some idea of what to expect along the way. Then, we're going to dyno John's Mustang and demonstrate how much power the Powerdyne XB-1 can make for you.

With the induction and some new Steeda injectors installed, we're ready to tackle the real meat and potatoes of this Powerdyne supercharger installation – the supercharger itself. Installing a supercharger isn't easy because so much changes about the engine's front accessory drive. We're going to relocate both the alternator and the air pump. If you're tempted to eliminate the air pump, forget it. Powerdyne has designed this system

with the Environmental Protection Agency and cleaner air in mind. Plus, the front accessory drive brackets and idler pulleys have been designed to work specifically with the air pump.

Why do we need to upgrade the fuel injectors when we install a supercharger? Because we need a richer fuel mixture to counterbalance the overwhelming amount of air coming into the combustion chambers. If we run the XB-1 supercharger with 7-8 pounds of boost without giving the mixture more fuel, it'll be an extremely lean mixture. Extremely lean mixtures run very hot, causing serious piston damage. And when you're pushing the throttle, engine destruction can happen in nanoseconds. Remember, pistons are made of aluminum, which melts at 1,300 degrees F. Exhaust gas temperatures need to be kept conservative when running a supercharger. Whenever you're running a supercharger, you need to know two critical measurements: boost pressure and exhaust gas temperature. Add these instruments to your engine's gauge package.

Upgrading the fuel system isn't just about high-flow injectors – it's about fuel delivery and pressure. We need a BBK high-performance electric fuel pump to replace the stock pump in the tank. We also need an adjustable fuel pressure regulator. The supercharger manufacturer will supply the information necessary for you to properly tune your engine once installation is complete. Boost directly determines what size injectors you will need. The more boost you intend to run, the greater the amount of fuel you're going to need. At 7-8 pounds of boost, we need the 36-lb/hr injectors that John has specified. If John were going to push it even higher, he would need 38- or 42-lb/hr injectors. Of course, he might later need an engine if he did.

Since we're adding a sizable accessory to our engine's front-dress, changes have to be made in order to make it work in a cohesive fashion. We need to install the brackets, supports, and spacers supplied by Powerdyne. We'll also need to remove the stock alternator/air-pump bracket, but don't throw it away. We learned this lesson the hard way with the classics. When vintage Mustangs were

purchased new and hopped up long ago, we threw away all of the stock parts, like air cleaners, valve covers, intake manifolds, carburetors, and the like, never thinking we'd need them again. We

6. Remove the radiator cover, electric cooling fan, coolant recovery reservoir, and fan controller. The fan controller is a microprocessor that controls fan operation and speed. When we turn on the air conditioning, the fan speeds up to increase airflow across the condenser. The microprocessor also varies fan speed with the outside air temperature.

7. This is the 5.0's front accessory drive-belt system. We're going to have to change this setup to accommodate the Powerdyne supercharger. Remove the factory serpentine belt. You will use this belt again.

8. Disconnect and remove the alternator.

9. This factory subassembly retains the alternator and air pump. Remove this sub-assembly and store it away for safekeeping. Remove the alternator pulley and unbolt the alternator case halves. Remove the front half of the case and relocate it as shown. Do not remove the rotating armature inside. Removing the armature will dislodge the brushes, which can be a pain. Make sure the armature stays put. Rotate the housing to the position shown and reinstall the three bolts.

learned during the restoration era what a mistake that was. Save all factory components, and put them away for safekeeping.

The front-dress becomes challenging whenever we're dealing with odd-duck components, like underdrive pulleys, aftermarket air conditioning, or a replacement engine with a different front dress. We cannot possibly cover all the bases on that one. A lot of it is trial and error, learning the ropes as you go. We've been there all too many times. And because we are dealing with Fords here, be prepared for running changes your mother never told you about.

In any case, your main concern should be proper pulley alignment. When belts are not in proper alignment, belt wear and tear becomes a huge problem. Serpentine belts must track nice and straight over their pulley grooves. Any side loading on the belt will shorten its lifespan considerably. Too much belt tension will also harm both the belt and the accessories. Accessories get harmed from excessive bearing and shaft loads, which cause premature wear.

To accommodate the Powerdyne XB-1 supercharger, we have to relocate the alternator and air pump. When we relocate the alternator, we have to rotate the back of the alternator to reposition the pivot point and connections. With the Powerdyne supercharger in place, the alternator fits snugly just below the

10. Install the Powerdyne crankshaft pulley. This is actually an off-the-shelf Ford crankshaft pulley with a Ford part number. It drives the supercharger. The factory 1994-95 crankshaft pulley closest to the harmonic balancer is the pulley you need to use for proper operation. The underdrive pulley will not work.

supercharger and above the air pump. Both the alternator and air pump are mounted on a small mounting plate attached to the right-hand cylinder head. They're further supported by the main supercharger mounting plate located in front. We'll get to this shortly.

11. Slide the air pump onto the studs as shown; then reinstall the air-pump hoses.

12. The alternator slides onto the studs as shown. Don't forget to reconnect all the wiring.

13. This is the Powerdyne main support plate. It attaches to the water pump and alternator/air pump studs. Spacers are used to shim things up. Note the adjustable idler pulley to the right. This is the supercharger belt's idler pulley, which slides up and down to control belt tension. The engine's accessory drive belt is controlled by a separate idler pulley.

This is where pulley spacing and fitment is so important to remember. Because we are going to spin these pulleys at high speed when the throttle is pinned, alignment is especially critical.

The air pump and alternator hang on a Powerdyne bracket bolted to the right-hand cylinder head. Threaded studs are

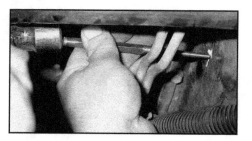

14. A 9/16-inch hole is punched into the side of the oil pan as shown. Start small and work your way up, but stop at exactly 9/16-inch inside diameter. Threads are cut into the hole's circumference. Once the hole is cleaned up with brake cleaner, the fitting is installed using either Teflon tape or sealer. The fitting should be tight. Drain the front sump of all oil, and then run a quart through it to get rid of all the metal shavings.

15. This is the correct serpentine belt drive routing for the factory belt. Note the changes in the idler pulleys. The factory idler pulley goes on the black Powerdyne bracket. The Powerdyne idler pulley goes at the factory idler-pulley's location.

screwed into the bracket. The air pump and alternator slide onto the studs. When we install the supercharger's main support plate, it slides onto these studs, securing the alternator and air pump. The alternator and air pump do not adjust.

The Powerdyne XB-1 supercharger is lubricated by the engine's oil fed by the oil pump. Oil gets to the supercharger through a reinforced, flexible hose supplied in the Powerdyne kit. This hose gets its pressure at the oil sending unit port near the oil filter at the left-hand side of the block. Powerdyne supplies us with a brass block and fittings that screw into the block where the sender is located at the factory. The brass block allows us to use the oil pressure sender and line at the same oil galley port.

Oil that flows to the supercharger has to return to the oil pan once it passes through the supercharger. At the bottom of the supercharger is a drain port where oil returns to the pan unpressurized. To get the oil back to the pan, we have to install a return fitting, which screws into the side of the pan near the front on the right-hand side. This can be performed a couple of different ways. You may remove the oil pan and have a fitting welded to the pan in this location. Because few people want to go through this procedure, we're going to show you Powerdyne's approach. We punch a 9/16-inch hole in the pan as shown, cut threads in the hole, and screw in a fitting. Use Teflon tape or Loc-Tite permanent sealer between the fitting and the pan. When you install the drain hose from the supercharger to the oil pan, make sure the hose doesn't rub anywhere.

When we reinstall the accessory drive, we're dealing with a different idler pulley setup for the factory accessory drive. Powerdyne provides a black idler pulley bracket that installs on the left-hand side of the engine near the power steering pump. Move the new Powerdyne idler pulley at the factory idler pulley location and use the factory idler pulley on the Powerdyne black bracket. Simply put, switch the factory idler pulley with the smaller Powerdyne idler pulley. Otherwise, the serpentine belt will not tighten. The Ford pulley adjusts into the serpentine belt for tension.

16. The XB-1 supercharger's oil drain hose runs from the bottom of the supercharger to the engine's front oil pan sump.

17. The XB-1 installs like this. Allen screws marry the supercharger and plate.

18. Powerdyne provides this brass block, which allows you to run the oil pressure sender and oil line to the supercharger off the same oil galley.

Earlier, we mentioned the need for fuel volume and pressure whenever you're running a supercharger. We begin with 36-lb/hr injectors from Steeda. Then, we pump up the volume and pressure with a BBK high-performance electric fuel pump. To install the BBK pump, we have to drop the fuel tank. For 1994-95 Mustangs, there are three bolts that retain the two fuel tank straps. Two are in front of the tank, and one is located in the right rear, behind the rear bumper. We suggest a very empty fuel tank when you're doing a fuel pump swap.

19. Remove the fuel tank so you can replace the fuel pump, located on the right-hand side. The fuel sending unit is located mid-tank.

The electric fuel pump is located on the right-hand side of the fuel tank at the top of the large hump. A rotating ring retains the pump, just like fuel sending units. The fuel-sending unit is located in the middle of the tank, retained the same way. You have a good opportunity to replace the fuel-sending unit while you're in the neighborhood.

The Powerdyne XB-1 supercharger has its intake at the center, where you'll see the centrifugal compressor blades. At the center, we want the compressor to receive unrestricted cool air via the intake duct, which leads to the mass-air sensor and air cleaner located in the right-hand fender well. The intake system is simple to set up and understand.

The Powerdyne XB-1 supercharger has plum set our '95 Mustang test mule on fire. At the rear wheels, it makes 353 hp and 373 ft-lbs of torque. John speculates that, with a little cam tweaking, power at the wheels could rise to over 400. How's that for real-world power – and from a tuner Mustang?

John took the liberty of computing "at-the-crank" numbers for us below. Because we are running a LenTech AODE (4R70W) transmission, rear-wheel numbers aren't going to be what they would be with a TKO or T-5. We lose power that it takes to turn the driveline. When we throw an automatic transmission into the equation, even more power is lost through the torque converter, clutches, and planetaries.

How does peak horsepower compute at the crank? John tells us it calculates out to 441 horsepower and a mind-bending 465 ft-lbs of torque at the crank. Not bad when you consider this is a stock bottom end with more than

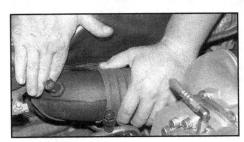

20. The air intake system begins with a 90-degree elbow at the compressor inlet. Our intake elbow needs a crankcase ventilation fitting. We bore a hole into the elbow and cut threads for the fitting. A non-collapsible hose is routed to the mass-airflow sensor and air cleaner in the fenderwell. The air cleaner and mass-airflow sensor are mounted to the body as shown.

80,000 miles on the clock by the time we wrapped up testing. John adds that he could have gotten even more power from this engine given electronics from a 1988-93 Mustang GT. The older electronics give us a greater range to work with, which means more power. To remain smog legal, John has to stick with the factory electronics. The Dyno Shop has taken the '95 about as far as it can go with factory electronics and stock displacement. But, just imagine how little it might take to push this one to the 500 mark.

We'll be watching John.

Supercharger Dyno Test

RPM	Horsepower	Torque
4,100	264	337
4,200	284	352
4,300	288	356
4,400	295	361
4,500	303	364
4,600	310	368
4,700	318	370
4,800	325	**373**
4,900	330	368
5,000	333	366
5,100	342	359
5,200	346	348
5,300	350	335
5,400	**353**	321
5,500	348	299

COOLING SYSTEM UPGRADE (1994-95)

One of the best gifts you can give your 5.0L Mustang is a better cooling system. From the factory, these Mustangs have an adequate cooling system, and run at normal operating temperatures during street use. It's when you turn up the flame and run them hard that the factory system won't cut it. Fluidyne can help with professional-grade radiators designed for hot Fox-5.0L use.

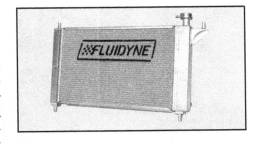

1. This is the Fluidyne all-aluminum radiator for 1994-95 Fox-5.0-liter Mustangs. It is a crossflow design, like factory equipment. You may use it without concern for end tank failure like we sometimes experience with stock radiators with plastic tanks. It offers us unequaled cooling power, but be advised that it's a pinch wider than the stock radiator.

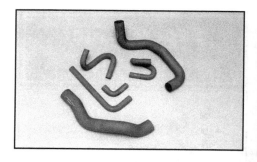

2. We've decided to go with blue heavy-duty Police package cooling system hoses to solidify the integrity of our '95 Mustang GT cooling system. These hoses, along with a new radiator, high-flow water pump from JMC Motorsports, and a new heater core, give us renewed confidence.

3. First, remove the radiator cover. Do not press on these plastic pseudo-screws. Lightly turn them counterclockwise to back them out. When it is time to reinstall them, simply push them into place.

4. Open the drain petcock on the right-hand side and drain the coolant. Properly dispose of the coolant. Disconnect the radiator hoses at both the engine and radiator.

5. Disconnect the coolant level sensor and remove the coolant recovery tank.

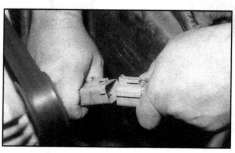

6. For 1994-95 the Mustang GT's cooling system is quite involved electrically. Since it has an electric cooling fan, there are sensors and a control module to be disconnected, not to mention the cooling fan itself.

7. Our '95 Mustang GT has an AODE (4R70W) transmission. You'll need to disconnect the two cooling lines need to be disconnected.

8. Lift out the factory radiator, which sits on two rubber mounts.

9. Remove the factory electric fan from the radiator. Transfer the transmission cooler line fitting from the factory radiator to the Fluidyne. Use Loc-Tite thread sealer or Teflon tape on the fitting threads.

10. Transfer the factory electric fan to the Fluidyne radiator. Some trimming is required.

11. Remove all remaining cooling system hoses at this time to make way for water pump removal. Yank the bypass and both heater hoses and throw them away. Unbolt and remove the factory water pump. Be gentle during the removal, as it is easy to permanently damage the timing cover. Despite all of the best factory corrosion protection, look at the pitting of the radiator hose attachment point.

12. Clean up the water pump contact surfaces and install the new gaskets. Use a light coat of high-heat silicone sealer for best results.

13. Water pump bolts get a dressing of ARP's Teflon sealer, which protects the bolts, water pump, and timing cover from corrosion and leakage. Install the new high-flow JMC water pump.

14. Replace the heater hoses between the engine and heater core. You'll need to disconnect the EGR sensor to service these hoses.

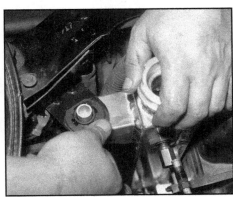

15. Install the new Fluidyne radiator. It sits on the same rubber mounts as the factory radiator. The rubber mounts on top hold the new radiator as well.

16. Connect the automatic transmission cooler lines to the new radiator.

17. Install and reconnect the coolant recovery tank.

18. Trim and install the bypass hose.

19. Install the upper and lower radiator hoses. Fill the radiator with a 50/50 mix of antifreeze and distilled water for best results. Fire the engine and allow it to rise to operating temperature with the radiator cap off. This allows all air pockets to burp and clear.

DRIVELINE

AND REAR AXLE

We tend to focus a lot of our attention on the engine in our Mustang projects. It's a shame most of us aren't more attentive to the area behind the power until mass destruction begins to occur at wide-open throttle. In this chapter, we're going to show you how to build reliability into your Mustang's all-important driveline and rear axle. Most of these items are common to both 1979-93 and 1994-95 Mustangs, so we're going to lump them into projects that apply to all model years.

FOX MUSTANG DRIVELINE BASICS

When the Fox Mustang debuted for 1979, there were two transmissions available: the SROD 4-speed manual and C4 Select-Shift automatic. This remained true through midyear 1983 when Ford introduced the Borg-Warner T-5 5-speed transmission as a Mustang GT option behind the 5.0L High Output V-8. At this time, Ford also introduced the C5 Select-Shift automatic, which was the C4 with a locking torque converter for improved fuel efficiency.

Beginning in 1984, Ford offered the optional automatic overdrive (AOD) with the 5.0L High Output V-8 with Central Fuel Injection (CFI). Because Ford didn't offer the C4 or C5 in any of the 5.0L High Output Mustangs, these transmissions will not be addressed in any detail here.

The T-5 was actually introduced for the first time in a light-duty application behind the 2.3L OHC four-cylinder engine in 1981. When Ford put the T-5 behind the 5.0L High Output V-8 in 1983, the internals had to be beefed up to handle the power (although that isn't saying much). In 1983-84, the T-5 struggled to handle the 5.0L V-8's power output, with a capacity of only 295 ft-lbs of torque. Quite a few of them failed, especially with modified engines making

This is the Ford C4 Select-Shift three-speed automatic transmission, first introduced in 1964. Back then, it was called the Cruise-O-Matic. In Mercurys, it was called the Merc-O-Matic. The C4 was offered in the Mustang from 1979 through 82. When Ford fitted the C4 with a locking torque converter in 1982, it became the C5. The C5 was a performance slug with one mission: fuel economy. (Photo courtesy Rob Kinnan, ProMedia)

more power. For 1985, Ford introduced the World Class T-5 with increased torque capacity and wide-ratio gearing. The World Class T-5 transmission shifted more easily and could handle greater amounts of punishment.

BUILDING A BETTER T-5

The Borg-Warner (now Tremec) T-5 has been in continuous production and service since 1981. What the T-5 has done for the Mustang cannot be underestimated. With four speeds plus one overdrive speed, the T-5 has enabled us to have our cake and eat it too. The lower gear ranges, including straight drive, allow us to have great fun with a 5.0L Mustang, while enabling us to cruise efficiently in overdrive. When you throw EFI into the equation, it spoils us rotten with both fuel economy and performance.

When the T-5 was introduced in 1981, it wasn't considered a transmission for high-performance applications. It was a quiet, easy-to-shift transmission that offered great efficiency. Who could argue with the logic behind overdrive? It significantly dropped engine RPM at cruise, saving us fuel, not to mention engine wear and tear. Admittedly, overdrive took some getting used to early on. We were used to engines taching 3,000 rpm at 70 mph. Slipping a 1983 Mustang

This is the Borg-Warner T-5 five-speed. Today, Tremec builds and markets this hardy transmission. Through the years, this transmission has evolved and been improved, beginning with the World Class T-5 in 1985. (Photo courtesy Rob Kinnan, ProMedia)

GT into fifth-gear (overdrive) lowered the revs enough that it didn't seem like we were doing 70 mph. In fact, 70 mph then meant a costly ticket from our nation's finest because the national speed limit was 55 mph – everywhere. That has easily been forgotten because 65- and 70-mph speed limits have been common for many years. Though we're certainly used to overdrive today, it took a lot of getting used to in the early 1980s.

As Ford began to turn up the flame in 1983, the 5.0L High Output engine began to ask more of the lightweight aluminum gearbox. Performance enthusiasts began to ask more as well. We power-shifted those early T-5 transmissions and learned quickly that they weren't up to the task – they broke.

Pro shifting is a concept that was started back in the 1960s by Liberty Gear to help 4-speed power-shifters find comfort and reliability with their transmissions. Back then, Liberty Gear worked mostly with GM Muncie M21 and M22 4-speeds, and Ford Top Loader 4-speeds. Today, their focus is more Tremec T-5s and T-45s.

What's the secret to having a better T-5 five-speed? Liberty Gear does its pro-shifting thing by grinding the teeth off the synchronizers and sliders, which enables the transmission to upshift into higher gears more smoothly. The synchronizer rings, keys, and springs remain to hold the transmission in the selected gear so you don't have to hold the shifter. This is a great process because it's cheap and easy to accomplish. Any savvy transmission builder can accomplish it in a matter of hours. You can even do it on your home workbench.

Although Liberty Gear is the centerpiece of this segment, we're also going to highlight other companies that offer high-performance T-5 components. You're going to see a lot of Tremec TKO and TKO II units in this segment, but the components we address here are available for World Class T-5 units as well.

Astro Performance's Tony Sarvis speaks of yet another approach to pro shifting where second, third, and fourth gears are removed, along with the synchronizers, sliders, and rings. Then, every other tooth on the gear, synchronizer, slider, and ring are removed. This allows for faster upshifts – and downshifts. There comes one penalty with this process, however: shifts are no longer smooth. But, they happen more quickly. This is one low-cost way of modifying the T-5 and TKO to achieve faster shifts.

A variety of companies have developed pieces you can buy that will make light work of an upshift. One of them is the face-tooth engagement modification, also called the dog-ring, which calls for the complete removal of the synchronizers. Then, the gears are modified or replaced completely with aftermarket gears. With the synchronizer eliminated from second gear, a dog-ring is welded in its place on one side of the gear. The first/second ring slider is then machined carefully to match the dog-ring's teeth. Then, third and fourth gear each are modified similarly, with a custom third/fourth gear slider employed. This process virtually eliminates fifth gear (overdrive), which makes it unwise for street use. However, if you're going racing, this is a great idea for quick upshifts.

One company familiar with T-5 and TKO pro shifting is Hanlon Motorsports in Elverson, Pennsylvania. Hanlon prefers the face-tooth engagement system of pro shifting. In the National Mustang Racers Association August 2003 *Race Pages* magazine, Hanlon said, "Where everyone else's stuff works on the inside of the slider, ours works on the side of the slider." He adds, "Instead of machining the teeth off the gear and welding on a pro-ring, ours has a drive sprocket on it. And, instead of machining every two teeth out of the middle of the slider, ours is stepped on the side of the slider, making it look like a full-race Jerico or G-Force transmission." He insists this is a better approach to pro shifting. Who can argue with him?

Another company that has pro shifting down to a science is ProMotion Performance Powertrain. ProMotion also subscribes to the face-tooth engagement approach to pro shifting. ProMotion President Walt Leaman says, "It's a stronger, less shock-producing shifting mechanism than traditional pro-shifting setups. With a traditional pro-shifted setup, you eliminate most of the teeth on the synchronizers, and this creates a lot of movement before everything engages, which generates into shock load into the transmission. With face-tooth engagement, you can ramp the face-tooth so that it slides into gear easier." Leaman adds, "It's less abrupt than a pro-ring. The face-tooth design is also easier to engage. It's almost a no-miss engagement and generates less shock load." Leaman speaks respectfully of his competition when he says, "We're all working on different methods of taking stock gear sets and putting face-tooth engagement on them."

ProMotion's modified Tremec is

In 1980, Ford introduced us to the AOD (automatic overdrive), first available in Lincolns and other high-end Fords. At the time, no one ever considered the AOD for performance applications. The AOD first appeared in the Mustang in 1984 behind the 5.0-liter H.O. with CFI (Central Fuel Injection). (Photo courtesy Rob Kinnan, ProMedia)

affectionately known in the industry as the "Baddest T-5 on the planet" because it works very well for racers. Leaman gives G-Force a lot of credit for the success of this transmission because G-Force makes the gear sets for ProMotion. Leaman tells *Race Pages* that G-Force makes it possible to put beefy, pro-shifted parts inside a T-5 transmission case. It's a low-buck way to get into pro shifting, without selling off the farm. You can get there for around $1,300. Because of the vulnerability of stock shifter forks, which tend to break in drag racing, ProMotion has developed forged 1-2 and 3-4 shifter forks that will take a pounding. These forks should be available by the time you pick up this book.

ProMotion also has another kind of system that falls somewhere in between harsh pro shifting and face-tooth. This method applies to ProMotion's Street Pro-Shifted Tremec T-5. Instead of every two teeth being removed from the stock synchronizer, only every other tooth is removed. Leaman sees this as a nice compromise between a pro-shifted transmis-

sion, which is very taxing to drive on the street, and a stock T-5 transmission. This method makes it possible to pro shift a T-5 on the street without the frustration of true pro shifting. Leaman adds that pro shifting does nothing to make the T-5 stronger. However, it does allow the T-5 to live up to its torque capacity.

Leaman tells us that we have no idea just how much stress we put on a T-5 during a power shift. The shifter multiplies our shift's torque. When we slam the shifter through the gear ranges, we are putting tremendous stress on the transmission's internals. To quote Leaman, "The synchro is trying to block the shift, which makes the gearset whip around. When you let go of the clutch and try to put the power back through the transmission, the gear teeth are now

Here are G-Force's T-5 synchronized, helical-cut 9310 steel gears, and 9310 steel shaft. This setup will take a lot of punishment and provide you with reliable service. Here's to smooth, fast upshifts. (Photo courtesy Rob Kinnan, ProMedia)

Also available from G-Force are T-5 gears that are a full 1/8-inch wider than stock cogs, made of super-tough 9310 steel. That's a stock T-5 gear on the left and the G-Force piece on the right. (Photo courtesy Rob Kinnan, ProMedia)

This is the dog-ring system with square-cut gears, available from ProMotion, G-Force, and Liberty. This isn't legal for some forms of drag racing. However, the choice is yours. (Photo courtesy Rob Kinnan, ProMedia)

These two images show us ProMotion's face-tooth (top) and pro-shifted sliders (bottom) installed in a T-5 transmission. (Photo courtesy Rob Kinnan, ProMedia)

These are G-Force's T-5 straight-cut 9310 steel gears with dog-ring engagement, including a 9310 steel shaft. (Photo courtesy Rob Kinnan, ProMedia)

The G-Force 25-spline input shaft (left) can take a lot more punishment than the stock 10-spline piece (right). (Photo courtesy Rob Kinnan, ProMedia)

mismatched or separated, and that's when you blow them up." What Leaman is telling us is simple. Whenever gearsets are out of synch and we try to throw power at them, failure is certain. Because it happens so quickly, it's impossible to right our wrong, and the transmission fails.

Whether or not you pro shift your T-5 depends on how you intend to use it, and how much cash you have to spend. Craig Liberty has suggestions that will save you money in the long run. He says, "Traditional pro shifting is more economical because you can use all of the stock pieces, including the sliders – even partially worn out ones." He adds, "You don't have to buy new hubs and sliders. We charge $66 to pro shift any stock gear, and $33 to modify the slider. For the average person, pro shifting is perfect." All you have to do is send your components to Liberty Gear and they will set you up. It costs approximately $264 to modify all of your gearsets in a T-5.

If you're going to get more serious about your personal drag racing program, Craig Liberty believes the face-tooth style is more suited to high-power, high-RPM Mustangs. The face-tooth approach is a stronger system, with less shock involved in the upshifts and downshifts.

Hanlon systems cost more, but there's more machine work involved. Hanlon makes all of its components from scratch, which involves tooling costs, not to mention a lot of research and development time. It's going to cost more, but it'll be worth every penny.

AOD TRANSMISSION BUILD TIPS

From 1984 to 1993, Ford offered an AOD behind the 5.0L High Output V-8. The "all-new" AOD transmission was new in case form only. Internally, the AOD used some off-the-shelf parts from the FMX transmission. The gearset's design was borrowed from the FMX cast iron automatic used in 1969-73 Mustangs. The gearset was a six-pinion design using a single planet carrier, like a lot of Ford automatics of the period. This was economical for Ford because very little research and develop-

ment was necessary for the heart of the transmission's design.

The AOD transmission was one of the first of its type in the industry, an automatic overdrive that would help fuel economy right out of the chute. We like the AOD for its healthy overdrive ratio, which makes it possible to cheat and run 3.73:1 or 4.11:1 rear end gears and still have conservative revs at highway speeds. With 3.73:1 gears, for example, the AOD's overdrive ratio keeps the revs around 2,200 rpm at 70 mph. The AOD also bypasses the torque converter in overdrive, giving us a direct link to the gearset and rear axle.

The AOD is a mechanically modulated (via the throttle valve cable) 4-speed automatic transmission with an overdrive unit. Earlier versions of the AOD were plagued with all kinds of reliability and performance issues because the AOD was never intended to be a performance transmission. When Ford put the AOD behind the 5.0L High Output engine in 1984, these problems only grew worse, making all kinds of upgrades necessary in the years to follow.

Those first AOD transmissions were available in the Lincoln Town Car, Thunderbird, and Cougar in 1980. The AOD delivered smooth upshifts – the kind of seamless performance we expect in luxury cars. However, those seamless upshifts are also the undoing of every type of automatic transmission. When we have a soft upshift, we're experiencing clutch and band slippage. With that slippage comes clutch and band material that finds its way into the fluid, wearing and cutting seals. Seal deterioration causes a loss in control pressure, which aggravates the slippage problem, leading to transmission failure.

The weakest area for early AODs is the direct-clutch (third gear) and overdrive drum/band. Other areas include the intermediate clutches, which were also never designed for high-performance applications. There were too few clutch discs and plates, and they were also too small. As a result, these clutches have also failed with great regularity behind the 5.0L H.O.

To improve reliability and performance, older AOD transmissions

need to be upgraded a number of ways. The first, and most obvious, is the wider two-inch overdrive band and clutch drum common with later AODE (4R70W) units. This is an expensive upgrade that can cost upwards of $1,000 for new parts. Ideally, you will find a used AODE overdrive drum and fit it with a new band for exceptional performance.

Installing an Art Carr or Precision Industries high-performance input shaft and torque converter will also improve reliability and performance in your AOD. The input shaft eliminates the lock-up feature in AOD models. That's the downside if you're interested in fuel economy as well as performance.

Another modification you can make is using the AODE's wide-ratio gearset in your AOD. This gearset offers great first- and second-gear holeshot performance while retaining the cruise features the AOD is appreciated for.

One of the most basic improvements you can make to your AOD and AODE is shift-improvement. Valve body calibration is what hurts the factory AOD/AODE performance. B&M, Art Carr, LenTech, and a host of others offer shift-programming kits that firm up the upshift. A firm upshift will extend transmission life by reducing clutch and band slippage. The better shift programming kits also raise upshift points, which improves performance at wide-open throttle. Too many of us are familiar with the premature upshifts of AOD transmissions, which cause 5.0L engines to fall on their faces at wide-open throttle. A good shift reprogramming will end all of that frustration. With the right shift programming kit, you can custom program your AOD's personality, getting those shift points in the right ballpark.

Another weak area for AOD transmissions is the direct clutch. To improve the direct clutch, we add clutch plates. Victoria Automatic Transmission (Victrans) offers a Power-Pack kit, which allows up to seven friction plates to be installed in the AOD's original five-clutch direct clutch drum. This improves performance dramatically. Some 1988-91 AOD units have a six-clutch direct clutch that will take up to eight clutches. By using the right combination of clutches, and the right snap ring, available from Ford, you can dial in your direct clutch using Victrans clutches and parts.

Victoria Automatic Transmission tells us a weak spot in the direct clutch is the input shaft spline area in the middle of the clutch hub. If you have a loose fit, or damage to the splines, toss it in favor of another one in better condition. The downside to this suggestion is the direct clutch's obsolete status with Ford. It's no longer available. The good news from Victoria Automatic Transmission is that AOD direct drums are available as a service kit from Ford called the Stamped Steel Drum Conversion Kit (F2ZE-7F283-A), which is included in the Ford Racing Performance Parts wide-ratio gearset.

What is the wide-ratio gearset? If you're building an AODE (4R70W), you already have it. If you're building an AOD, you need the wide-ratio gearset available from Ford Racing Performance Parts (FRPP). Here's how the wide-ratio gearset stacks up against conventional AOD thinking.

Gear Range	Standard AOD	Wide-Ratio AODE
First Gear	2.40:1	2.84:1
Second Gear	1.47:1	1.55:1
Third Gear	1.0:1	1.0:1
Overdrive	0.67:1	0.7:1

As you can see, the wide-ratio AOD/AODE gearset gives a nice, broad range and thus a mechanical advantage out of the hole through second gear. But, we still get the overdrive range of 0.7:1 once we're cruising. The 2.84:1 first and 1.55:1 second allow us to accelerate smartly from a stop to straight 1.1:1 drive, which is perfect for drag racing.

Since Ford has been building wide-ratio AODE (4R70W) transmissions since 1993, you have a wide range of cores and parts to play with. Whenever you order the Ford Racing Wide-Ratio Upgrade Kit, you get the four-friction

(clutch plate) intermediate clutch pack and special Dynmax clutches. If you install the F3LY-7B066-A intermediate pressure plate, any AOD or AODE can be upgraded to add a greater number of clutches. The Dynmax clutch discs became standard equipment in all AODE transmissions beginning in 1994. They help ensure longer clutch life.

If you're going to install an AODE in your pre-1994 Mustang, you're going to need the Baumannator TCS electronic transmission controller from Baumann Engineering in order to make it work properly. The TCS controller allows you control of all shift points in any application, according to Victoria Automatic Transmission. On top of that, the TCS controller enables you to dial in the AODE to any application – regardless of vehicle type or axle ratio.

Whenever you install the wide-ratio kit in your AOD, there's a lot to consider, because the transmission's personality changes. The AOD upshifts into second gear at wide-open throttle at 4,900 rpm, and it upshifts to third at 4,500 rpm. Whenever we install the wide-ratio setup, 1-2 upshifts occur at 5,680 rpm. The 2-3 upshift happens at 4,750 rpm. If the 1-2 upshift is too high at 5,680 rpm, install an E2AZ-7C063-B or E8AZ-7C063-A governor on the tailshaft to change the transmission's upshift points. The E2AZ-B will lower the upshift RPM speed somewhat, while the E2AZ-A governor will lower it significantly. You may have to test both governors to arrive at the upshift speed you desire.

When we're thinking about upshift points, thoughts aren't often far from the throttle valve (TV) cable used only with the AOD transmission. Because the AODE transmission is controlled by the engine's electronic control module (ECM), there is no TV cable. The TV cable is tied to the throttle linkage for much the same reason as the kickdown linkage on older automatic transmissions. All the kickdown linkage did was control upshift and downshift points based on where the throttle was positioned. At wide-open throttle, the kickdown linkage position delayed the upshifts until the maximum speed allowable. If that engine speed was 5,200

rpm, that's when the transmission would upshift at wide-open throttle in drive. If you came off the gas, the kickdown linkage would move enough to "tell" the transmission to upshift.

In the old days, if you held the shifter in 1 or 2, that's where the transmission stayed until your engine failed. The AOD and AODE are different. To prevent engine failure, the AOD/AODE is designed to upshift, regardless of shifter position, to protect the engine from an over-rev.

The TV cable does the same job as the kickdown linkage in C4, C6, and FMX transmissions. Because it's tied to the throttle linkage, it modulates the transmission's shift programming. It does this by controlling line pressure. More importantly, proper adjustment of the TV cable is critical to transmission life. Misadjust the TV cable and you will burn up the transmission.

MORE AOD UPGRADES

Two input-shaft upgrade packages are available from Art Carr and Precision Industries for AOD transmissions. The Art Carr input shaft employs both a solid input shaft and a special torque converter available only from Art Carr. This input shaft kit eliminates the lock-up feature, which causes a loss in fuel efficiency. If your goal is drag racing only, the Art Carr system is for you. The Art Carr torque converter employs a C6 input shaft spline, which only works with the Art Carr input shaft. What does this mean for driveability? It means a more seamless 2-3 upshift at wide-open throttle, keeping your 5.0L engine from falling on its face.

Another important upgrade for early AOD transmissions is the rear lube output shaft. AOD transmissions built prior to 1988 don't have this output shaft. This shaft is called the seven-tooth, speedometer-geared, rear-lube output shaft. Available from Baumann Engineering, this shaft works with the E8ZZ-7C063-A governor, located on the tailshaft. This governor will allow you to raise your shift points to 4,900 rpm. The rear-lube feature keeps critical planetaries lubricated.

It's important to mention while we're on the subject of AOD and AODE transmissions that the overdrive band and drum are prone to failure in older AOD transmissions. There are three basic types of overdrive servos and drums used in AOD transmissions. The smaller "C" servo is common with older lo-po AOD slushboxes. The "C" is cast into the servo cover, and is visible whenever we drop the transmission pan. The larger "B" servo is common with 1985-up V-8 applications. The best servo is the largest "A" servo used in 1992-up AOD and AODE transmissions. If you already have the "B" servo, Victoria Automatic Transmission tells us the "A" servo won't make much difference in shift quality. Ideally, you'll include the larger 2-inch overdrive drum and band with your servo upgrade.

AOD/AODE Identification

When you're shopping the salvage yards and transmission parts places for a suitable AOD/AODE core to build, identification is everything. Because Ford has been using the AOD/AODE behind a variety of engines since 1980, quick identification is important. Quickest rule of thumb is the two-bolt/three-bolt starter rule. All 5.0L engines have a two-bolt starter. No exceptions. The newer 4.6L/5.4L SOHC/DOHC V-8s use a three-bolt starter.

If you're looking for a wide-ratio gearset, look closely. All AOD and AODE transmissions built prior to 1996 have the standard gearset, with the exceptions being 1994-95 Thunderbird/Cougar, E- and F-series trucks, 1995 full-size Fords and Mercs, and 1993-95 Lincolns.

Some AOD valve bodies are different because they lack the overdrive switch common to most AOD transmissions, which means their shift pattern will be P-R-N-OD-D-1 instead of the P-R-N-D-2-1 pattern we're used to seeing.

Don't accidentally pick up an AOD from a 3.8L V-6. It doesn't have the full complement of clutch plates in the direct clutch assembly like the V-8 AOD. Whenever you're shopping for an AOD transmission, make sure you measure

your application before going shopping. You want to measure overall length, mount location, and more before laying down the cash. It's a good idea to stay away from pre-1988 AOD transmissions for reasons of evolution. The AOD simply became a better transmission after 1988. Baumann Engineering tells us the 1992-96 E- and F-series trucks are equipped with the toughest parts, including the super-wide 2-inch overdrive drum and band, and the "A" servo. Don't be fooled by the AOD behind the 3.8L-supercharged V-6 in the Thunderbird SC. It still has the lame 1.5-inch overdrive drum and band. Another important issue is transmission size. Some of the Lincolns have longer output shafts, which make them a "no-fit" gamble for the Mustang enthusiast, so check overall transmission length before buying.

LenTech AOD Swap

We're going to show you how to do a simple swap – from one AOD to another. But this isn't just any swap, because we're stepping up to a LenTech automatic overdrive – a virtually indestructible AOD engineered and built for high-performance Fox-body Mustangs.

What makes the LenTech AOD so different? The LenTech AOD we're about to install is the Street Terminator for 1984-93 Mustangs with the 5.0L High Output engine. This transmission is good for up to 400 horsepower. It features the 1-2 3/4-shift pattern pioneered by LenTech. It also has engine braking in manual second, along with electric overdrive delete. This makes for an AOD transmission you can live with for all kinds of driving and weekend racing.

LenTechs are high-end AOD transmissions that cost between $2,000 and $3,000, depending on how you want it built. LenTech begins with a quality-selected core that is completely stripped and inspected. The front pump is modified for improved lubrication flow and pressure. Clutch drums are modified to take on additional clutches. Some 26 modifications are made throughout the transmission to improve performance. Six redlined 3-4 clutches. Three redlined intermediate (second gear) clutches. Five

or six redlined forward clutches. Three or four reverse clutches. New redlined overdrive band. All new seals, gaskets, and filters. New bushings and thrust washers. New intermediate one-way clutch. New low one-way clutch. LenTech 1-2 3/4 valve body with electronic overdrive delete. New transmission pan and bolts. Assembled, with all critical clearances adjusted and checked. New 12-inch torque converter. All LenTech AOD and AODE transmissions are dyno tested and inspected before shipment and delivery. Best of all: you get a one-year warranty with every LenTech AOD. Cost is $2,195 for US customers.

1. This is the LenTech Street Terminator AOD transmission for 1984-93 Mustangs with the 5.0-liter H.O. V-8. The Street Terminator won't make your engine more powerful, but it will make the most of your engine's power output.

2. This is the LenTech 12-inch torque converter, which features a one-piece billet steel front cover for strength and durability. Here are some other things your speed-shop torque converter doesn't have – Torrington needle thrust bearings throughout, and furnace-brazed construction. Stall speed for this one is in the stock range, depending on your order specifications. We want our LenTech converter to come on around 2,500 rpm.

3. First, disconnect the O2 sensors and remove the H-pipe. This improves access to the transmission.

4. With the transmission properly supported, remove the crossmember and bellhousing bolts at the engine.

5. Remove the driveshaft and cap the tailshaft housing to prevent fluid loss. Ideally, you will have drained the transmission sump of all fluid. Did you know the AOD's torque converter has a drain plug?

7. Remove the starter. Have you disconnected the battery cable? That should happen first.

8. The torque converter cover plate is next. Remove the cover and unbolt the torque converter. Drain the torque converter now to keep the mess to a minimum.

6. The shift and throttle valve linkages need to be disconnected, as does the neutral safety and backup light switch located on the left-hand side. Don't forget to disconnect the speedometer cable while you're over there.

9. The AOD transmission is carefully lowered out of the tunnel. Have you capped the tailshaft housing to keep fluid in and dust out?

10. Some hardware items, like transmission cooler fittings, shifter and throttle valve linkages, and the like have to be transferred to the LenTech transmission.

11. Fill the torque converter with one quart of automatic transmission fluid. Do not use Type F with the AOD. Use MERCON III. One area in which we need to exercise extreme caution is torque converter installation. Because the AOD and AODE have a shaft within a shaft, it's very easy to improperly seat the torque converter, which can be a very costly mistake. Rotate the torque converter and gently push it until it seats completely.

Tremec TKO Installation

We're going to quickly go over the Tremec TKO 5-speed transmission. We're all familiar with the Borg-Warner/Tremec World Class T-5 our Mustangs have been equipped with from the factory, which is a great street/strip transmission. It takes a lot of punishment and comes back for more. As we have already shown you, the T-5 can be tricked up to do great things. But, every manual transmission has its limits, and the T-5 is no exception. We can't throw much more than 400 horsepower at the T-5 without certain destruction.

The TKO and TKOII are relatively new high-performance 5-speed transmissions from Tremec. The TKO and TKOII are the same except for overdrive ratio. The TKO has an overdrive ratio of .68:1. The TKOII has an overdrive ratio of .82:1. The 3550 and 3550II are close cousins to the TKOs, and are the same except for torque capacity. And before we forget, Borg-Warner is now called TTC, which stands for Transmission Technologies Corporation, also known as Tremec. Let's talk about the TKO and TKOII.

The TKO transmission series is a big step up from the World Class T-5 because it's designed to take a lot more punishment – in excess of 400 ft-lbs of torque. In comparison, the 3550 and 3550II will take up to 350 ft-lbs of torque. Like the TKO and TKOII, the 3550 has an overdrive ratio of .68:1 and the 3550II has an overdrive ratio of .82:1. So what does this overdrive ratio mean to you? Plenty. An overdrive ratio of .68:1 offers much better cruise than the .82:1, because the .68:1 keeps the engine at lower revs. If you're seeking a TKO or 3550 series transmission for good, economical cruising, you've chosen correctly. These transmissions will take a pounding without complaint.

The difference between the TKO and 3550 is clear. The cause of the 350-ft-lb torque capacity of the 3550 becomes apparent when you look at the input shaft. The 3550 has a 10-spline input shaft and a 26-spline output shaft. The TKO, with its 400-ft-lb torque capacity, has a 26-spline input shaft and a 31-spline output shaft.

12. Lift the LenTech AOD into position and carefully mate it to the engine and flexplate. Check the torque converter for smooth rotation. If there is any binding, remove the transmission and check the torque converter for proper installation. The converter should rotate smoothly if it's properly seated.

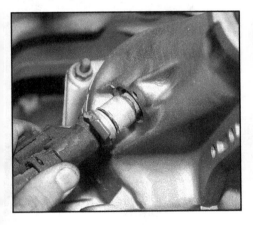

13. Install the speedometer cable and bolt. Use transmission fluid on the speedometer drive gear and seal.

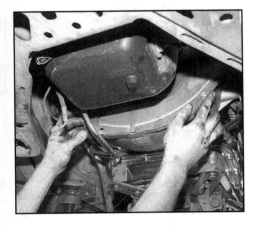

14. Install the torque converter bolts and tighten them up. Then install the starter and the torque converter cover.

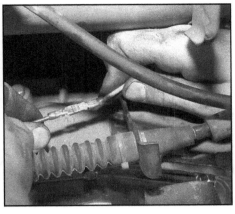

15. One feature the LenTech AOD brings us is electrically controlled overdrive lockout. We have installed a switch in the console that enables us to lock out the overdrive. Here, we are connecting the overdrive lockout feature.

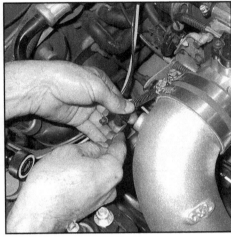

16. With everything underneath out of the way – transmission crossmember, driveshaft, shifter linkage, throttle valve (TV) cable, neutral safety and back-up light switch, and transmission cooler lines – we're ready to dial in our LenTech AOD. Once the engine has been running for 15 minutes and transmission sump temperature is warm, we can adjust the TV cable. Seasoned transmission professionals know to install a pressure gauge and adjust the cable until control pressure is where it belongs. This is the best way to adjust the TV cable. A good rule of thumb is this: upshifts should be firm and on time. If the upshifts happen too late, the cable is too tight. If upshifts happen too soon, the TV cable needs to be tighter.

The TKO and TKOII enable you to shift from three different locations, depending on the type of vehicle you intend to install them in. Both transmissions are a perfect drop-in replacement for the indestructible Ford Top Loader 4-speed. This works very well for classic Mustangs, not to mention 1979-95 Fox-body Mustangs that came with the T-5. The only challenge may be input shaft length, which can be customized whenever you order your TKO from Tremec. The real beauty of the TKO is driveshaft length. Your T-5 or Top Loader's driveshaft will spline right into the TKO and TKOII, reaching the differential yoke with ease.

With the basics out of the way, let's get down to what a TKO really is. It has a single-rail design that moves three shift rods internally. The three rods have spring-loaded detents that make this transmission feel notchy during shifting. This is the hallmark of a high-performance transmission, so expect nothing soft about the TKO – it has an attitude. Instead of those carbon-lined synchronizer rings in your T-5, the Tremec TKO has solid bronze synchronizers. Although it's a super-tough gearbox, it doesn't like being pushed beyond 6,500 rpm, according to Tremec. You can get into the TKO for under $1,500. Not bad considering the transmission you're getting for the money. The TKO and TKOII weigh 100 pounds each.

How do the TKO/TKOII and 3550/3550II stack up?

We're going to show you a quick TKO install in a '93 Mustang GT.

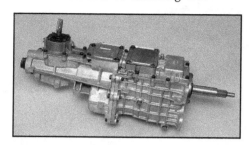

1. This is the Tremec TKO five-speed transmission. With 26-spline input and 31-spline output shafts, this transmission can take 400+ foot-pounds of torque from your small-block Ford. Gear ratios are 3.27, 1.98, 1.34, and 1.00, with a choice of either .68 (TKO) or .82:1 (TKOII) overdrive ratios.

2. Inside the bellhousing, we're installing a Centerforce Dual-Friction clutch, along with a new Centerforce flywheel. Anytime you are stepping up to a TKO, or even a new World Class T-5, opt for the Centerforce clutch.

3. Steeda's adjustable clutch cable is a must for any installation. Since it's fully adjustable, it will last your Mustang a lifetime.

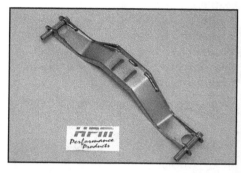

4. You're going to need this crossmember from HPM Performance Products, designed specifically for the TKO and TKOII. You may order it through JME Enterprises.

5. Because we are converting from an AOD to a TKO, we need the pedal assembly from a manual shift Mustang. This is the entire pedal assembly, which fits up under the dashboard behind the instrument panel. You'll need to drop the steering column to access the pedal support assembly.

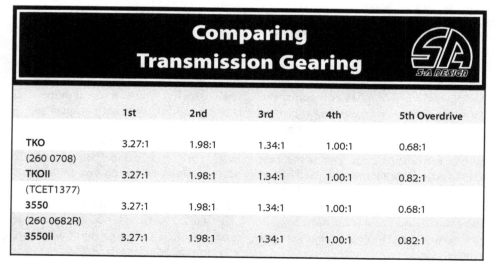

Comparing Transmission Gearing

	1st	2nd	3rd	4th	5th Overdrive
TKO (260 0708)	3.27:1	1.98:1	1.34:1	1.00:1	0.68:1
TKOII (TCET1377)	3.27:1	1.98:1	1.34:1	1.00:1	0.82:1
3550 (260 0682R)	3.27:1	1.98:1	1.34:1	1.00:1	0.68:1
3550II	3.27:1	1.98:1	1.34:1	1.00:1	0.82:1

6. The Pro 5.0 shifter for the TKO makes things nice and crisp, with tight throws and quick action. This shifter is easy to install in a matter of minutes. Don't forget to lubricate the ball and rail with transmission lube or wheel bearing grease before seating the shifter.

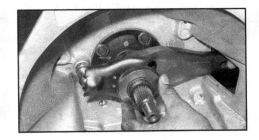

7. The Centerforce throwout (clutch release) bearing installs like this. Lubricate the pivot ball and contact surfaces with wheel bearing grease. We suggest wheel-bearing grease because it is very durable.

8. The new TKO manual transmission takes a different separator plate than the old AOD. Note the difference shown here.

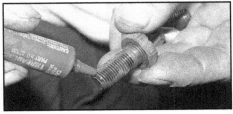

9. Installing the flywheel begins with a new clutch pilot bearing from JMC Motorsports. Since the flywheel fits only one way, we won't be able to screw this one up. The crankshaft flywheel bolt holes are of a single pattern that works only one way. Use Loc-Tite on your flywheel bolt threads. Torque the bolts to factory specifications.

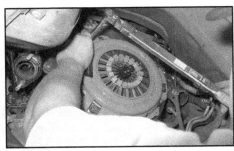

10. We're installing a new Centerforce Dual-Friction clutch in our '93 Mustang GT. The beauty of a Centerforce is its common-sense approach. Flyweights help the clutch grip the disc as the RPM increases. The faster you spin it, the tighter the clutch's clamping force on the disc.

11. When you're installing the TKO, it's like this thing was born for a Mustang. It's a perfect fit. The only challenge is the backup light/neutral safety switch wiring, especially when going from an AOD to the TKO. You will have to find a donor car or your local Ford dealer for the correct harnesses.

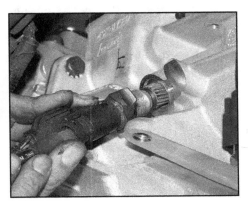

12. Another surprise for us was the speedometer drive gear. The teeth on a TKO's output shaft are different than the factory speedometer drive gear. See JME Enterprises for the correct speedometer drive gear for your TKO application.

13. The HPM Motorsports crossmember from JME Enterprises is designed specifically for the TKO.

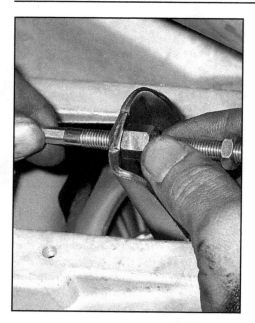

14. The TKO bellhousing and clutch work identically to the T-5 setup. Install and adjust it just like you would with any T-5 application. The Steeda adjustable clutch cable makes it easy.

REAR AXLE BASICS

There are three basic types of integral carrier differentials you can expect to find out there for late-model Mustangs. At a glance, they tend to look the same, which is why you need to be careful when you're shopping. The 7.5-inch rear end was standard equipment in all 1979-85 V-8 Mustangs. When we say "7.5-inch," we're referring to the ring gear diameter. Four-cylinder models were fitted with the 6.75-inch integral carrier differential, which was very inadequate for sixes and V-8s. The 6.75-inch rear end was very common in the 1974-78 Mustang II with four-cylinder power. If you find one of these with leaf-spring mounts, you've found one from a Mustang II, Pinto, or Bobcat.

For many years, the Ford 9-inch removable carrier rear axle was the weapon of choice for Mustang racers. And for many, it still is. Never underestimate the strength of a 9-inch Ford because it remains an unbeatable differential. Dozens of professional racers, including those who race Chevrolet and Dodge, who run the 9-inch Ford, understand its value. The 9-inch removable

carrier Ford is legendary in its performance and reliability.

When the Mustang GT rolled onto the scene in 1982, it had a woefully inadequate 7.5-inch integral carrier differential that could barely tolerate the torque of a 5.0L High Output V-8 with two-barrel carburetion. As horsepower and torque began to increase in the years to follow, Ford had to develop a durable differential that would stand up. In 1986, Ford introduced the 8.8-inch integral carrier differential in the Mustang GT. According to Ford, the 8.8-inch carrier is 35 percent stronger than the 7.5-inch unit it replaced.

One reason more and more performance enthusiasts are going to the 8.8-inch rear axle over the 9 inch is efficiency. The 9 inch creates more internal friction, so it takes more power to turn a 9 inch than it does an 8.8. The 8.8 also weighs less than a comparable 9 inch. Unless you're planning extreme amounts of power, you can run an 8.8-inch rear end with confidence.

Here are some upgrades you might want to consider for your 8.8. Because C-clips tend to fail under extreme conditions, we've found ways to eliminate them and keep our axle shafts. The Ford and Jegs C-clip eliminator kits (#M-4220-A or #873-A1092) allow you to weld 9-inch axle flanges onto your 8.8-inch housing. They also permit you to install the right axle shafts. All you need is a reputable shop and/or welder to get the job done.

Another upgrade is an axle girdle, which gives the differential housing much-needed support. Ford's part number is M4033-G. Jegs' is 6-9-101-8.8. We're going to show you how to install the girdle shortly.

One popular upgrade with the 9 inch, as well as the 8.8, is the Detroit Automotive No-Spin differential; i.e. the Detroit Locker. The Detroit Locker helped Ford to race to success 35-40 years ago at Le Mans, and again at Sebring. You can be successful too, with a variety of locker-type differentials.

The Detroit Locker is a time- and race-proven differential that provides a fail-safe system of traction. It remains locked at all times, ratcheting as you

turn corners. When traction is paramount, the Detroit Locker is one of your best choices. But for street use, this isn't always the case. That ratcheting noise is a pain in the neck on the street.

Another choice you have today is the ARB Air Locker, which uses compressed air to lock the two sides of the differential. The Air Locker allows you to lock and unlock the differential, depending on the kind of driving you're doing. This technology and convenience isn't cheap though.

The Lock-Right differential from Powertrax is more of a Johnny-come-lately for the 8.8. This differential offers smooth operation because it engages only as needed, which makes it quieter and smoother than the Detroit Locker.

While you're thinking about how to improve traction, also consider how much traction enhancement you're going to need. For street use, the 8.8-inch Traction-Lok does its job quite well. Although the name implies a locking differential, the Traction-Lok is little more than a clutch-type limited-slip differential. It offers two-wheel traction while cruising down the road. Whenever you turn a corner, the clutches slip, allowing a "differential" in axle rotation.

Gear selection depends on how you intend to drive the vehicle. Daily drivers, with overdrive transmissions, can get away with 3.27:1 or 3.55:1. Weekend racers need something more liberal, like 3.55:1, 3.73:1 or 4.11:1. Probably the best choice for the daily driver/weekend racer is 3.73:1. This is a nice compromise because it keeps the revs conservative. At 70 mph, with 3.73:1 gears, you can expect 2,200 rpm, depending on wheel/tire size. A set of 3.55:1 gears puts your small block somewhere around 2,000 rpm at 70 mph. Axle ratios for the 8.8 as high as 5.13:1 are available, but most racers opt for 4.11:1 or 4.56:1 gears with 31- or 35-spline axles.

8.8-INCH GEAR SWAP

We're going to show you a simple 8.8-inch gear swap in a '95 Mustang GT. Jason Hughes, of Differential Systems in San Diego, California, is going to show us how to get there.

1. These are 3.73:1 gears from JMC Motorsports, provided by Ford Racing Performance Parts. We were impressed with the quality; these gears lapped right in nicely.

2. First, disassemble the brakes and remove the rotors. If you have drum brakes (prior to 1994), you will have to completely disassemble the brake and remove the backing plate.

3. Remove the differential cover and drain the lube.

4. Disconnect the driveshaft and tie it out of the way.

5. To remove the axle shafts, you must first remove the roll pin. Remove the roll pin retainer bolt as shown. Then slide the pin out.

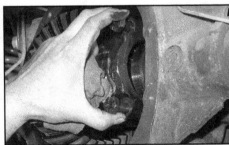

7. Next, remove the differential by removing the bearing cap bolts. Be careful on this one. The differential is heavy.

6. (Left) Slide the axles inboard. Remove the C-clips located at the differential at the ends of the axle shafts. Then remove the axle shafts.

8. The drive pinion is next. Remove the yoke-retaining nut, and then drive the pinion out as shown.

9. On the workbench, we remove the ring gear by extracting all of the bolts. Set the differential assembly on a thick cloth. Drive the ring gear off with a punch and a hammer. Be careful not to damage the ring gear.

10. This is the Traction-Lok differential assembly. The clutches should be inspected for wear while you have the rear end apart. Differential side bearings should be replaced. Ditto for the drive pinion bearings. Start fresh with new parts.

11. If you're on a tight budget, you may want to inspect the bearings and press them back into service. Look closely at the roller bearings and the bearing cups. All should be free of scoring and obvious wear. Any bluing of the bearing surface is cause for replacement.

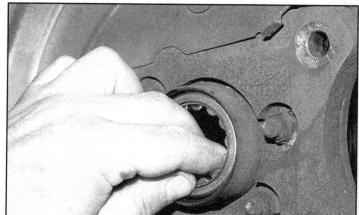

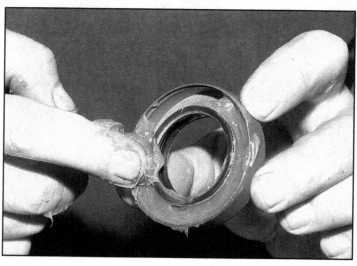

12. Axle bearings should always be inspected closely. The same is true for axle shafts. Any indication of wear is cause for replacement. Axle seals get packed with grease to keep the spring from popping out during installation. New bearings need to be packed with grease before you install the axle.

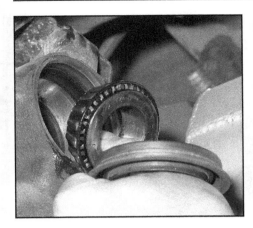

13. Drive pinion bearings need close inspection because they get extraordinary amounts of wear. We suggest replacing them in every case. Bearing cups are pressed into the axle housing.

15. With the differential and drive pinion installed, we're ready to lap gears. This process tells us how happy the gears are with each other. The ring and pinion gears must mate smoothly. We get there by painting the ring gear teeth and running the gears through. The pattern should look like this. Do this before you install the crush sleeve for best results. A dial-indicator really isn't necessary, according to Jason. The dial-indicator tells us about backlash. We want to allow room for gear growth as they get hot during use. See your Ford Shop Manual for backlash specifications.

14. The new ring gear is drawn onto the differential as shown. Once the ring gear is in place, the bolts get Loc-Tite. Crisscross the torque pattern.

16. We're installing a differential cover girdle to stiffen up the case. Once the cover is properly installed, the girdle bolts get torqued to approximately 25 ft-lbs.

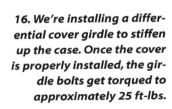

SUSPENSION AND BRAKES

If you're going to build power into your Fox Mustang, you need to plan in a suspension and braking system that can handle the power. Few things are more dangerous than a powerful automobile with no brakes and a crummy suspension. An uncontrollable vehicle can get you killed. Before getting started on a 400-horse small block, ask yourself – will it stop? Will it handle? Then get to work on a power management system that'll keep you safe and alive. Remember, power is only beneficial when it's properly managed. Here are some important points to think about.

BUILD IN SAFETY

Ford designed the Fox-body Mustang for exceptional handling during its development in the 1970s. MacPherson struts and coils in front, and a sophisticated four-link, coil spring, shock arrangement in the rear made for an excellent handling foundation to begin with. This system was a quantum leap in technology over the leaf- and coil-spring-suspended Mustangs of 1965-78. Both front and rear sway bars were used from the beginning. The Fox platform was a simple package that was good from the start. Our job as enthusiasts is to make it better – and safer.

The Fox suspension system hasn't changed much since its inception in 1978. Beginning in 1982, Ford incorporated tubular traction bars into the new Mustang GT to help keep the 7.5-inch rear end in place during hard acceleration. This traction bar system was used through 1984, after which it was replaced by Quadra-Shock traction enhancers.

In 1979-81, there were three basic suspension levels: one for bias-ply tires (believe it or not), one for radial tires, and the TRX handling suspension equipped with metric radials and wheels. The TRX suspension was offered from 1979 to 1984. Because few enthusiasts have any interest in retaining the TRX wheels and tires, those won't be covered here. After 1984, there were two basic suspension types: standard and performance. The standard suspension system had steel wheels and modest underpinnings. For example, the standard Mustang did not have Quadra-Shock rear suspension. Coils weren't as stiff either. Despite these facts, it was still a suspension system that worked quite well. Chances are good you won't be building a 2.3L four or 3.8L V-6 Mustang with the standard suspension system for your Mustang project. Your platform will likely be a 5.0L V-8 Mustang of some sort. Our goal is to show you how to improve on a winner.

So how do we improve on an already outstanding suspension package? We begin by upping the spring rates to keep tires glued to the pavement. Stiffer springs work better when we stiffen the shock and strut dampening. The body will remain more level in hard turns with thicker sway bars. If we want to spend more money, we can alter the suspension's geometry with aftermarket control arms that are fully adjustable. Camber plates above the struts give us even more options in terms of suspension tuning.

If you're on a limited budget, begin your suspension tuning with springs, struts, and shocks. This stiffens the suspension, which improves the tire's relationship with the pavement. Struts and shocks that dampen with a stiffer personality work hand-in-hand with the stiffer springs at all four corners. We suggest replacing all four springs at once. When you do the fronts or the rears first, it tends to throw your Mustang's suspension out of tune because spring rates vary too much from front to rear.

If you have a more generous budget, you can replace the control arms with adjustable control arms that allow you to tune your suspension and change pinion angle. Aftermarket control arms, also called trailing arms, not only improve suspension tuning but also stiffen up the rear end and limit its movement. If you mix in a panhard bar, which limits side-to-side movement, you can greatly reduce axle movement.

When you step up to a Griggs, Maximum Motorsport, or Ford Racing Mustang suspension system, you change everything for the better. The front-end cradle, which supports the engine and front suspension, can be replaced with a bulletproof cradle that properly modifies suspension geometry and makes the front end stronger. These are high-end systems that are expensive but very effective on a race track. We're going to talk more about these in the pages ahead.

When it comes to the braking system, you must first decide what you can afford. The Mustang's stock braking system can be improved through the use of high-performance friction materials and slotted brake rotors. Slotted and cross-drilled brake rotors help the pads gas off more effectively, which keeps the pad in contact with the rotor under the greatest braking conditions. We slot the rotors to help heat and expanding gasses from the pads escape. Under really hard braking, pad and rotor temperatures can run upwards of 900 degrees F. Rotors actually become red hot under these conditions. When rotors are not slotted, heat and pressure build between the rotor and pad, which hurts braking effectiveness. Think of this like you would wet brakes. Instead of water between the pad and rotor, we have gasses from the superheated pads.

An important part of a braking upgrade is knowing what kind of friction material to use. We spoke with Baer Braking Systems, which gave us the lowdown on brake friction materials. Because Baer has invested untold amounts in the development of some of the best braking systems in the industry, we listened closely. Todd tells us that SBS, which provides Baer with brake pads for its braking systems, offers three basic types of friction materials for disc brakes. The Touring pad performs very well for street-driven vehicles. What makes this a great street pad is the quiet operation coupled with superb braking performance. As you brake with this pad, it grows, increasing braking effectiveness.

The Pro Track pad is more of a race compound that may also be used as a street pad. Because they're harder pads than the Touring pads, there's more noise. When we use harder pads, they're harder on the brake rotors. What makes these pads harder is the carbon ceramic compound that is capable of handling temperatures up to 1,292 degrees F. This is an excellent pad for lighter-duty racing. It's not recommended for the daily driver – unless your daily driving is road racing.

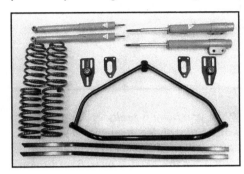

Suspension upgrades begin with the basics – springs, shocks, and struts. We also add a brace to the front-end assembly to stiffen the platform. Subframe connectors make a very significant contribution to platform stiffness. Upgrade as your budget permits.

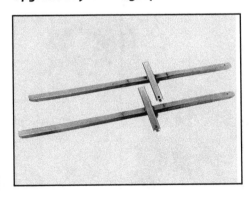

Subframe connectors stiffen up the Fox platform nicely. These must be welded in. When they're welded in, we strongly suggest removing your Mustang's seats and carpeting to prevent fire. Subframe connectors keep your Mustang's body from flexing in hard cornering. Remember that you can make a platform too stiff, which makes the ride hellish for a daily commuter. Unless your Mustang is fully committed to road racing, don't go too extreme.

Baer and SBS offer us yet another pad with a state-of-the-art compound recommended for serious racing. The Pro Race pad stands up to the worst punishment you could ever throw at a disc brake pad. Because this is a dual-carbon pad, it can stand up to fierce temperatures courting 1,500 degrees F. Needless to say, this is not a street pad.

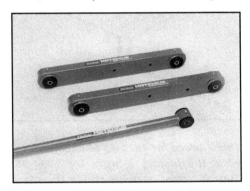

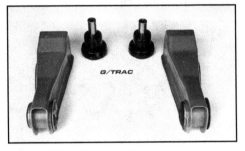

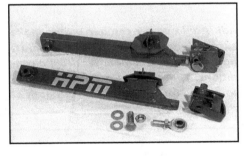

Once we have installed high-performance springs, shocks and struts, the next logical step is to improve suspension geometry. We tighten up the rear with meaty aftermarket control arms and perhaps a panhard bar. The panhard bar keeps the rear axle centered in hard cornering. Our objective with aftermarket control arms is to keep the rear end where it belongs under hard acceleration and hard cornering. Urethane bushings add to the stability. For daily driving, you want polyurethane bushings, which are more flexible than straight urethane.

The reason you should never use a race pad on the street is comfort and convenience levels. Race pads make a lot of black dust, which winds up all over your Mustang's wheels. Because these pads work their best when they're very hot, they complain a lot when they are

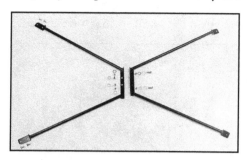

This X-brace for 1979-93 Mustangs does what the factory X-brace for 1994-95 Mustang does. It helps stiffen the platform for better stability and handling.

Adjustable caster/camber plates make suspension tuning easy. You can adjust both caster and camber for driving conditions. These are affordable and easy to install. Toe is adjusted underneath at the tie-rod ends.

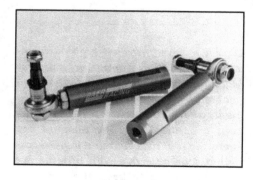

Bump-steer kits improve stability by allowing the steering linkage to articulate smoothly as we travel over irregularities in the road. Plus they're easy to install and adjust.

When you have a really uptown suspension system dialed in, or even if you don't, you need good brakes to stop your Mustang after the blast is over. Baer Brakes, out of Phoenix, Arizona, has been building high-performance disc brakes for Fox-body Mustangs for many years. Our point here is simple. Plan in the best braking system for your investment dollar. We say "investment dollar" because this is your life, so invest in good brakes.

This is the complete JMC Motorsports disc brake package for Fox-body Mustangs. Huge front disc brakes with a near-equal rear discs will make you spit out your gum during hard braking. Boost these powerful disc brakes with the JMC dual-master-cylinder package, which not only performs very well, it looks great too. This is a master cylinder that means business.

cold. In street use, race pads never get hot enough to do their job well.

When you buy a Baer Claw braking system, the system is turn-key and simple. Everything is there to get you into disc brake performance in a matter of hours. When budget limits your options, consider Eradispeed, Baer's upgrade system for factory disc brakes. Eradispeed consists of slotted and cross-

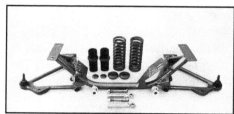

If you can afford it, you can completely replace the factory front suspension system with something from Griggs or Maximum Motorsports. This totally tubular system improves front suspension geometry for race-level handling. It doesn't come cheap, but again, it's an investment in your life.

Here's another example of a fully adjustable rear suspension package. The adjustable Heim joints on the upper control arms control the pinion angle. This is a nice feature for a high-performance Fox-body Mustang. Note the super-thick sway bar, which keeps body roll to a minimum.

drilled rotors that give your factory disc brakes improved performance on par with Baer's own Baer Claws. Of course, the factory disc brakes won't outperform the Baer Claws – even with Eradispeed rotors and SBS pads.

JMC Motorsports has a respected line of high-performance disc brakes for Mustangs. In fact, these disc brakes are designed specifically for Mustangs. If you're seeking high-end braking performance, the JMC Motorsports six-piston front disc brakes will get the job done at 13 x 1.25 inches. In back, JMC Motorsports will set you up with four-piston, 12 x 1.25-inch disc brakes to match. This makes the JMC disc brake package unequalled in the industry. A very clever dual-master cylinder setup makes installation easy, with reservoirs that are easy to service and maintain.

Let's look at some examples of what can be done to enhance your Mustang's handling and braking.

BUDGET FRONT SUSPENSION UPGRADE

We're going to begin with the most basic suspension upgrade you can make: springs, struts, and sway bars. These elements, all by themselves, will improve handling in a weekend. Our platform is a '93 Mustang GT hatchback; call it a factory stocker with modest mileage. It handles as well as can be expected from a factory original Mustang GT.

We're going to begin our upgrade with MAC springs and Koni struts. We're sticking with a stock front sway bar in front, with fresh polyurethane bushings. We're going with polyurethane bushings instead of urethane bushings because we want flexibility and quiet ride. Urethane bushings make the ride stiff and noisy. Polyurethane, as its name implies, offers us some give in its design. Unless you want a brick-like hardness to your ride quality, specify polyurethane.

3. To remove ball joints and tie-rod ends, you don't always need a removal fork, which can sometimes damage the rubber boots. A sharp whack with a hammer can jar the tie-rod end or ball-joint loose. You must first remove the cotter pin and loosen the nut, then give it a whack.

4. Strut removal must be done carefully. The weight of the vehicle needs to be on the spring and strut while you remove the top strut fastener. The strut is what keeps the coil spring compressed. When you remove the nut at the top, you are releasing the coil spring's pressure. The body will tend to lift off the strut.

Tires are sometimes a more important issue than suspension and brakes. The contact patch your Mustang's tires have with the road is critical to handling and braking. The contact patch is our only link keeping us glued to the road, and staying alive. The more rubber we have in contact with the pavement, the more control there is.

1. This is the 1993 Mustang GT front suspension. We want to replace the McPherson struts and coil springs with a setup that will improve handling and can be installed in a day.

2. After safely supporting the front end, the stabilizer links are removed first. We're opting for new polyurethane bushings and links.

5. The coil spring must be removed carefully because there it's under a lot of pressure. Although some folks use a coil spring compressor, you don't need one for removal or installation. Let the weight of the engine and powertrain do the work for you. Lower the Mustang body carefully onto the jack stands. Slowly back the jack down and allow the spring to relax.

6. Unbolt and remove the strut as shown here. Be cautious with the coil spring.

7. Install the new coil spring insulator and fit the coil as shown. Apply upward pressure with the jack under the control arm to seat and compress the spring.

8. Install the Maximum Motorsports camber adjustment plate. The camber adjustment plate makes front-end alignment easy and fully adjustable.

9. The Koni adjustable strut works like the older Koni adjustable shock absorbers. You can dial in the strut's stiffness and dampening rate.

10. The new Koni strut attaches to the spindle with two bolts. At the top, it fits through the Maximum Motorsports camber plate. Install the top retaining nut and tighten everything up. You have to work a plan between the Mustang and the jacks. The strut goes in with the weight off the lower control arm. To get the strut through the camber plate, gradually put weight back on the suspension until the strut comes through the camber plate.

11. Install the stabilizer links once you have the vehicle at rest.

12. The Koni struts are fully adjustable, which means you can dial them in to whatever your driving conditions are. With their adjustments easy to access, the Koni strut makes it simple to tune your suspension.

BUDGET REAR SUSPENSION UPGRADE

We're going to tackle the rear suspension of our '93 Mustang GT with new MAC control arms and coil springs, a thicker sway bar, and Koni adjustable shock absorbers. MAC control arms, with their rigid design and polyurethane bushings, keep the rear axle correctly positioned in all kinds of conditions. MAC suspension system components are good for street and track because they don't limit you to either. They improve handling for the commute without making you feel like you're driving a brick-hard race car. Yet, when you're ready to do some weekend racing or chase a canyon road, MAC control arms are up to the task. MAC control arms provide solid stability for the tightest of budgets.

When we install the MAC rear sus-

1. This is the MAC suspension upgrade system, including the front coil springs and caster/camber adjustment plates, which obviously do not apply to our rear suspension installation. We're going to show you how to install these components and get down to the business of handling and safer driving.

2. The upper control arms and Quadra-Shock system are removed first. Vehicle weight needs to be on jack stands underneath the rear axle. At this time, we want controlled vehicle weight adjustment. We want it where we can slowly jack the vehicle off the lower control arms and coil springs. Remove the shock absorbers at this time, with vehicle weight off the shocks, yet without the axle weight on the shocks. Shock stress must be neutral.

pension system, we're eliminating a lot of excess baggage. The factory Quadra-Shock system, which was factory installed on 1985-93 Mustang GTs and the Cobra, becomes unnecessary because we are installing MAC control arms, which are designed to enhance traction by themselves. Stiffer coil springs also improve handling significantly.

As we did up front, we're fitting the rear end with MAC coils and Koni adjustable shocks for flexibility. We can dial in our Koni shocks, from firm to soft, depending on how we want the ride and handling. The Koni shocks are adjusted through access panels over the rear wheelhouses. Let's get started.

3. Slowly jack the body up off the rear axle, allowing the rear axle to sit on the jack stands. Now you can easily remove the coil springs.

4. Remove the lower control arms as shown.

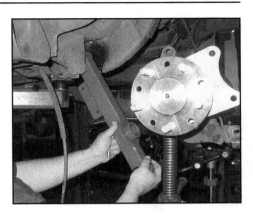

5. The new MAC lower control arms install like this. Because these arms are stiff, they eliminate the need for the factory Quadra-Shock system.

6. Upper control arm installation is simple and easy. Just bolt them in and lubricate the bushings and bolts for flexibility and corrosion prevention.

7. The new MAC coil springs will improve handling and reduce body roll. They install by setting them in the coil spring pockets. Don't forget the coil spring insulators. They're important for keeping things quiet.

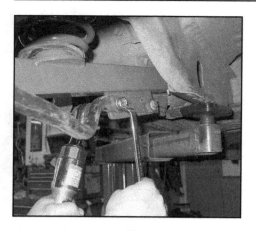

8. Install the new MAC sway bar and tighten the fasteners.

9. Koni adjustable shock absorbers install the same way the factory shock absorbers did. Top attachment points are located behind small plastic access panels in the rear quarter-trim panels. Adjustment is easy to get to via the small access panels. We suggest soft and medium settings for street use. Dial in stiff when it's time to road race or blast through a canyon.

MAXIMUM MOTORSPORTS SUSPENSION

Now we'll look at a couple of high-end suspension systems for late-model Mustangs for an idea of how far you can take your 1979-95 Fox-body Mustang. When it comes to safety and stability, one of the wisest investments you can make in yourself and your Mustang is a high-tech, fully tunable suspension system. Granted, it's a lot of money, but how much is your life worth? A good suspension system, along with honed driving skills, can get you steered out of trouble, and it can save your life.

The Maximum Motorsports suspension system we're about to show you does't have to be purchased and installed as shown. You can order some of it, or if you're going to do some serious road or drag racing, you can order all of it. The choice is yours. Julio Mayen of JME Enterprises in San Diego, California, who owns the '85 Mustang we're about to tackle, is going road racing. He has specified a full-bore Maximum Motorsports suspension system for his Mustang.

Let's begin in front and explain these engineered components from Maximum Motorsports. Then, we're going to show you where they're located and how they're installed.

Maximum Motorsports tells us it spent more than two years developing its K-member for 1979-95 Mustangs, also known as the cradle. These folks didn't just sit down and pencil out a tubular version of the factory K-member. They engineered and refined this design by taking it out on the race track and giving each development test fixture a workout. Where other manufacturers focused on saving weight, Maximum Motorsports compromised between weight and durability. This means the Maximum Motorsports K-member isn't the lightest out there, but it's the strongest.

What makes the Maximum Motorsports K-member different from your body-colored stocker? It's certainly lighter. We know. We've checked. It lengthens your Mustang's wheelbase by 3/4 inch. This improves weight distribution and increases caster. Maximum

Motorsports, as the name implies, maximizes the potential of your Mustang's front suspension geometry. It does this by optimizing the vertical location of the control-arm pivots. This improves the camber curve on lowered Mustangs. It also improves the roll center height.

So, what does all of this fancy chitchat mean? When we speak of the camber curve, we're talking about the front tire relationship with the pavement as we roar down the road. As we enter a turn, we want lots of negative camber. Negative camber is when the top of the tire points in and the bottom points out. Positive camber is when the top of the tire points outward and the bottom points inward, causing the outer sidewall to roll against the pavement, causing tire scrub. It also causes the vehicle to roll over away from the direction of the turn. So, when we have positive camber, we're going to tend to skid to the outside of a turn, especially if we're going at high speed.

Negative camber keeps the tread in contact with the pavement in a hard turn. The contact patch keeps us on the road. The more contact patch we have with the road, the safer we are. When we speak of camber curve, we're talking about how camber behaves as we negotiate a turn. As we roll straight down the road, we want approximately 1/2-degree of negative camber. This half degree of negative camber keeps most of the tread squarely on the pavement. Camber curve happens when we enter a turn. How well does the tire contact patch stay constant with the pavement in a turn? Good camber curve keeps contact patch pretty constant through a turn. The other part of this equation is driving skill. You can overcorrect in a turn and lose contact patch quickly, regardless of how much negative camber you have.

The Maximum Motorsports K-member actually has two available locations for control-arm pivots, which allows you to choose the best location for your expected driving patterns. Another desirable feature of the Maximum Motorsports K-member is the revised location of the steering rack. It reduces understeer and tire wear.

Maximum Motorsports gives Ford a

lot of credit where credit's due with the Mustang's front suspension. Maximum Motorsports extensively tested the factory K-member, and its own K-member, for anti-dive characteristics. Maximum Motorsports has stayed with Ford's geometry here. When it comes to engine location, Maximum Motorsports gives you choice. There are two engine mount locations available for your 5.0L engine – one farther back for improved weight distribution. If you're building a 1996-up Mustang, you can put the 4.6L SOHC or DOHC aside and install a 5.0L engine using the Maximum Motorsports K-member. This works for off-road or in some states that have passive smog legislation.

Another nice feature is the abundant oil pan clearance Maximum Motorsports has designed into its K-member. Header clearance is also maximized, and access to the starter is improved as well. Did you know the Maximum Motorsports K-member is pre-drilled for a plumb bob tool for easy and accurate squaring during installation? When you install the Maximum Motorsports K-member, you're shaving 14 pounds off your Mustang's front end. Add this to other weight savings, like aluminum heads or a fiberglass hood, and the result is improved handling.

With all of this wind out of the way about the K-member, it's important to mention the tubular front control arms from Maximum Motorsports. If you're thinking about bolting your stock control arms to the Maximum Motorsports K-member, forget it. They won't fit. But, why would you go to the trouble and expense of a specially-engineered K-member, only to bolt on stock control arms? Doesn't make much sense, does it? Maximum Motorsports didn't think so either, which is why it engineered not one, but two types of front control arms for its K-member. Its control arms are a true "A" arm, rather than the "V" arm we see from the factory. The "A" design provides maximum rigidity, which places equal forces on the K-member. The Maximum Motorsports control arm is gusseted to ensure the entire arm will bend in a mishap before a weld breaks. Tough? You bet.

The Maximum Motorsports control arm vastly improves suspension geometry by allowing the tires to steer in a tighter turning radius. This is a tighter turning radius than a stock control arm will deliver. Urethane and Delrin bushings are available. Julio is opting for Delrin bushings for greater stability. Urethane is hard stuff, but Delrin is even harder, allowing zero deflection in turns. The Delrin bushings are not a recommended street bushing because they make the ride harder.

We mentioned the availability of two control arm types and here's why. The first is for zero-offset suspension geometry. The zero-offset control arm gives us the same relationship between the control arm pivots and the ball-joint. The alternative is the forward-offset control arm. This approach moves the ball-joint forward. When we combine this control arm with the Maximum Motorsports K-member, we move the front wheels forward 3/4 inch. In some applications, we will have to modify the fender well opening. For street applications, we suggest sticking with the stock geometry.

When we install the Maximum Motorsports control arms, we save another six pounds up front. If you cannot afford the Maximum Motorsports K-member, you can still install the control arms. However, you must go with coil-over struts. You can also go with another brand of coil-over struts if Maximum Motorsports struts aren't to your liking.

Maximum Motorsports has thought completely through the Mustang's front suspension, reviewing every detail. Take the ball-joint dust boot, for example. Urethane dust boots outlast the factory rubber boots, which split and crack, allowing contaminates to get in and damage the ball-joint. This is especially true in desert and high-ozone environments like Los Angeles, Phoenix, and Las Vegas. The blistering desert heat, coupled with air pollution issues, will ruin a rubber ball-joint dust boot in less than a year. We've seen this happen too many times in the dry and dusty Southwest. Once the ball joint's protection is gone, deterioration and failure are

inevitable. Urethane boots will stand up to the harsh elements that destroy rubber.

Urethane front control arm bushings from Maximum Motorsports stand up to hard use because they are full-floating, with a steel insert. When we use the lubricant included in every Maximum Motorsports urethane kit, the bushings will serve us quietly and effectively for years to come. Expect a shorter lifespan if you do a lot of racing. Rough roads also take a toll.

Whenever you're upgrading your Mustang's front end with Maximum Motorsports components, don't forget the sway bar and bushings. Depending on the driving you're going to do, you don't always have to replace the sway bar. The thicker the sway bar, the less body roll you will experience. Remember, a thicker sway bar affects ride quality. Sometimes we can get the sway bar too thick and beat the daylights out of ourselves on the way to work. Find a nice compromise for your streeter and go with it. Sometimes, the factory sway bar is the best choice. Don't discount Ford's judgment here.

When we step up to a Maximum Motorsports front suspension, we need to know we're making a lot of choices, both conscious and subconscious. When we install the Maximum Motorsports control arms, we are eliminating the stock coil springs, meaning we'll have to go to coil-over struts. There are a lot of coil-over strut designs out there. The Maximum Motorsports coil-over strut kit is designed specifically for this suspension system. Think of it as you would matching valvetrain components. If you're building an engine, you should specify all Comp Cams or all Crane Cams, for example. Mixing it up isn't always a good idea. The same can be said for suspension components that are engineered to work happily together. Our underpinnings for this project will be all Maximum Motorsports.

Maximum Motorsports has maximized bump travel in its coil-over struts by providing an assortment of spacers in the kit. You really can fine-tune the Maximum Motorsports coil-over strut to your specific application. The upper spring perch has been designed for optimum strength, so you don't have to worry. We're talking proper clearance and bump travel. There are O-rings in the thrust bearing to keep out dust and moisture. These coil-overs are easily adjusted using the spanner wrench provided in the kit. You may also adjust ride height by adjusting the coil-over springs surrounding the strut. Simply adjust spring positioning with the spanner wrench. Raising and lowering the spring adjusts ride height. Compressing or decompressing the spring controls handling and ride quality. If you opt for the Bilstein struts available from Maximum Motorsports, it doesn't get any better.

The only consequence of coil-over struts is tire/wheel clearance issues with some applications. This is something you need to confirm before spending money on wheels, tires, and coil-overs. Make sure, before buying, that it will all work together peacefully.

On top, Maximum Motorsports has developed caster/camber plates that are fully adjustable. These sliding, fully-adjustable caster/camber plates carry the Mustang's front-end weight. Factory caster/camber supports don't provide the flexibility provided by good aftermarket plates. The Maximum Motorsports caster/camber plate has a spherical bearing that allows the strut to articulate under all kinds of conditions. Maximum Motorsports uses steel, whereas other manufacturers use aluminum and/or urethane. Thanks to a lot of research and development time, Maximum Motorsports has achieved what is likely the best caster/camber plate in the marketplace.

We make this claim by knowing the design. The Maximum Motorsports caster/camber plate rolls with front suspension movement, making for smooth operation across the triangular attachment points (1979-93) and quadangular points (1994-95). Each attachment bolt carries the load evenly. This, in turn, spreads the load evenly over the strut towers. You may use the Maximum Motorsports caster/camber plate with a stock suspension system. Your front-end alignment professional will love it.

Front-end alignment issues are challenging on nearly every type of vehicle

made. For example, static alignment is your Mustang's alignment at rest. This can vary a lot, depending on ride height. Maximum Motorsports tells us that when we lower our Mustangs, we're dialing in more negative camber. The factory caster/camber adjustment does not allow us much adjustment room. This means we may wind up with too much negative camber, with no way out. As a result, the Maximum Motorsports caster/camber plate becomes a mandatory accessory that we need in order to get a full spectrum of alignment tuning. We don't want too much negative camber. When we have too much negative camber, we create excessive wear toward the inner tread and sidewall.

We've learned that static alignment is our Mustang's alignment while at rest. Dynamic alignment is what happens to our Mustang's alignment when we are rolling. Did you know the Dearborn, Michigan assembly plant, which has been building new Mustangs since 1964, does a rolling front-end alignment? It's done with a chassis dynamometer, which gets the front wheels in motion; the Mustang gets set up for the real world out there. Getting a dynamic front-end alignment isn't always possible. In fact, it's rarely possible, given the demographics of alignment shops out there. Most are fixed, static-alignment shops.

Please remember something else about alignment shops. Just because they have the latest alignment technology doesn't mean they know how to align your front-end. Choose an alignment shop based more on know-how and less on the latest technology. Does your alignment shop know what it's doing? Marlon Mitchell, who owns Marlo's Frame & Alignment in Chatsworth, California, has been aligning front ends since he was 10 years old. Marlon doesn't have the latest technology. He uses the old-time bubble fixtures and measuring rods, and he follows his gut instincts about front-end alignment. He practices his craft very well, drawing business from hundreds of thousands of motorists all over Southern California. Our point? Technology, lasers, and computers don't always make the alignment shop. Know-how does.

Dynamic alignment really is the proper assessment of what your Mustang's alignment will be in motion. Suspensions with a lot of give won't remain the same as they were during a static alignment. So, we have to align a front-end based on what we know the front-end will do in motion. We may have to crank in additional camber or caster based on what we know the suspension

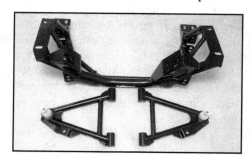

1. *Fitting your Mustang with a Maximum Motorsports suspension is literally redesigning your Mustang's suspension system, without having to hire engineers and suspension tuners. Maximum Motorsports has done the design work for you. This is the front suspension cradle and control arms. Maximum offers two types of control arms, depending on how you want your front suspension geometry. Heavy-duty bushings keep things in spec.*

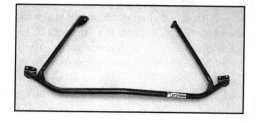

2. *This is the strut tower support from Maximum Motorsports. Install this assembly to stiffen up the front end considerably.*

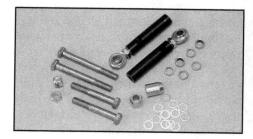

3. *This bump-steer kit offers us stability in all kinds of road conditions.*

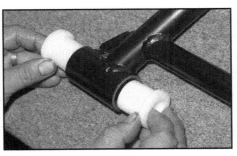

4. *Urethane bushings and stabilizer links work well on the track because they give us precision under all kinds of conditions. Regardless of how rough road conditions become, and how much the road challenges us, urethane bushings and stabilizers keep control arms and sway bars properly located.*

6. *Assemble the front control arms using the bushings provided in the kit. A special lubricant is provided to help quiet the control arm bushings.*

8. *Caster/camber adjustment plates are installed to make alignment and strut flexibility easy. Caster and camber are adjusted here. Toe is adjusted underneath at the tie-rod ends.*

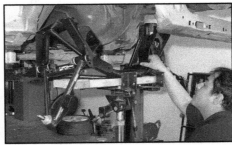

5. *Our Maximum Motorsports kit is designed for conventional springs, struts, and shocks. However, because we are going racing with these components, we're spending the extra money for coil-overs. These adjustable coil-overs have to be assembled. Complete instructions, included in the kit, enable us to properly assemble the coil-over shocks and struts. Super stiff urethane bushings replace the soft rubber shock bushings.*

7. *The front suspension cradle is installed as shown. This assembly is bolted to the front frame rails. Needless to say, the factory cradle is long gone. Space prohibits us from showing you the removal of the original cradle.*

will do during hard cornering. If we know it's going to move a degree or so more toward positive camber in a corner, we're going to need to dial in more negative camber to make up the difference. It takes a very savvy alignment specialist to know what the suspension will do under actual driving conditions.

Seasoned alignment people understand that we need more negative camber for a race car because we're going to be cornering harder in the turns. We want the tire tread squarely on the pavement in a hard turn. This is where additional negative camber becomes

necessary before racing. For street driving, we need less negative camber 1/2 degree. This makes our Mustang user-friendly in mild turns, yet it doesn't cause excessive tire wear. If we're doing both street driving and racing, we need to change camber for the racing part. We need more negative camber for racing, and less of it for the street – commit that to memory. With the Maximum Motorsports caster/camber plates, you can change alignment settings yourself with a minimum of fuss. However, we suggest the sharp insight of an alignment specialist for best results.

9. *The Maximum Motorsports struts are installed with the top studs routed into the caster/camber plates. The bottoms use two bolts each at the heavy-duty spindles.*

Maximum Motorsports didn't forget the fundamentals in back. These folks went back to the drawing board, improving the Mustang's get-along with a variety of components designed to improve handling. The most basic, of course, is the four-link suspension support system.

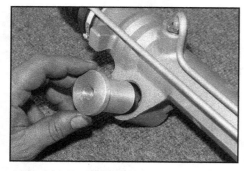

10. We're installing a new power steering rack from JME Enterprises using the aluminum bushings from Maximum Motorsports. These bushings give the steering rack additional stability.

11. Our Maximum Motorsports suspension system includes subframe connectors, which stiffen the Fox Mustang platform. These subframe connectors are raw steel and must be welded onto the unit body.

From the factory, the four-link support system needs some support. Ford called that support system the Quadra-Shock traction enhancement system. With four hydraulic dampers designed to reduce axle hop and improve tire contact, the Quadra-Shock system was a nice idea, but certainly excessive. It consumed too much space, and it added unnecessary weight to the rear end.

Maximum Motorsports looked at the factory rear suspension and knew instinctively there had to be a better way. The Maximum Motorsports system eliminates the upper control arms and the Quadra-Shock traction system completely. How can they do this? With rock-solid lower control arms sporting urethane bushings. There is also an optional ride height adjustment feature available for these super-tough control arms. These are nice features you have a right to expect in a good aftermarket control arm.

Maximum Motorsports tells us that wheel rate refers to the rate of roll stiffness as measured behind the wheel. We get total wheel rate from what the sway bar and suspension do in a turn. Suspension movement comes from how much the springs, bushings, shocks, and sway bar move. The harder the bushing, the stiffer the suspension. We call this bind. This, and other dynamics, determine how much the suspension will move. Maximum Motorsports has developed bushings that have just the right amount of give, which gives the suspension predictable performance. At the chassis side of a Maximum Motorsports rear control arm, we have a four-piece urethane and steel bushing designed to afford us the right amount of movement. The softer outer portions allow the angular motion necessary to prevent bushing bind. At the axle end, a Teflon bearing makes for stiff connection, yet it prevents binding. This bushing is different because the axle takes a greater pounding than the chassis.

With Maximum Motorsports control arms and shocks out of the way, you

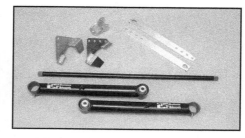

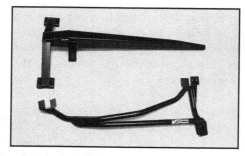

12. The rear suspension is decidedly complex because we're doing so much with it. We'll eliminate the upper control arms entirely, since the Maximum Motorsports lower control arms do the work with urethane and steel bushings. The panhard bar with Heim joints will keep the rear axle stable. A torsion-style sway bar consumes less space than the stock bar and is fully tunable. A torque arm is tied to the subframe connectors and rear axle to help with stability. We can control pinion angle using the adjustable torque arm.

still have decisions to make. Coil-over shocks and stiff lower control arms provide new levels of stability, which is great for street and occasional racing. Street Mustangs also need something else – roll stability. The Maximum Motorsports rear sway bar isn't the result of conventional sway-bar thinking. This is a fully-adjustable, tubular torsion bar that doesn't work like a conventional sway bar. It's hollow, for one thing, and it works like a vintage Chrysler/Plymouth/Dodge torsion bar – its twisty nature is what provides stability. The more twist we crank into the torsion bar, the stiffer the roll. In other words, the more we twist the sway bar, the less it will allow the body to roll. When we move the sway bar end links closer to the bar, we stiffen up sway bar adjustment. When we stiffen up sway bar stiffness, we reduce the vehicle roll rate. This is a revolutionary sway bar system.

When it comes to street Mustangs, this is about as far as you want to go with the Maximum Motorsports rear suspension. If you're going road racing, or like to blast through canyons, stay with us. The next area of consideration is the panhard bar. The panhard bar is tied to the rear axle housing and the frame rail. Maximum Motorsports gives you the goods to stabilize the rear axle. There is a subframe, with an eyelet on the right-hand side. And, there is a bracket that attaches on the left-hand side of the rear axle. The aluminum panhard bar with adjustable Heim joints at each end ties to the subframe and rear axle. The panhard bar

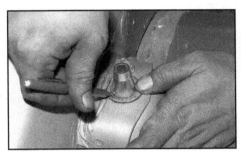

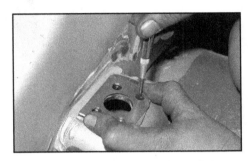

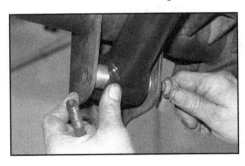

13. Rear lower control arms are all you need with the Maximum Motorsports suspension system. These arms stabilize the rear axle. Bushings at the body have to be lubricated and installed first. The bushings are already installed at the axle.

14. Spherical upper shock mounts are installed as shown. We have to open up the shock mount hole in the chassis and drill holes for the spherical joints. The coil-over shocks are inserted into the joints. This allows the shocks to articulate.

enables us to dial in rear-end alignment. Then, once rear-end alignment is where it needs to be, it keeps the rear axle permanently fixed. This means you can cut the meanest of apexes and know your rear-axle alignment will remain true.

Another rear-end alignment fixture and traction enhancer is the big Maximum Motorsports torque arm that ties

15. Rear coil-over shocks are installed as shown. The tops will articulate smoothly thanks to the spherical joints we've already installed.

16. The torque arm makes our rear axle adjustable, yet rigid. This arm is tied to a crossmember, which is tied to the subframe connectors. It keeps the rear axle very stable in high-power conditions.

17. This is the subframe designed to hold the panhard bar. The panhard bar is designed to keep the rear axle centered. It's also fully adjustable, thanks to Heim joints at both ends.

18. *Julio Mayen of JME Enterprises installs the panhard bar. This lightweight tubular aluminum bar adjusts the rear axle from side to side and keeps the rear axle stable. The subframe that the panhard bar is tied to bolts to the rear frame rails. It's a lot of work, but well worth the time invested. The tubular sway bar, yet to be installed, is actually a torsion bar that is fully adjustable for tuning.*

the rear end to the unit body. With the torque arm, we're able to adjust drive pinion angle and prevent rear-axle hop when the throttle is wide open. We don't recommend the torque arm for street use because it does make for a stiff ride since it limits axle movement.

Another thing to consider whenever you're entertaining the use of a torque arm is spring stiffness. Torque arms mandate the use of springs that are not as stiff. Otherwise, ride quality and even vehicle stability will suffer. You need a nice balance of stiff and flexible – even when you're going racing full time.

GRIGGS GR-40 SUSPENSION UPGRADE

Earlier, we showed you how to install a complete Maximum Motorsports suspension system on a 1979-93 Mustang. The Maximum Motorsports system is designed for all-out racing if you opt for the whole package. It's a system you can order in whole or in part. The same can be said for heavy-hitter Griggs Racing out of northern California. Griggs needs no introduction in racing and performance circles. These avid racers produce one of the best racing suspension systems in the industry. This is why John Da Luz of JMC Motorsports in San Diego, California, specified the Griggs GR-40 system for his '94 Mustang race car that'll be campaigned in the

American Iron Series in the years ahead.

John has completely gutted his Mustang GT. Inside is a full cage built by CDB Fabrications in Southern California. On the engine stand is a 331-ci stroker currently under construction. A Tremec TKO is waiting in the wings. Underneath is a Currie 8.8-inch groundpounder. You get the idea. The Griggs name is a natural for something like this.

So, what can Griggs do for your Mustang? In a word – plenty! To quote Griggs, "Griggs GR-40 chassis components are simply the finest chassis components available for the Mustang. No competitors, regardless of price, offer the same level of performance." The folks over at Maximum Motorsports might put up a good argument, because both companies bring very competitive and race-proven suspension systems to the marketplace. We've had the good fortune of experience with both manufacturers. Who can argue with their status in the industry? Certainly not us. We're talking some of the best components made anywhere in the world.

Griggs tells us the Mustang was never a purpose-built car, like the Corvette or Mazda RX-7. The 1979-95 Mustang was based on the Fox-platform, the same platform used for the Fairmont, Zephyr, Granada, Monarch, Thunderbird, Cougar, Lincoln Continental, and Mark VII. Call this well-engineered platform long on potential, but from the factory, it was pitifully lame.

We know from years of observation that the Fox-body Mustang struggles with structural integrity. Prior to 1994, the Fox was especially weak, with a lot of body flex and twist. Ford revisited the Fox platform during SN-95 development and created a better Mustang body for 1994. Even 1994-95 Mustangs need to be stiffer for racing purposes. If you're building a weekday commuter and weekend racer, you'll have to find a comfortable compromise between stiff and flexible.

A good rule of thumb to keep in mind when you're building a Mustang is this: too stiff is too much. To keep things comfortable for vehicle occupants in a street driver, we need a platform and body that have a certain amount of flex.

We want the body and chassis to absorb some of that road shock. To accomplish this, keep your structural mods to a minimum. Full-time racers need to be stiff in order to maintain proper chassis alignment and structural integrity under severe-duty conditions.

What does Griggs Racing suggest for structural modifications that will improve your Mustang's integrity? Let's begin with the platform. Most suspension component manufacturers opt for stiffer springs, shocks, and struts. They also go with harder bushings. Griggs has completely visited the Mustang's underpinnings and come up with a user-friendly system of suspension management. You can install part of it or all of it, depending on how you intend to drive your Mustang.

The most important thing when ordering your Griggs suspension is knowing how far to go. We're going to show you what each element of a Griggs suspension and chassis system does. Then, you decide how aggressive you need to become with your Mustang.

Griggs has focused on the Mustang's platform shortcomings and gone back to the drawing board with components that enhance a Mustang's handling and performance qualities. Let's take a closer look at what Griggs Racing is all about. When it comes to the 1979-95 Mustang platform, Griggs professionals agree there is too much body flex. Rear upper control arms don't do the job they were designed to do very well. The upper control arms were designed to locate the rear axle housing laterally as well as controlling its rotation (pinion angle, for example), but they give the Mustang a high roll center and they bind when a Mustang enters a turn. Griggs tells us this binding causes a sudden increase in the wheel rate, which causes that typical Mustang "snap" oversteer that startles the daylights out of those that aren't ready for it.

In front, the Fox platform offers but two degrees of caster, which, Griggs adds, was designed for those skinny biasply pizza cutters that the Fairmont and Zephyr were designed for. It's surely not enough for today's low-profile high-performance tires. Also in front, there is a very low roll center, which can get us into all kinds of trouble out there. The front control-arm angle promotes too much brake dive, and bumpsteer is way out of hand in Fox-body Mustangs from the factory. What may surprise you even more is steering rack geometry. Factory steering rack positioning does not provide enough toe, causing the outside edge of the outside tire to drag in turns.

While this might not apply much to street use, it certainly has merit on the race track and twisty canyon roads. A torque-arm and Panhard bar have been incorporated into the Griggs engineering process to eliminate the rear upper control arms. Doing this, Griggs has eliminated the oversteer shortcoming that Mustangs have long been famous for. Subframe connectors stiffen up the body without being too obvious. In front, Griggs has redesigned the K-member, relocating the control arm attachment points. This yields better high-speed stability, decreases brake dive, raises the roll center, improves steering geometry, and more. The Griggs bumpsteer kit reduces bumpsteer. Good springs, shocks, and struts make a huge difference in handling.

The Griggs GR-40 Suspension Kit equips a Mustang for professional-level racing. In fact, we're about to install the Griggs GR-40 kit in two days. One day for the front, and one day for the back. Let's talk about all of the elements.

What do we accomplish with the Griggs front half of the GR-40 system? The GR-40 tubular K-member lowers the front end without disturbing the geometry. The SN-95 (1994-up) spindles give us even more. The Griggs K-member reduces the scrub radius and corrects

Ackerman (steering rack to steering components relationship). It revises caster for better straight-line performance. Control arm locations have been changed to reduce body roll, update camber, and reduce brake dive.

In back, the Griggs TorqueArm (trademarked TorqueArm by Griggs), panhard bar, and rear lower control arm bushings are what make a clear difference in suspension performance. What does each of these elements accomplish? If you're building a powerful, high-performance Mustang, you're going to need a system of traction control when the throttle is pinned. Fox-body Mustangs get squirrelly when we mash the throttle, especially from a standstill. Ford tried to correct this with traction bars (1982-84) and the Quadra-Shock system (1985-95), but neither has done much for traction and stability issues.

The installation of the TorqueArm and panhard bar does a lot for traction and stability. The TorqueArm keeps the rear axle stable by eliminating axle hop and twist. The panhard bar keeps the rear axle centered under acceleration and cornering. The torque arm, in general, is not a new idea. General Motors has been using a torque arm on its F-body Camaro and Firebird for many years. The torque arm does a nice job of providing stability on all fronts. Griggs takes this concept a step further with meaty urethane bushings on its lower control arms, which also eliminates wheel hop. The TorqueArm and panhard bar are suitable for both road racing and drag racing. The only reason we tend to discourage their use for street driving is some ground clearance issues

you might find on public roads and private parking lots. Access to some lifts and alignment racks out there might also be an issue with these modifications.

Springs, shocks, struts, and caster/camber plates are another area we need to address. Griggs suggests matching these items whenever you upgrade the suspension. We can adjust ride height by how we choose and adjust our springs and rates. Griggs suggests being very careful about how you choose components and tune the suspension. You can crank too much spring into the tuning and ruin the ride. You can also have too little spring in there and ruin handling quality. In any situation, including racing, we need to have a compromise between ride quality and handling.

One of the greatest benefits to the Griggs GR-40 is weight reduction and the ability to move the engine for improved weight distribution. Installing the Griggs K-member and control arms knocks the better part of 20 pounds off the front end. Coil-over struts eliminate those heavy coil springs. The TorqueArm actually adds weight to the platform, but it adds it where we need it most, improving the center of gravity to some degree.

We don't often think of Griggs for braking systems. However, Griggs is a good source for complete chassis systems, including the brakes. Big 13-inch disc brakes get the job done nicely, with PBR calipers like we find with Baer brakes. Whenever you're ordering large 13-inch brakes, you're going to need 17-inch wheels. If you're fitting the Mustang with 16-inch wheels you're in for a rude awakening, because they will not fit over 13-inch brake rotors. Griggs

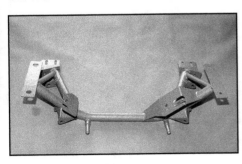 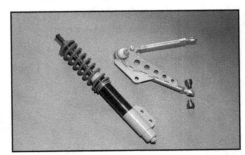 

1. John Da Luz has opted for the full Griggs Racing system. The kit includes the K-member, Koni coil-overs, and lightweight control arms for the front. The complete package in back includes the TorqueArm, panhard bar, subframe connectors, heavy-duty control arms, and more. None of this comes cheap for anyone, especially the amateur racer on a budget.

suggests the 17-inch Cobra R wheels as one option for late-model Mustang performance. At the same time, Griggs strongly endorses the SN-95 spindle for any late-model Mustang project for strength and five-lug convenience.

If you're doing a 1979-93 Mustang, Griggs suggests the P255/40 x 17 wrapped around a 17 x 9-inch rim. For 1994-95 Mustangs, step it up to P275/40 x 17. If you intend to push the 1979-93 platform to this tire size, be prepared for fender lip mods to squeeze the rubber in.

If you're wondering about Griggs' racing experience, listen up. Griggs has been in business for 24 years as of this publishing, with vast experience around both amateur and professional racing venues. In fact, the first Griggs Racing TorqueArm was installed in 1979 on a 2.8L V-6 RS-series Mustang. Racing experience for Griggs includes AMA, GATR, IHRA, NASCAR, NHRA, SC, SCORE, USAC, and WoO. Needless to say, all this experience can be very beneficial to your personal racing program.

We're going to install the Griggs GR-40 suspension on John Da Luz's '94 Mustang GT turned road-racer. Step by step, we will show you what's involved.

2. John has completely stripped the body to the bone. We're removing the bolt-on factory K-member at this time. There's no need to support the engine from the bottom, just use a hoist or an engine support that sits over the inner fenders.

3. Two healthy guys can hoist the Griggs K-member into place. The Griggs K-member bolts to the frame rails in four places, two bolts hold each side of the K-member. At the rear of the K-member, where the frame rails run down to the floor pan area, there are two bolts on each side. Ascertain proper K-member alignment, and then torque all of the bolts to Griggs specs.

4. The Griggs front control arms are installed using solid aluminum bushings for stability. You wouldn't use these bushing for street use.

5. John is installing a new steering rack with Griggs solid aluminum bushings between the rack and K-member. The factory uses rubber bushings for insolation. Installation begins with these aluminum washers for the rack to seat against.

6. Here, we're installing the steering rack with aluminum mounts from Griggs.

7. Here's the SN-95 hub being installed onto the Griggs control arm.

8. Coil-over Konis do the dampening and suspending in front. They're fully adjustable, plus, with the coil-overs, you can adjust ride height and spring pressure.

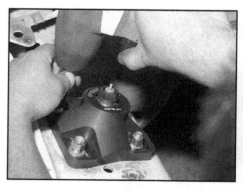

9. Griggs takes a different approach to its caster/camber plates. This is a spherical caster/camber adjustment plate that moves with the strut. The adjustment for the Koni strut is clearly visible on top.

10. With the steering rack installed, we're ready for the Griggs bumpsteer tie-rod ends. The bumpsteer tie-rod ends stabilize the steering over a variety of road conditions.

11. John Da Luz wraps up the front end by connecting the steering shaft to the rack. The steering shaft and universal joints also come from Griggs.

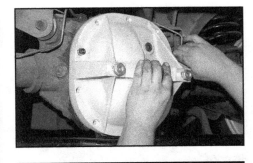

12. We will begin at the rear by installing the bearing support and cover. John uses The Right Stuff to seal the cover. Bearing supports are screwed in and torqued to 25 ft-lbs. Not only does this casting from Griggs look sharp, it also performs some important functions: holding the rear end together and radiating heat.

13. John installs the TorqueArm from Griggs Racing. The TorqueArm ties to the rear-axle center case and is adjustable at the crossmember. At the end of the TorqueArm, there will be a crossmember tied to the subframe connectors. A bushing will isolate the arm and the crossmember.

14. Subframe connectors from Griggs stiffen up the platform and have to be welded in place. They tie the front and rear frame rails together.

15. Rear lower control arms install with ease, as John Da Luz demonstrates here. Because we're installing coil-over shocks, there will be no coil springs between the control arm and frame.

16. Coil-over adjustable Koni shocks install like factory equipment. Top attachment points are accessed through the quarter-trim panels. The Konis are also adjusted at the top. Attachment points at the axle are the same as factory.

17. The panhard bar installation begins here, with this bracket and support assembly on the right-hand side of the rear axle.

18. The bracket we've just installed on the right gets a big brother above, which is welded to the rear frame rails. This subassembly is pushed forward to where it stops and will go no further forward. The Griggs instructions are very specific about location and measurement.

19. John welds the panhard bar support in place at each of the two frame rails. He has removed the powder coating at the joint for welding.

20. John installs and static adjusts the panhard bar. As you can see, the panhard bar keeps the rear axle centered and provides stability. There is a Heim joint at the right-hand end of the panhard bar for adjustment.

DISC BRAKE UPGRADES

Probably one of the greatest investments you can make, even with a tight budget, is an upgrade to a better disc brake system. You may invest, first, in larger front disc brakes. Then, upgrade the rears as your budget permits. If a set of Baer or JMC disc brakes keeps you out of one accident, they have more than paid for themselves.

The 1979-93 Mustang never had much of a braking system. This is the standard four-lug disc brake common to everything but the SVO and Cobra for 14 years. It wasn't until 1994 that Ford fitted the Mustang with better disc brakes on all four corners. If you want better braking, there are some quick-stopping answers from Baer and JMC Motorsports.

This is the Baer Brake Systems four-wheel Baer Claw setup. The Baer Claws are a great value and arrive at your doorstep ready to install. Note the axle shafts shown here as a nice upgrade to five-lug wheels. You get these for front and rear. Or, you can start with the front, and do the rear later, as budget permits.

This is the 13-inch front disc brake with a six-piston caliper from JMC Motorsports. When you are installing aftermarket disc brakes, such as Baer, JMC, or Wilwood, install a new heavy-duty Cobra spindle. Baer disc brakes arrive assembled. All you have to do is install the brake assembly. Installing the JMC Motorsports six-piston disc brake shown here begins with the hub.

This six-piston monster from JMC Motorsports is easy to install. Once the hub and spindle are properly installed, the rotor and caliper go on. The caliper is retained with two bolts and torqued to specs using Loc-Tite. High-performance brake pads drop in like this, retained with two machine screws.

JMC Motorsports enables you to step up to even larger disc brakes with the 13 x 1-1/4-inch rotors and six-piston calipers. This is one of the best high-performance disc brakes in the Mustang world.

1. Removing the factory front disc brakes is easy. Begin by removing the caliper, it only takes the removal of two bolts.

2. Remove the dust cap, cotter pin, castle nut, and outer wheel bearing. Then the rotor can come off.

3. Remove the dust shield. Depending on the kind of aftermarket disc brake you're going to run, you may have to change the hub. Baer front disc brakes come with new hubs and spindles. So do JMC Motorsports brakes with four- and six-piston calipers. If you're rebuilding your factory hubs and spindles, you can keep the dust shields.

INSTALLING BAER REAR DISC BRAKES

From 1979-93, the Mustang was factory-fitted with front disc brakes and rear drum brakes. Front and rear, Mustang brakes have been pitifully small. Even in 1994, when Mustang brakes grew larger, they still weren't big enough. Baer Brakes offers us a nice rear disc brake conversion kit for the 1986-93 Mustang GT. This kit's designed for five-lug axle shafts, which we intend to install here. Because we have limited space, we're not going to cover every detail of a rear disc brake conversion. We're going to cover the basics and allow your skills and the Baer Brakes instructions to do the rest.

Because the 1979-93 Mustang has four-lug spindles and axle shafts, this is a configuration we would normally go back with. In fact, Baer has both four- and five-lug configurations for late-model Mustangs. When you're interested in installing five-lug wheels, it becomes necessary to change the front hubs and rear axle shafts. Changing the front hubs is easy. You can update the spindles and opt for heavy-duty SN-95 (1994-up) spindles. This is also a swap that involves disconnecting the strut, tie-rod ends, and ball-joint. All are easy to do.

Swapping the axle shafts entails pulling the differential pan, roll pin, and C-clips. We remove the roll pin by removing the retaining bolt at the differential, sliding the pin out, then sliding the axles inboard enough to remove the C-clips. With the C-clips removed, the axles slide out with ease.

Let's look at the Baer Claw brake we're about to install. Baer uses PBR calipers in all of its high-performance disc brakes. These calipers are available in a variety of finishes, depending on your desire. The Baer Claws have 12-inch rotors that are slotted and cross-drilled to dissipate heat and gasses. These rotors have a limited lifetime warranty against warping. A wide variety of brake pads are available for Baer brakes, depending on how you're going to drive. As mentioned earlier, use street pads for the street – race pads for the track.

Because the '93 Mustang has a different parking brake cable system than 1979-92, Baer offers an appropriate cable system for the '93. If you're putting Baer disc brakes on the rear of your '93 Mustang, always remember to specify model year. You'll have to change the cables to achieve proper fit and operation.

Not only do you have pad options, but other options as well. When you order your discs from Baer, you have a choice of slotted, cross-drilled, zinc-washed, two-piece, HPC-coated, and optional ARP studs for strength.

1. We're installing a Baer dual master cylinder. Master cylinders should be bench bled before they're installed on the vehicle. This gets all of the air out of the reservoir and cylinder. While we're focused on hydraulics, we're also installing an adjustable proportioning valve, which modulates braking pressure to the rear disc brakes. Too much brake pressure to the rear brakes is a bad thing because it can cause you to lose control of the vehicle.

2. Since we're swapping from four-lug to five-lug axle shafts and spindles, we've got to remove the axle shafts. First remove the roll pin. Then slide the axle shafts inboard to access the C-clips shown. Each shaft has a C-clip.

3. Both axle shafts slide out with ease. While you're at it, replace the axle bearings and seals.

4. The drum brake assemblies are connected to the axle-housing flange, just like we find with conventional axle assemblies. It's just four bolts to take them off.

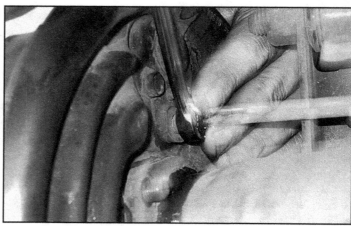

5. Disconnect the brake line at the wheel cylinder. Parking brake cables need to be disconnected at this time since the Baer disc brakes arrive with their own parking brake cables.

6. The rear drum brakes come out as an assembly. You don't even have to disassemble them.

7. The installation begins with brackets that fasten to the axle flanges. These brackets point toward the rear of the vehicle. Note proper positioning.

8. The new axle shafts are installed as shown. Lubricate the bearing contact surfaces with wheel bearing grease. Do the same thing with the new bearings and seals. Pack the seals heavily with wheel bearing grease to protect the springs.

9. Install the C-clips with the axle shafts in place. Reinstall the roll pin and retainer bolt.

10. This is where the job gets easier. Slide the new rotor into place on the axle flange. We suggest a thin layer of grease between the rotor and axle flange for corrosion prevention. You want to use a heavy graphite or molybdenum that won't spread outward across the rotor. Check with Baer Brakes if you aren't sure which type. You need a protective layer between the rotor and axle flange.

11. The Baer/PBR calipers slip into place. Torque the fasteners to the appropriate torque in the Baer instructions.

12. Baer has provided us with the correct parking brake cables. Installation begins at the body and works its way down to the brake shown.

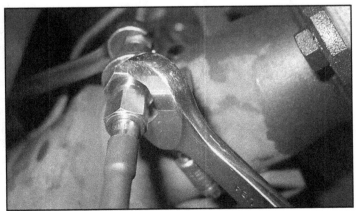

13. Brake hydraulic pressure comes via hard lines from the distribution block to the calipers. Instructions and hardware are included in the kit.

WHEELS AND TIRES

Whenever there's shop talk about performance, wheel and tire issues can't be far behind. Tires are an integral part of a Mustang's performance system. They allow our powerful 5.0L engines to hook up with the pavement for improved quarter-mile times, and traffic-light-to-traffic-light performance. They also affect our Mustang's relationship with the pavement in terms of handling. The more rubber we put in contact with the road, the better our Mustangs handle. When we have a better understanding of tire design and construction, we're better able to make an informed decision when it's time to buy tires.

The same can be said for buying wheels – your decision needs to be an informed one. When we're shopping for wheels, our first consideration needs to be style, followed quickly by fit. Does the wheel's styling work with your Mustang's body style? Once we pass that juncture, the next consideration is proper fit. Proper fit means offset, backspacing, and wheel-well clearance. Will the wheel and tire combo fit comfortably in the wheel well without body and chassis interference? You would be amazed how many of us make this mistake. And when we make it, it's typically a costly one. Wheel and tire dealers rarely exchange or refund when a selection is made in error. And, the stuff is

never worth used (even one-day old) what you paid for it. So, let's get it right going in and save a lot of money.

CHOOSING A TIRE

Whenever you're shopping for tires for your Mustang, carefully consider how the car will be driven. We drive late-model Mustangs all kinds of ways. Most of them get used for the daily commute and weekend motorsports activities. This means we have to fine-tune our driving expectations. Regardless of how we drive our Mustangs, we want handling. We want the beast to turn on a dime. We also want tire life.

In the real world, it's hard to achieve both handling and tire life. If you want handling, you're going to sacrifice tire life. Tires that handle well are made of softer rubber compounds that "give" with the road and the vehicle. They not only give, they stick to the road. Soft rubber compounds give us the flex we need for great handling. But, softer compounds cost more and wear out more quickly. When you corner hard, you're leaving a lot of rubber crumbs and dust in your wake. Tread life fades quickly.

When we think of great-handling tires, with wide profiles and low sidewall height, we think of the BFGoodrich Comp T/A radials. The Comp T/A was born for a 5.0L Mustang GT and Cobra.

It holds the road very well and gives us acceptable tread life for a high-performance tire. The same can be said for the

This is the BFGoodrich Comp T/A radial tire. If you study the tread design and the width, it's apparent why it handles so well. A good, wide footprint gives your Mustang its adhesion with the road. Water channels reduce the risk of hydroplaning. A low sidewall profile provides good cornering capability. These are just two of the features you should consider in a high-performance tire.

Like the BFGoodrich Comp T/A, the Goodyear Eagle is another great-handling, low-profile tire that holds the road very well. Handling is this tire's greatest asset – long life isn't. In regular use, with rotations, balancing, and proper care, this tire will live for 30,000 to 40,000 miles. Run it hard and you can expect less.

This is the BFGoodrich Radial T/A. Its profile is what makes this tire considerably different from the Comp T/A. The Radial T/A has more sidewall and less tread surface. It is also made of a harder rubber compound, so it lasts longer. Because there's more sidewall, the Radial T/A delivers a more comfortable ride. It's a good tire for the daily commute, but not a good tire for autocrossing or road racing.

Goodyear Eagle GS, which is a comparable tire to the Comp T/A.

Tire handling really is all about that small area between the tire tread and pavement called the contact patch. The greater the contact patch, the better our Mustang will hold the road. As this word implies, grip sums up our tire's relationship with pavement and vehicle. As we cruise down the road, there are a lot of forces working on our tires. There's vehicle weight, side loads when we negotiate a turn, and aerodynamic loads that come from air moving over the surfaces of the body. If it's windy, aerodynamics becomes even more unpredictable, putting all kinds of stresses on the tires.

Tire adhesion is likely the most critical issue facing us in tire selection and use. We want good adhesion for reasons of safety and handling. We want our rear tires to hook up when the throttle is opened. And, we want good adhesion when we're entering a turn at speed. Driving without tire adhesion is like driving on ice – it gets us nowhere.

When we enter a turn at speed, the vehicle will tend to keeping going straight into and past the turn – translated: into the trees. Tire adhesion is what keeps the vehicle directed and on course. We get tire adhesion through good contact patch. We also get it from a flexible sidewall that allows the vehicle to go with the tire in a turn. When vehicle velocity overwhelms the tire sidewall and contact patch, we lose adhesion. If we are operating at a handicap, such as wet pavement, ice, or sand, we lose adhesion there too.

WHEEL SELECTION AND FIT

Choosing the right wheel for your Mustang is a matter of personal taste, function, and fitment. If you have a 1987-95 Mustang GT or Cobra, most of the decision has already been made for you in terms of size and style. These cars were fitted with low-profile tires and 16-inch wheels to begin with. This means you're married to 16 inches and larger. It also means you should go with a tire/wheel combination that these cars were designed for.

Undoubtedly the most popular wheel design for late-model Mustangs is just about any five-spoke rim. The Cobra-R rim from Steeda is quite popular. The Torq-Thrust wheels like we see on the Bullitt Mustangs are also in style. One of the newest wheels available is the Magnum 500 rim on the Mach 1. This is a great-looking wheel that will fit your 1994-95 Mustang. If you want to understand what's most popular out there, just look around. Attend car shows and racing events. You can glean a lot of good ideas just looking around at how enthusiasts are equipping their Mustangs.

Aside from the obvious (looks), you need to be very attentive to how the wheels will fit. You want to look at backspacing and offset. Does the wheel clear the inner wheelhouse and suspension components? And does it clear the wheel well lip at all angles? This is the sort of thing you need to ascertain before buying. You need a wheel dealer interested in properly fitting your wheels. It's a good investment of time to mount a tire on a rim and check for fit. This costs the dealer little more than time, which is important, and so is the time it takes to correct an expensive mistake.

When you go shopping for wheels, choose the wheel and the wheel dealer carefully. No one wants the sting of a fly-by-night dealer they won't be able to count on in the future. If pricing seems too good to be true, then it probably is. Opt for proven dealers that have been around for a long time and have customers lined up at their doors. There's a reason why people keep coming back. Always opt for a dealer that understands your wheel needs and wants.

Wheel fitment begins in two places: off-set and backspacing. Here, John Da Luz checks offset and backspacing with a tool designed just for this purpose.

Backspacing is shown here. Does the wheel and tire assembly clear the inner wheelhouse and suspension components? In back, we want the tire sidewall and rim to clear everything on the inside. On the outside, we are concerned mostly with the fender lip and wheelhouse.

In front, run the steering wheel lock-to-lock and check clearances. The tire may clear, but will it clear during a dip in the road, or with your Mustang full of people? How much room do you have at all extremes?

Another important issue we don't often think about is brake clearance. Will the wheel clear the brake rotor and caliper? If you've installed huge 12- and 13-inch disc brakes, 16-inch wheels won't always clear the calipers.

The five-spoke Cobra-R wheel from Stee-da remains one of the most popular Mustang wheels out there. It's made for a Mustang, and looks great on a Mustang.

This Torq-Thrust five-spoke design from Performance Wheel Outlet comes in the proper offset and backspacing for a Mustang in sizes ranging from 16 to 18 inches.

The new Ford Mustang Mach 1 comes from the factory with this Magnum 500-style five-spoke wheel, available from Performance Wheel Outlet in San Bernardino, California. Put a set of these on your 1994-95 Mustang. If you're building a 1979-93 Mustang, you'll need five-lug hubs to use this wheel.

BODY TUNING AND TIPS

When you have most of the mechanical issues out of the way, you're going to want a good-looking Mustang to round out your efforts. There has never been a better marketplace for aftermarket bolt-on goodies like there is now for 1979-95 Mustangs. Fiberglass body upgrade kits and parts make it easy to transform your vanilla road rocket into something exciting to be seen in. Having a hot-performing Mustang isn't just about speed; it's certainly also about good looks. You can improve your Mustang's looks with some great low-buck bolt-ons. A billet grille can be bolted on in less than one hour for less than $100. Custom taillights can be installed in the same amount of time for under $200. A cowl induction hood can be delivered to your door for under $400. Installation, fiberglass work, and paint can be covered for under $600. How about a wilder rear deck spoiler for under $400? These are just a few of the quick and easy bolt-ons that can affordably change your Mustang.

We're not going to give you as much info on installing body upgrades as we are going to show you what's available. The main thing to remember about body kits and bolt-ons for late-model Mustangs is integrity. It may be cheaper, but is it solid? Is it easy to install? Will you have to spend a fortune in body-work and massaging because the fiberglass and molded plastic is junk because you tried to save a few bucks? We've seen this all too often with Mustang body bolt-ons. You don't want a ground-effects kit that will leave the body at 120 mph, nor do you want something flimsy that won't hold up in normal use.

When you order and receive a Mustang body kit, the next big step will be contracting the installation work out to qualified personnel. Just because it's a body shop does not mean it's qualified to install a ground-effects kit. For example, mass production crash shops that do a lot of insurance work can't always be counted on to do the best custom work. They're looking for the quick-turn-around insurance job, and your custom work is a time-consuming pain in the butt. Regardless of what most of the production crash shops will tell you going in, their work will be hurried. So, in the best interest of your Mustang project, spend a little more money, and opt for the best shop. You want a computer-matched color that matches your Mustang's finish exactly. Some colors we can cheat with, like white, off-white, some solid colors and black. Others, like metallics, mandate a perfect color match. Without it, your Mustang will look ridiculous and "bolt-on." If you're going to go to all the trouble and expense of a body kit, do it right

A couple of tasteful body mods can set your 'Stang apart from the crowd. Like many aspects of building a car, having too many body mods is not necessarily a good thing.

all the way with the right kit, the right shop, and a perfect color match.

Maybe ground effects or wheel-well flares aren't to your liking. But, you want something that will make your Mustang distinctive. Rear deck spoilers are generally easy bolt-ons you can do yourself. So are front chin spoilers. These are striking bolt-ons you can take to a body shop for scuffing and painting, and then install them yourself in an afternoon. The most important thing to remember with body bolt-ons like these is proper preparation. You can't just scuff them and lay down a coat of paint. Front chin spoilers, especially, need aggressive preparation if you're concerned about paint chipping and peeling. You want a good primer coat that will ensure solid paint adhesion. Ideally, you will have a body shop that can bake the paint at the appropriate temperature. This is how the factory does it with mass-production Mustangs, which is why paint adhesion and durability is always so much better.

Ground-effects kits need extra special attention because they're so close to the ground, where debris can do so much damage. Stray stones, speed bumps, and a host of other threats can undo your efforts in seconds. When you have installed a ground-effects kit, front-chin spoiler, or side exhaust system with a special rocker panel, protecting the paint becomes your greatest

challenge. This is why laying down the paint properly in the first place counts.

Paint manufacturers have urethane finishes designed to flex with urethane body components. These finishes allow the paint to flex or give with the bumper or air dam. The problem is that some states, like California, have banned the use of flex agents and flexible finishes due to a perceived threat to the environment. Using an inflexible finish on urethane and flexible plastics just about ensures doom for your finish.

If body bolt-ons, like hoods, spoilers, and ground-effects kits are outside of your budget, there is still a lot to choose from that will fit your pocketbook: billet fuel doors and grilles; vinyl graphics; custom taillights and mirrors; bolt-on hood and side scoops, and even Cobra emblems that will dress up your Mustang without costing you a fortune. When you're considering vinyl graphics and stick-on emblems, be smart about place-

How about a high-wing spoiler from JBA? You can bolt this high-altitude airfoil onto your 1979-93 Mustang hatchback.

SEMO Classic Mustang caters mostly to the vintage Mustang crowd. However, they have a lot of exciting accessories for late-model Mustangs. This cowl-induction hood is just what the doctor ordered for 1994-95 Mustangs. Here, it looks sharp painted like a 1969 Mustang Mach 1 hood.

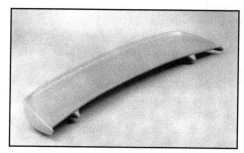

Late-model 1979-95 Mustangs enjoy a wealth of exciting fiberglass and plastic body panels. Cervini's, for example, designs, develops, and manufactures a wide variety of body kits, hoods, and deck-lid spoilers for late-model Mustangs. See Cervini's at all of the major Ford events around the country, including the Carlisle All Ford Nationals every June.

Rear-deck spoilers are among the most affordable body mods you can make. They're easy to install and can be painted any color. Saleen Autosport has quite a variety of exciting body bolt-ons, which help you make your Mustang look like a Saleen. California Mustang is an excellent source for great body bolt-ons for late-model Mustangs.

Here's another fiberglass hood from SEMO Classic Mustang. It takes the cowl induction approach and gives it "snort."

ment. We see a lot of really hokey placement out there in our travels. You can have too many stick-ons – or two kinds of graphics messages that make no sense. For example – why send a GT and Cobra message? Send one or the other, but not both. The positioning of your vinyl

Here we revisit the rear deck spoiler, this time from Steeda. This completes the lazy rear deck of the 1979-93 Mustang hatchback and coupe. Call this one an easy bolt-on you can do in an afternoon.

Steeda offers this cowl-induction-style hood for 1994-95 Mustangs with air extractors to release underhood heat.

Here's something really sharp from Steeda for 1979-93 Mustangs. This cowl-induction hood has twin air extractors on each side to get rid of intense underhood heat, especially right over the exhaust headers. This makes the hood functional, as well as good-looking.

graphics can wind up decidedly poor and get you a lot of laughs. Err on the side of conservatism whenever you're planning graphics. It's easy to go overboard and wind up removing most of what you've installed. Think your graphics trip out before installation and wasted money. And, don't be afraid to start over if it doesn't work out. The best part of a mistake is what you learn from it.

INSTALLING A CERVINI'S HOOD (1994-95)

Here's an easy one you and a friend can handle in an hour. The most time-consuming part here is working it and having it painted. This is the Cervini's cowl induction hood for 1994-95 Mustangs. This hood bears similarity to others shown in this chapter. We just happened to catch John Da Luz and Julio Mayen installing one of these in San Diego, and with camera in hand, we captured the event. Installation is a cake walk because Cervini's quality is outstanding. This cowl induction hood is a perfect fit. And when you consider the zero-adjust build quality of the 1994-04 Mustang, installing a high-quality Cervini's hood is easy.

John took his black '95 Mustang GT down to a body shop, had them work the hood and lay down computer-matched black basecoat and clear coat. After several weeks, we had almost forgotten John had replaced the factory hood.

1. John preps the hood for installation and body shop. He wants to remove all contaminants prior to installation. Once the hood is properly adjusted, he doesn't want it disturbed. The body shop primed and painted the hood on the car.

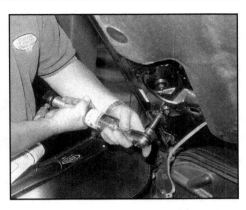

2. John Da Luz and Dave Toth of JMC Motorsports unbolt the factory hood and put it away for safekeeping.

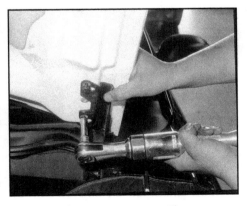

3. The new Cervini's cowl-induction hood is installed, adjusted, and tightened.

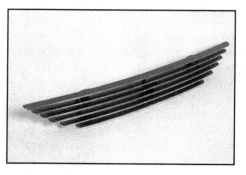

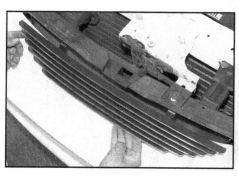

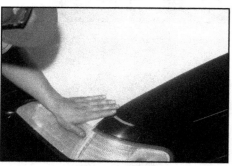

2. This is the aluminum billet grille from Brothers Performance Warehouse. It's retained by four bolts and is easy to install.

5. To install this grille, you need to drill four 5/16-inch holes in the Mustang's grille support. This happens where the four L brackets are.

4. John and Julio check the hood for proper fit, and both are impressed. All it needs now is professional prep, black basecoat, and clear coat.

INSTALLING A BILLET GRILLE (1994-95)

Here's a quick and dirty, low-buck way to change your Mustang's identity in about one hour. Brothers Performance Warehouse has billet aluminum grilles for 1994-95 Mustangs that are affordably priced and easy to install. These grilles are available in brushed aluminum, polished aluminum, and black. Four brackets anchor them to your Mustang's grille opening. Here's a quick play-by-play.

1. This is the '95 Mustang Cobra. Aside from the snake, we're unimpressed with the stark grille. Show us some honeycomb. Show us some lines. Show us anything.

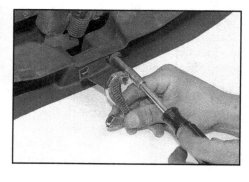

3. First, remove the Cobra logo. A single screw is all it takes.

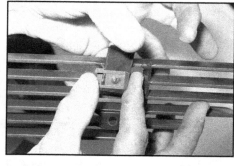

4. The billet grille has four "L"-shaped brackets that are fastened with four sheet-metal screws and tinnerman's nuts. Make sure they're square with the grille bars top and bottom.

6. The billet grille looks sharp, adding a new dimension to our Cobra coupe. Remember, these custom grilles are available in brushed aluminum, polished aluminum, and black. With a little imagination, you can pin the Cobra or the galloping horse to this grille.

INSTALLING A BILLET FUEL DOOR (1994-95)

This is a great, easy-to-install, cheap body bolt-on. And, it gives your 1994-95 Mustang a competitive persona in a matter of 15 minutes. The Bullitt billet fuel

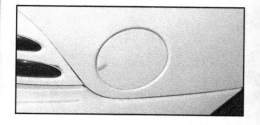

1. Not much to look at, is it? This is the stock, garden variety, slap-open 1994-98 Mustang fuel door. No need for security devices because – who'd want to steal it?

door has been hotly pursued ever since we first saw it on the Bullitt concept Mustang at the Los Angeles Auto Show years ago. Everyone saw it and just had to have it. Now, you can. One place to find it is from UPR products.

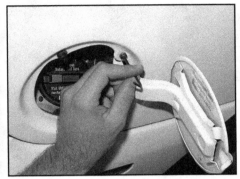

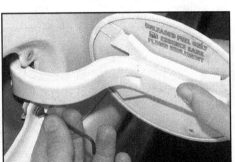

2. The stock fuel door removes with two Allen-head screws.

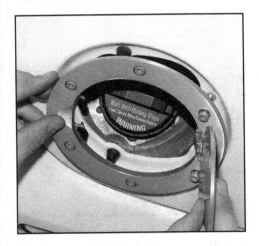

3. The new Bullitt billet fuel door from Brothers Performance Warehouse is easy to install. Two Allen-head screws get the job done. This striking body bolt-on is designed for the 1999-04 Mustang body. But it also fits the 1994-98 Mustang quarter panel quite well.

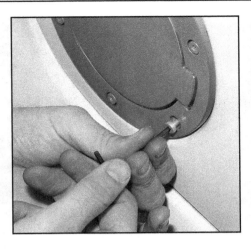

4. Running the two Allen screws down finished the job.

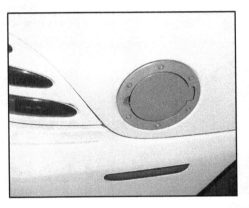

5. Our Bullitt fuel door looks sharp, was easy to install, and didn't cost much.

GRAPHICS PACKAGES

One of the most affordable ways to dress up your Mustang is the application of a graphics package. With today's technology you can apply virtually anything to your Mustang that your mind can dream up. If you're crazy about your girlfriend or boyfriend, you can probably apply their face to the hood if you search hard enough for a graphics specialist.

Classic Mustang enthusiasts like Shelby stripes. The late-model crowd likes anything Saleen, Steeda, or Roush, for example. Brothers Performance Warehouse in Southern California has just about any kind of graphics dress-up image you can think of — and more. We're going to clad both sides of a '95 Mustang Cobra with a "Mustang" graphics kit from Brothers Performance Warehouse. Here's how to get there.

1. Before applying our body graphic, Bryan Rogers of Brothers Performance Warehouse thoroughly cleans the surface with a mild solvent. All wax and debris must be removed for good graphic adhesion. Even a tiny speck of dust will show in your graphic.

2. Apply soapy water to the clean surface to keep the graphic positionable during installation. With a wet surface, we can position the graphic and get it where we want it. As the soapy water dries, positioning becomes permanent.

3. With a wet surface, the graphic is positioned and taped in place. The horse's mouth should be positioned at the lower region of the front fender beneath the Mustang logo. The mane and tail should run along the top of the quarter panel.

4. Before applying the graphic, Bryan lays down more soapy water. Because Southern California is a dry, desert environment, the water evaporates quickly. This is an ongoing process.

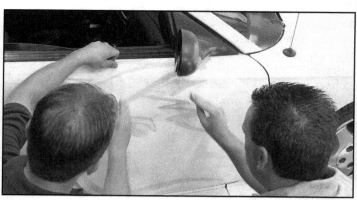

5. Beginning at one end of the graphic, ideally the nose, we start peeling the protective paper off of the adhesive vinyl. We stress laying down the graphic in one-inch segments, rubbing down the graphic with a body filler spatula or old credit card. You need firm pressure, one inch at a time, to achieve solid adhesion with the surface. The soapy water must evaporate before adhesion is possible.

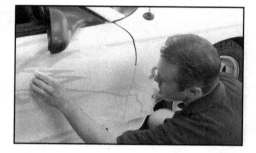

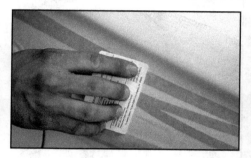

6. Be prepared for a long, tedious trek across the side of your Mustang. The graphic must be applied slowly and carefully in one-inch segments. Work the vinyl only with the protective covering in place. Make sure you have adhesion with the surface before moving on. Few things are more frustrating than a vinyl graphic that lifts off and wrinkles. Once you stretch it or distort it in any way, the battle is lost. It will never lie down correctly again.

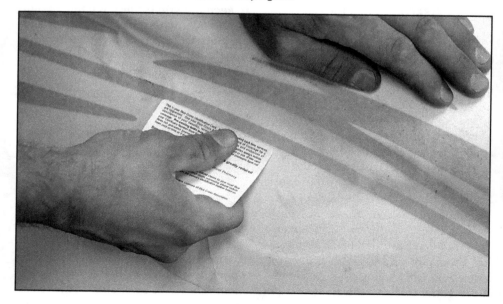

7. Work your way across the body as shown. Again, leave the protective cover in place until most of the graphic has adhered to the surface.

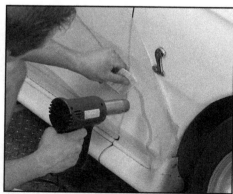

8. Using a heat gun, carefully warm the graphic and protective paper. This helps the soapy water evaporate more quickly. Work the graphic to ensure good adhesion. Keep that credit card or body filler spatula moving over the surface with gentle pressure. When the surface is wet, the graphic can lift, so be careful.

9. Slowly and carefully, Bryan peels back the protective paper and examines his work. The soapy water must be completely gone before we are ready for this step; otherwise, the graphic will lift.

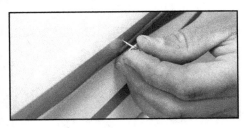

10. Air bubbles are inevitable in the vinyl graphic. Here, we are using a pushpin to pop the air bubbles. However, we suggest a fine-point sewing needle for best results. A small pinprick allows air to escape without damaging the vinyl.

11. At the door gaps, cut the vinyl as shown with a razor blade and fold the ends back. Be careful here because the vinyl can lift.

12. This is our installed graphic from Brothers Performance Warehouse.

INSTALLING EURO TAILLIGHTS (1979-93)

When Ford introduced the redesigned '87 Mustang GT, few of us cared for the fluted taillights. We weren't all that thrilled with the Mustang LX taillight either. What we would have given for the aftermarket Euro taillights now available for the 1979-93 Mustang from Brothers Performance Warehouse! These taillights are as easy to install as stock units because, like the stockers, they are modular. Our subject vehicle is a '88 McLaren Mustang roadster. The factory taillights are fogged from the intense Southern California sun.

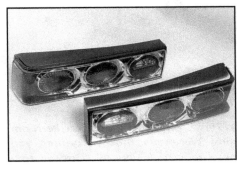

1. The 1987-93 Mustang Euro taillights from Brothers Performance Warehouse completely change a Mustang's personality. Some like them – some hate them. Whatever your opinion, I'm sure you're passionate about it. They're priced at around $230, and they install in about one hour.

2. The original 1988 Mustang taillights have become milky and foggy from the sun. Time to spruce up the place with fresh Euro taillights from Brothers Performance Warehouse.

3. We're removing the interior trunk panels. These are McLaren trunk panels, which are different than those from Ford. Plastic fasteners retain the Ford panels, while the McLaren panels are retained with screws.

4. Taillight sockets are a push-and-twist affair. Remove all of the sockets, taking note of their location.

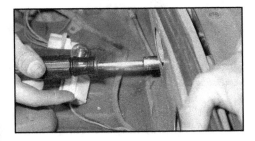

5. The factory taillight modules are retained with nuts as shown. The taillights are nothing more than modular units fastened to the body.

6. Remove the taillights as shown.

7. The new Euro taillights install just like the factory units. Just fit them into place.

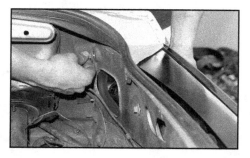

8. Install the factory nuts and washers. Tighten them until the taillight module is snug, but don't over tighten them. Check and make sure the seals are where they need to be.

9. Install the taillight sockets, and check the bulbs for proper operation. Reinstall the trunk panels.

10. Euro taillights freshen up an aging Mustang. These are a nice touch for an old steed. If the Euro taillights aren't to your liking, Brothers Performance Warehouse also has OEM-style taillights in stock.

INSTALLING 1996-98 TAILLIGHTS IN YOUR 1994-95

When the SN-95 Mustang was introduced just before Christmas in 1993, we liked the retro styling, which reminded us of the classic Mustang. Ford told us, "It's what it was – and more..." And so it was. The redesigned, Fox-body Mustang coupe and convertible were very sharp. They caught on fast and sold very well. Sales records shot up well above 200,000 units. Despite how overjoyed we were

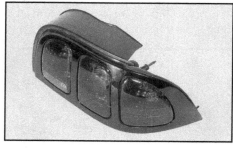

1. This is all it takes. Brothers Performance Warehouse has everything you need to install 1996-98 Mustang taillights in your 1994-95 Mustang. They also have exciting aftermarket taillights available that will dress up any 1994-98 Mustang.

with the new Mustang, the taillights tended to underwhelm us. They were the traditional three-element design, sort of, but the three elements ran horizontally instead of vertically, like the 1965-70 Mustang. Even at a glance, the 1994-95 Mustang taillights just didn't whinny "Mustang!"

When Ford face-lifted the Mustang for 1996, giving the GT and Cobra those high-tech overhead cam V-8s, the taillights changed, too. We liked the more classic three-element design. Those who purchased 1994-95 Mustangs just had to have them. Here's how you can.

2. As you can see here, there isn't much difference between the 1996-98 taillight module and the 1994-95. They're interchangeable and use the same harness. No special modifications are required.

3. This is the 1994-95 Mustang rear fascia with the original horizontal three-element taillights. Although these were nice lamps, they just didn't say "MUSTANG!" like the 1996-98 module did.

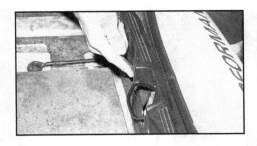

4. To get to these taillights, even to just change a light bulb, you must first remove most of the trunk liner. Begin at the trunk threshold.

5. Remove this thumbscrew on each side, which screws onto the taillight stud.

6. Remove the rear trunk liner, which lifts right out. Most of the trunk liner is retained via the nip-and-tuck method, so it's easy to remove and reinstall. The side liners come right out on both sides.

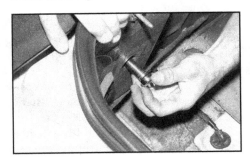

7. Each taillight module is just that – a removable module. Four studs retain the module. Remove four nuts, like this, on each module.

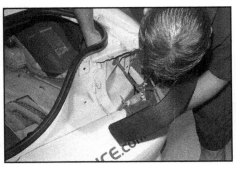

8. Pull each module out from the body like this. The taillight harness remains with the body. Simply remove each socket from the module and remove the module.

9. After you install all of the sockets in the appropriate positions, then install the module. Check the lights for proper operation before completely installing the module.

10. Install the four nuts and snug'em down.

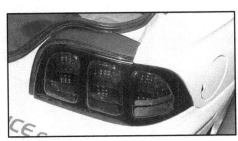

11. This is a nice improvement for 1994-95 Mustangs. You may paint this module to match body color. We decided to stay with the Saleen look on this one.

INSTALLING SEQUENTIAL TAILLIGHTS (1994-95)

When the '96 Mustang was introduced, Classic Design Concepts in Detroit wasn't far behind with a great idea – sequential, three-element taillights, like the classic Thunderbirds and Cougars. While we were upgrading a '95 Cobra to 1996-98 three-element taillights, we decided to install the sequential taillights as an afterthought. Brothers Performance Warehouse stepped up with the sequential, three-element taillight kits from Classic Design Concepts.

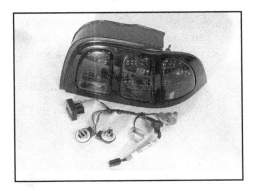

1. The Classic Design Concepts three-element, sequential taillight conversion kit comes in a simple package, with the harnesses and instructions only. The 1996-98 three-element module is extra and, needless to say, necessary for this sequential turn signal kit to work properly. There is one type of kit for 1994-95, and another for 1996-98. The 1996-98 kit will not work properly on a 1994-95 Mustang. Guess how we know?

2. The stock taillight harness disconnects here inside the trunk area on both sides. This harness comes through the taillight panel from the module. Simply push the grommet through when you remove the module.

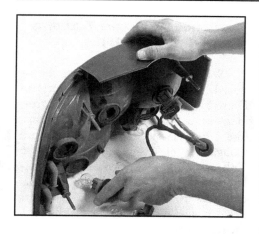

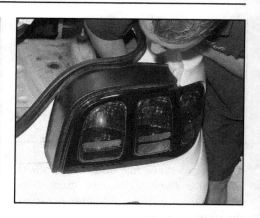

3. We've already shown you how to remove and install the taillight module. Here, we have the module in a studio to show you how to swap the stock taillight harness for the Classic Design Concepts sequential taillight kit.

6. The installed sequential turn signal harness looks like this.

9. Bryan Rogers checks the taillight for proper operation. If you use the 1996-98 harness on a 1994-95 Mustang, only one lamp will light, as Bryan has discovered. The specially modified 1994-95 harness is designed to work with the 1994-95 system. Don't bother picking one of these 1996-98 harnesses up at a swap meet and trying it on your 1994-95 Mustang.

INSTALLING NEW HEADLIGHTS (1987-93)

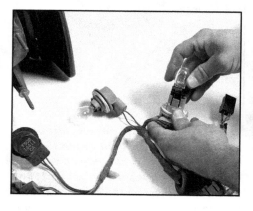

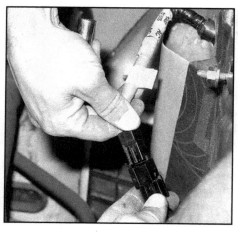

4. All bulbs are swapped from the stock harness to the Classic Design Concepts harness. The process seems easy enough.

7. The new harness enters the tail panel, just like the factory harness. Inside the trunk, it connects just like the factory harness. No cutting or splicing here, just an easy modification you can do in 30 minutes.

In this book, we're focusing a lot on easy, inexpensive improvements you can make on your Mustang. Believe it or not, headlights and taillights are one of the nicest cosmetic improvements you can make in the wake of a paint job. Even if you've had to go the economy paint job route to improve your Mustang, you would be amazed what a color sanding and rubout will do when coupled with new headlights and taillights. You can change virtually everyone's opinion of your Mustang with these easy, simple steps you can knock out in an afternoon. Again, we look to Brothers Performance Warehouse for answers.

Introducing the Projector Headlights from Brothers Performance Warehouse. This is not a low-buck mod, at a cost of more than $300. However, you can always opt for headlights that don't cost as much but look brand new. Stock aftermarket headlights, for example, retail for under $100 each. The Projector headlights give your Mustang that European look – an outlaw persona that's intimidating for those going too slow. They also light the road ahead nicely. Whether you're installing Projector headlights or OEM replacements, the procedure is the same.

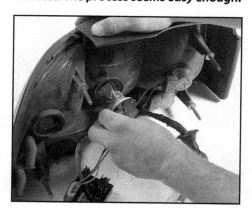

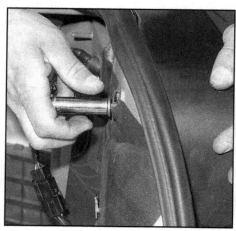

5. The new Classic Design Concepts taillight harness is installed in the 1996-98 module. Each socket is numbered for ease of installation. The back-up light stands alone.

8. The taillight module reinstalls with ease. Four nuts will do it. Don't over tighten them though.

1. Most 1987-93 Mustangs suffer from age. These Lexan plastic headlights looked very futuristic when they debuted for the first time on the 1987 Mustang. But since then, the sunlight and weather have taken a toll on the plastic, making it milky and unattractive.

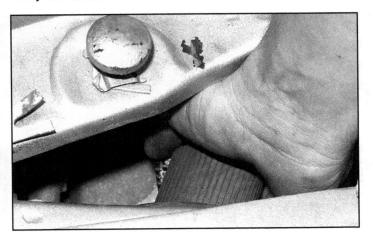

2. First, we remove the halogen lamps, but don't touch the glass. The oil from your fingers will create hot spots on the surface of the lamps and cause them to fail.

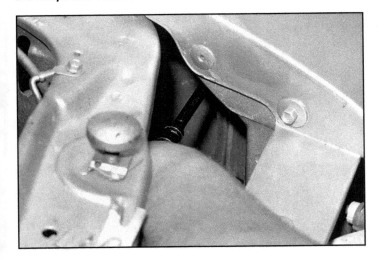

3. The first lamp we remove is the side marker. Two nuts retain the lamp; they can be removed with a deep-well socket.

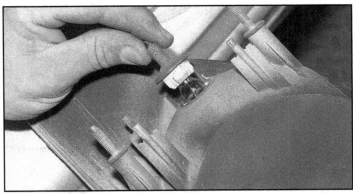

4. Remove the side-marker lamp with a twist and pull.

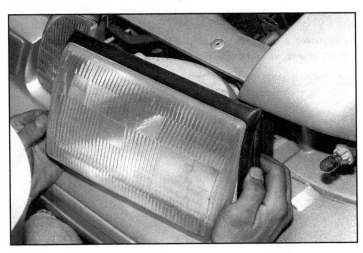

5. The original composite headlight is retained from behind with four nuts. Remove the nuts; then remove the lamp assembly.

6. This is the Projector headlight from Brothers Performance Warehouse. The Projector will completely change your Mustang's attitude. In addition to the regular halogen headlight, the Projector has a separate driving lamp that projects a beam of light. This lamp has to be wired in a separate circuit with a switch and relay, protected by a fuse or circuit breaker.

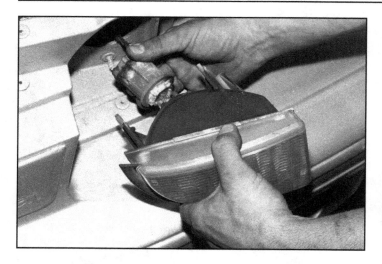

7. Remove the parking lamp by extracting two nuts from behind. Remove the socket with a twist and yank.

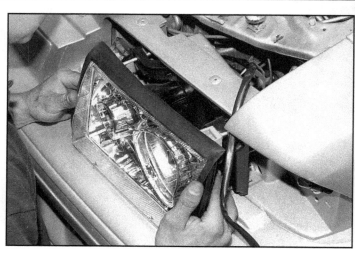

10. The Projector headlight fits right in place of the OEM headlight. Four nuts retain the lamp, just like OEM.

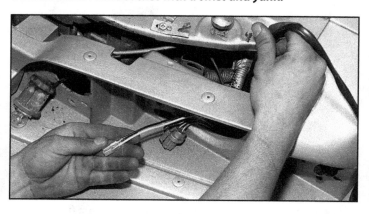

8. The Projector lamp lives off a separate circuit that you must create. You're going to need a relay and a switch, but Brothers provides the wiring. We suggest getting your power from the cigarette lighter circuit or directly from the battery. Always use circuit protection in the form of a fuse or a circuit breaker.

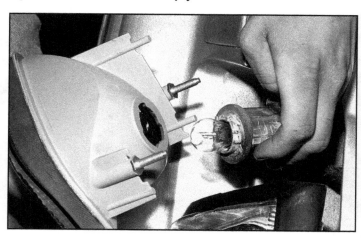

11. While you're in the neighborhood, install new parking and side marker lamps. Hey, they're affordable. Here, we're installing the parking lamp.

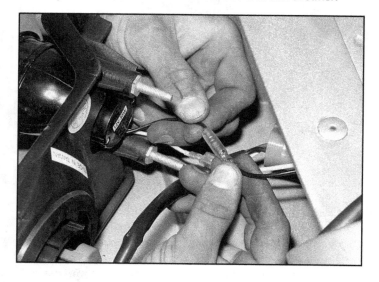

9. Bullet connectors tie the projector lamp to the wiring.

12. We have kicked the old parking lamp to the curb. The new one is seated and tightened via the two nuts from behind.

INDUSTRY SOURCE GUIDE

ARB 4x4 Accessories
20 South Spokane St.
Seattle, WA 98134
206/264-1669
www.arbusa.com

Art Carr Performance Transmission
19 Windmill Circle
Abilene, TX 79606
888/526-5868
www.artcarr.com

Astro Performance Warehouse
601 E. Alfred St.
Tavares, FL 32778
800/343-0956

B&M Racing & Performance s
9142 Independence Ave.
Chatsworth, CA 91311
818/882-6422
www.bmracing.com

Baer Brakes, Inc.
3108 W. Thomas Rd., Suite 1201
Phoenix, AZ 85017-5306
602/233-1411
www.baer.com

Bennett Racing
P.O. Box 593
Highway 5 S.
Haleyville, AL 35565
205/486-8441
www.bennettracing.com

Brothers Performance Warehouse
2012 Railroad St.
Corona, CA 92880-5432
909/735-8880
www.brothersperformance.com

C&L Performance
207-G Green Cove Rd.
Huntsville, AL 35803
256/882-6813
www.cnlperformance.com

California Performance Transmissions
5502 Engineer Dr.
Huntington Beach, CA 92649
800/278-2277

Centerforce Clutches
2266 Crosswind Dr.
Prescott, AZ 86301
520/771-6422
www.centerforce.com

Cervini's Auto Designs
3656 N. Mill Rd.
Vineland, NJ 08360
800/488-6057
www.cervinis.com

Coast High Performance
2555 W. 237th St.
Torrance, CA 90505
310/784-2977
www.coasthigh.com

D.S.S. Competition Products
960 Ridge Ave.
Lombard, IL 60148
630/268-1630
www.dssracing.com

Differential Systems
3585 Hancock St.
San Diego, CA 92110
619/298-3568
E-Mail: Jaytool_2000@yahoo.com

Edelbrock Corporation
2700 California St.
Torrance, CA 90503
310/781-2222
www.edelbrock.com

Fluidyne High Performance
174 Gasoline Alley
Mooresville, NC 28117
888/FLUIDYNE
www.fluidyne.com

Ford Performance Solutions
1004 Orangefair Lane
Anaheim, CA 92801
714/773-9027
www.f-p-s.com

Ford Racing Performance Parts
44050 N. Groesbeck Highway
Clinton Township, MI 48036
586/468-1356
www.fordracing.com

G-Force
1525 S.R. 934
Annville, PA 17003
717/867-4352
www.gforcetransmissions.com

Griggs Racing Products
29175 Arnold Drive
Sonoma, CA 95476
707/939-2244
www.griggsracing.com

Hanlon Motorsports
3621 St. Peters Rd.
Elverson, PA 19520
610/469-2695

JMC Motorsports
2277 National Avenue
San Diego, CA 92113
619/230-8866
www.johnsmustangs.com

JME Enterprises
619/575-5667
2256 Main St., Suite #8
Chula Vista, CA 91911
www.jmeenterprises.com

Koni North America
1961 International Way
Hebron, KY 41048
859/586-4100
www.koni-na.com

LenTech Automatics
3487 Joy's Rd.
Richmond, Ontario K0A-220, Canada
613/838-5390
www.lentechautomatics.com

Liberty's Gears
6390 Pelham Rd.
Taylor, MI 48180
313/278-4040

Lunati Cams
4770 Lamar Ave.
Memphis, TN 38118-7403
901/365-0950

MAC Performance Products
43214 Blackdeer Loop
Temecula, CA 92590-3473
800/367-4486
www.macperformance.com

Maximum Motorsports
3430 Sacramento Dr., Unit D
San Luis Obispo, CA 93401
800/839-092
www.maximummotorsports.com

MSD Ignition
1490 Henry Brannan Rd.
El Paso, TX 79936
915/857-5200
www.msdignition.com

Nowak Racing Engines
249 E. Emerson Ave.
Orange, CA 92665
714/282-7996

Performance Automatic Transmissions
8174 Beechcraft Ave.
Gaithersburg, MD 20879
800/767-8174

Performance Automotive Warehouse
21001 Nordhoff Street
Chatsworth, CA 91311
818/678-3000
www.pawinc.com

Performance Wheel Outlet
195 E. Redlands Blvd.
San Bernardino, CA 92408
909/825-5363
www.performancewheeloutlet.com

Powered By Ford
1516 S. Division Ave.
Orlando, FL 32805
407/843-3673
www.poweredbyford.com

Powertrax
P.O. Box 238
1208 Old Norris Rd.
Liberty, SC 29657
864/843-9231

Powerdyne Automotive Products
104-C East Avenue K-4
Lancaster, CA 93535
661/723-2800
www.powerdyne.com

ProMotion Performance Powertrain
4766 NE 12 Ave
Ft. Lauderdale, FL 33334
954/771-5575

ProPower
4750 N. Dixie Highway, No. 9
Fort Lauderdale, FL 33334
954/491-6988
www.propowerparts.com

Race Pages
ProMedia Publishing
3518 West Lake Center Dr., Suite D
Santa Ana, CA 92704
714/444-2426
www.promediapub.com

Scat Crankshafts
1400 Kingsdale Ave.
Redondo Beach, CA 90278
310/370-5501
www.scatcrankshafts.com

Speed-O-Motive
131 North Lang Ave.
West Covina, CA 91760
626/869-0270
www.speedomotive.com

Steeda Autosports
1351 N. Steeda Way
Pompano Beach, FL 33069
954/960-0774
www.steeda.com

TracTech Inc.
11445 Stephens Drive
Warren, MI 48089
800/328-3850

Trans Am Racing
13307 S. Manhattan Place
Gardena, CA 90249
310/323-5417
www.taracing.com

Transmission Technologies Corporation
23382 Commerce Drive
Farmington Hills, MI 48335
800/355-0086
www.ttcautomotive.com

Unlimited Performance
(UPR Products)
750 South East Coast Street
Lake Worth, FL 33460
561/588-6630

Victoria Automatic Transmission
800/668-7270 / www.victrans.com

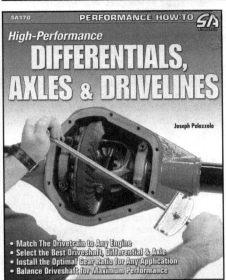
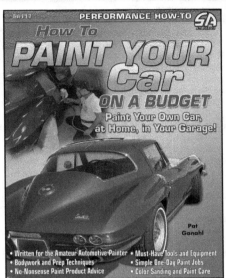
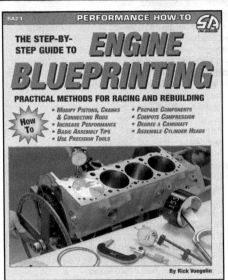
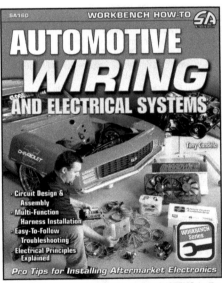

CPSIA information can be obtained
at www.ICGtesting.com
Printed in the USA
FSHW020850050121
77325FS